LANGUAGE AND CULTURE IN EU LAW

AF782682

Law, Language and Communication

Series Editors
Anne Wagner, Lille University – Nord de France, Centre for Legal Research and Perspectives of Law, René Demogue Group, France and
Vijay Kumar Bhatia, City University of Hong Kong

This series encourages innovative and integrated perspectives within and across the boundaries of law, language and communication, with particular emphasis on issues of communication in specialized socio-legal and professional contexts. It seeks to bring together a range of diverse yet cumulative research traditions related to these fields in order to identify and encourage interdisciplinary research.

The series welcomes proposals – both edited collections as well as single-authored monographs – emphasizing critical approaches to law, language and communication, identifying and discussing issues, proposing solutions to problems, offering analyses in areas such as legal construction, interpretation, translation and de-codification.

Language and Culture in EU Law

Multidisciplinary Perspectives

Edited by

SUSAN ŠARČEVIĆ
University of Rijeka, Croatia

Routledge
Taylor & Francis Group
LONDON AND NEW YORK

First published 2015 by Ashgate Publishing

Published 2016 by Routledge
2 Park Square, Milton Park, Abingdon, Oxfordshire OX14 4RN
711 Third Avenue, New York, NY 10017, USA

First issued in paperback 2016

Routledge is an imprint of the Taylor & Francis Group, an informa business

Copyright © Susan Šarčević 2015

Susan Šarčević has asserted her right under the Copyright, Designs and Patents Act, 1988, to be identified as the editor of this work.

All rights reserved. No part of this book may be reprinted or reproduced or utilised in any form or by any electronic, mechanical, or other means, now known or hereafter invented, including photocopying and recording, or in any information storage or retrieval system, without permission in writing from the publishers.

Notice:
Product or corporate names may be trademarks or registered trademarks, and are used only for identification and explanation without intent to infringe.

British Library Cataloguing in Publication Data
A catalogue record for this book is available from the British Library

The Library of Congress has cataloged the printed edition as follows:
Language and culture in EU law : multidisciplinary perspectives / By Susan Šarčević.
pages cm. -- (Law, language and communication)
Includes bibliographical references and index.
ISBN 978-1-4724-2897-4 (hardback)
1. European Union countries--Languages--Law and legislation. 2. Law--Translation--European Union countries. 3. Law--European Union countries--Language.
4. European Union--Language policy. I. Šarčević, Susan, editor.
KJE5306.L36 2015
341.242'2014--dc23

2014030037

ISBN 13: 978-1-138-63756-6 (pbk)
ISBN 13: 978-1-4724-2897-4 (hbk)

Contents

List of Tables

Notes on Contributors

C.J.W. (Jaap) Baaij is Assistant Professor at the University of Amsterdam Law School and LL.M. candidate at Yale Law School, class of 2015. He teaches European Contract Law and Contract Law Theory and holds training seminars for translators and lawyer-linguists in the EU institutions, as well as seminars on legal integration and multilingualism across Europe and in the United States. He is editor of *The Role of Legal Translation in Legal Harmonization* (2012).

Martina Bajčić is Senior Lecturer at the Faculty of Law of the University of Rijeka in Croatia where she teaches Legal English and Legal German. She holds a PhD in Linguistics and has completed a Postgraduate Specialist Study Programme in European Integration. Her research focuses mainly on legal translation and legal terminology. She is a sworn court interpreter for English and German and a member of the Croatian Translators Association.

Maja Bratanić is Professor and Head of the Department of General, Comparative and Computational Linguistics at the Institute of Croatian Language and Linguistics in Zagreb, where she is chief coordinator of the Croatian Special Field Terminology Programme and the Croatian national term bank *Struna*. Her main fields of research include lexicographical theory and practice, terminology and terminography, corpus linguistics, anthropological linguistics and English for specific purposes.

Mattias Derlén is Doctor of Laws and Senior Lecturer at the Department of Law at Umeå University in Sweden. His areas of interest include the multilingual interpretation of EU law and constitutional issues of EU law relating to the Court of Justice. He is the author of the widely cited book *Multilingual Interpretation of European Union Law* (2009) and has published a series of articles on the CJEU case law.

Jan Engberg is Professor of Knowledge Communication at the Department of Business Communication and the School of Business and Social Sciences at the University of Aarhus in Denmark. His areas of research include the study of texts and genres in the academic field, cognitive aspects of domain specific discourse and the relations between specialized knowledge and text formulation. He has published widely in the area of law and language and is currently co-editor of the international journal *Fachsprache*.

Annarita Felici is Associate Professor of Translation at the Faculty of Translation and Interpreting of the University of Geneva. Her fields of special interest include legal translation, the comparative analysis of legal texts, discourse in institutional settings and the application of corpus linguistics to translation and specialized language. She was previously 'Juniorprofessorin' of legal linguistics at the University of Cologne in Germany and spent over 10 years in the UK lecturing translation, general linguistics and Italian as a foreign language.

Michele Graziadei is Professor of Comparative Law at the Law Department of the University of Torino. As a member of the terminology team of the *Acquis* Group, he co-edited the text of the *Principles of Existing EC Contract Law*. His current research focuses on comparative law, the cognitive approach to the study of legal cultures and individual agency in the law.

Anne Lise Kjær is Professor of Law and Language at the Faculty of Law of the University of Copenhagen and Director of RELINE, the Danish based Network for Interdisciplinary Studies in Language and Law. She is also senior researcher at the Centre of Excellence, iCourts, which investigates the autonomization of international law from cross-disciplinary perspectives. She is co-editor of *Linguistic Diversity and European Democracy* (2011) and *Paradoxes of European Legal Integration* (2008).

Maja Lončar is Research Assistant at the Department of General, Comparative and Computational Linguistics of the Institute of Croatian Language and Linguistics in Zagreb. She has worked as an ECQA certified terminologist on several Croatian Special Field Terminology projects, including 'Croatian Terms for Concepts of EU Law'.

Barbara Pozzo is Professor of Comparative Law at the Insubria University Law School in Como (Italy) where she teaches Introduction to Legal Systems of the World and Legal Translation. She is editor of the book series 'Languages of the Law' published by Giuffrè, Milano, and edited, among others, a special issue of *European Review of Private Law* entitled 'Impact of Multilingualism on the Harmonization of European Private Law' (2012).

Colin Robertson recently retired after almost 25 years of service in the EU first as a legal translator at the Court of Justice in Luxembourg and from 1993 as a legal-linguistic reviser (lawyer-linguist) at the Council of the European Union. He holds a law degree from Aberdeen University and worked as a lawyer in the UK public service. He has knowledge of several languages, including English, French, German, Italian, Czech, Slovak and Bulgarian, and is currently studying Chinese.

Ingemar Strandvik is quality manager in the European Commission's Directorate-General for Translation, where he previously worked as a translator. He has a

Master's degree in EU Law and is a (Swedish) state-authorized translator and court interpreter. His background is in translation didactics at Stockholm University and as chief editor for a major lexicographical project at the publishing house Norstedts.

Susan Šarčević is Professor and former Head of the Department of Foreign Languages at the Faculty of Law of the University of Rijeka where she taught Legal English, Legal German and EU Terminology. She publishes extensively and lectures worldwide on legal translation and comparative legal terminology. Her best-known work is *New Approach to Legal Translation*. She is Research Professor at the Research Centre for Legal Translation of the China University of Political Science and Law in Beijing.

Acknowledgements

First of all I would like to thank the authors for their valuable contributions providing multidisciplinary perspectives on the role of language and culture as driving forces in the dynamics of EU law. Special thanks go to Nada Bodiroga Vukobrat, Director of the Jean Monnet Inter-University Centre of Excellence Opatija and Professor of European Law at the Faculty of Law of the University of Rijeka, for her assistance in organizing the conference which served as the starting point of this book. Organized in cooperation with the Department of Foreign Languages of the Rijeka Faculty of Law, the conference was a key activity in the Jean Monnet Programme of Professor Bodiroga Vukobrat's EU Lifelong Learning Project and was also supported by my national research project 'Strategies for translating the EU *acquis*'. I am especially grateful to the Jean Monnet Inter-University Centre of Excellence Opatija, the Hanns Seidel Foundation and the municipality of Opatija for their financial support which made the conference possible. Thanks are also due to Martina Bajčić and Adrijana Martinović for their dedicated work in organizing and coordinating the conference logistics.

Susan Šarčević
Zagreb, Croatia

List of Abbreviations

ABGB	Allgemeines Bürgerliches Gesetzbuch (Austrian General Civil Code)
BDÜ	Bundesverband der Dolmetscher und Übersetzer (German Federal Association of Translators and Interpreters)
BeVReStG	Gesetz zur Stärkung der Verfahrensrechte von Beschuldigten im Strafverfahren (German Act on Strengthening Procedural Rights of Accused Persons in Criminal Proceedings)
bg	Bulgarian
BGB	Bürgerliches Gesetzbuch (German Civil Code)
BVerfGE	Entscheidungen des Bundesverfassungsgerichts (Decisions of the German Federal Constitutional Court)
BVerwG	Bundesverwaltungsgericht (German Federal Administrative Court)
CESL	Proposal for a Common European Sales Law
CFR	Common Frame of Reference
CISG	UN Convention on Contracts for the International Sale of Goods
CJEU	Court of Justice of the European Union
CMLR	Common Market Law Reports
Cr.App.R.	Criminal Appeal Reports
CRC	Coordination and Revision Centre (Czech Republic)
cs	Czech
da	Danish
DCFR	Draft Common Frame of Reference (Principles, Definitions and Model Rules of European Private Law)
de	German
DG	Directorate-General
DGT	Directorate-General for Translation
EAEC	European Atomic Energy Community
EC	European Commission
EC	European Community
E.C.C.	European Commercial Cases
ECHR	European Convention on Human Rights
ECJ	Court of Justice of the European Communities (pre-Lisbon)
ECLI	European Case Law Identifier
ECR	European Court Reports
ECSC	European Coal and Steel Community

ECtHR	European Court of Human Rights
EEC	European Economic Community
ELF	English as a *lingua franca*
EMT	European Master's in Translation
en	English
EP	European Parliament
es	Spanish
et	Estonian
EU	European Union
EULITA	European Legal Interpreters and Translators Association
Euramis	European Advanced Multilingual Information System
EWCA Civ	England and Wales Court of Appeal (Civil Division)
FG	Finanzgericht (German Financial Court)
fi	Finnish
fr	French
GVG	Gerichtsverfassungsgesetz (German Court Constitution Act)
HGB	Handelsgesetzbuch (German Commercial Code)
hr	Croatian
hu	Hungarian
IATE	InterActive Terminology for Europe (EU's Multilingual Term Bank)
IEHC	High Court, Ireland
ISO	International Organization for Standardization
it	Italian
JVEG	Justizvergütungs- und Entschädigungsgesetz (German Judicial Remuneration and Compensation Act)
K.B.	King's Bench
LSP	Language(s) for Specific Purposes
MEP	Member of the European Parliament
MT@EC	Machine Translation at European Commission
nl	Dutch
OJ	Official Journal of the European Union
PCC	UNIDROIT Principles of International Commercial Contracts
PECL	Principles of European Contract Law
pl	Polish
pt	Portuguese
Q.B.	Queen's Bench
ro	Romanian
sk	Slovak
sl	Slovene
StGB	Strafgesetzbuch (Criminal Code, Austria and Germany)
StPO	Strafprozessordnung (Code of Criminal Procedure, Austria and Germany)
sv	Swedish

TC of LAS	Terminology Commission of the Latvian Academy of Sciences
TCU	Translation Coordination Unit
TEAEC	Treaty establishing the European Atomic Energy Community (EURATOM Treaty)
TEU	Treaty on European Union (post-Lisbon)
TFEU	Treaty on the Functioning of the European Union
TransCert	Trans-European Voluntary Certification for Translators
TTC	Translation and Terminology Centre (Latvia)
UfR	Ugeskrift for Retsvæsen, Denmark
UKHL	United Kingdom House of Lords
UKSC	United Kingdom Supreme Court
UN	United Nations
VAT	value added tax
VGH	Verwaltungsgerichtshof (German Court of Appeal for Administrative Matters)
vol.	volume

Chapter 1
Language and Culture in EU Law: Introduction and Overview

Susan Šarčević

Introduction

The accession of Croatia to the EU on 1 July 2013 provided an opportune occasion for European scholars and EU practitioners to gather at the Jean Monnet Inter-University Centre of Excellence in Opatija for a multidisciplinary conference to discuss the vital role of language and culture as driving forces in the dynamics of EU law. The chapters in this volume are based on the papers presented at the conference although all of them have been expanded and fine-tuned. Each chapter examines certain aspects of the unique role of language and culture in shaping EU law, which is founded on the principles of linguistic and cultural diversity. The goal therefore is not only to investigate the multilingual and multicultural character of EU law, but first and foremost to show how multilingualism and multiculturalism have influenced its development.

Since EU law is made by the EU institutions but must be integrated into national law and applied by the national courts, the linguistic and cultural processes at work have a direct impact on both EU and national law. The pluralistic character of the authorship enables the multi-levels of these interactive processes to be examined from a multitude of perspectives. First, there are 'insider' and 'outsider' perspectives. Quite logically, the insider perspectives are provided by the practitioners who work in the EU institutions and have a hand in shaping these processes from within, while the scholars from European universities present the perspectives of 'outsiders' who are active participants in these processes at national level. Second, the views presented are multidisciplinary in nature thanks to the mixed backgrounds of the authors who include both lawyers and linguists representing a wide variety of specialist domains. The academic authors on the legal side are from the areas of European private and public law, comparative law and philosophy of law, on the linguistic side from translation studies, terminology studies, cultural studies and communication studies. The practitioners from the EU institutions also have mixed backgrounds: a lawyer-linguist from the legal department of the Council and a linguist from the Commission's Directorate-General of Translation (DGT) who is a specialist for quality management.

The individual chapters cover a broad spectrum of topics, all of which shed light on two complementary but also contradictory strands running throughout the book – the linguistic and cultural diversity of EU law, on the one hand, and the desire and need to build unity in diversity, on the other. Two dynamic processes of Europeanization are at work to achieve this goal: the creation of a common language for expressing EU law that will be equally 'foreign' to all Member States (chapters 5, 6, 7, 8)[1] and the construction of a common European legal culture of shared values and standards (chapters 2, 6, 10).[2] Another common leitmotif that stands out is the vital role to be played by educators and universities in shaping these processes with the aim of building a 'common culture' through the Europeanization of legal education (chapters 2, 5 and 10).[3] From the insider point of view, a 'shared culture' already exists and is founded in the treaties of primary law (Chapter 3). At the level of secondary law, outsiders, especially comparative law scholars, have joined forces throughout Europe in an attempt to create a common terminology in areas of private law as a precondition for achieving greater harmonization aimed at removing barriers to cross-border transactions (Chapter 2).[4] As a result, considerable progress has been made over the past decade by the completion of the academic Draft Common Frame of Reference (DCFR),[5] which has been followed up by the Commission's Proposal for a Common European Sales Law (CESL) (Chapter 5).[6]

These efforts have resulted in a new variety of a neutralized English[7] which is taking on the role of a *lingua franca*. Instead of diminishing the need for translation, the use of a neutral *lingua franca* opens up new frontiers for legal translation in which EU translators have the task of deculturalizing their national

1 See Dannemann (2012: 96–119); also Pozzo (2012: 184–200).

2 See Helleringer and Purnhagen (2013: 3–15) on the impact of a European legal culture; also Smits (2007: 143–51) who describes legal culture as 'mental software'.

3 On the Europeanization of legal education, see Arzoz (2012), also Simantiras (2013), who discusses the possibility of building a common culture through legal education. Citing the advantages of the McGill Law School's programme of trans-systemic law teaching, De Mestral suggested over a decade ago that students would 'cease to think in terms of a single national legal paradigm' if law were taught from a multi-systemic perspective at European universities (2003: 805–6). In this context the Europeanization of higher education in other areas should also be mentioned, especially the EMT – European Master's in Translation (see Chapter 13).

4 See Dannemann et al. (2007: XXXIII–XL); also Ajani and Rossi (2006: 90).

5 In light of the DCFR and other events since the publication of his celebrated book *A New European Legal Culture* (2001), Hesselink speaks about a transformation from a 'rather formal, dogmatic and positivistic legal culture into a more substance-oriented and pragmatic European legal culture' (2013).

6 See Perfumi's analysis of the DCFR and the CESL and their role in the emergence of a common contract law terminology which could lead to a 'shared European culture'. As she puts it: 'In striking a balance between unity and diversity, a common terminology should express at the same time a shared European culture and the respect of diversity in language, culture and traditions' (Perfumi 2013: 135).

7 Robertson (2012: 1233) regards EU legal English as a new genre.

languages in order to create a common EU legal terminology to express uniform concepts Union-wide (chapters 5 and 8). An insider explains how EU translators are dealing with this problem in a case study of the translation of the CESL (Chapter 9). Different approaches are taken on the issue of translation strategy and the role of comparative legal analysis in EU translation (chapters 7 and 9).[8] Although insiders boast of 'absolute concordance'[9] between the equally authentic texts of EU legislation, obviously such equivalence cannot be achieved in practice. As a result of the inherent imperfections of legal translation, the Court of Justice of the European Union (CJEU) must strike a proper balance to ensure the uniform interpretation and application of EU law, while respecting linguistic and cultural diversity and the right of EU citizens to legal certainty (chapters 2 and 4). In practice, the main burden of applying EU law falls on the national courts, some of which have come up with innovative methods of coping with the increasing number of official languages (Chapter 4).[10] Uniform law can be achieved only by establishing autonomous EU concepts. However, the multilingual and multicultural character of EU law raises serious questions as to the viability of the autonomy of EU concepts, a premise of EU law established by the case law of the CJEU (chapters 6 and 10). Judges of new Member States face multiple problems when called upon to apply EU law,[11] which provides a testing ground for the reliability of the translations of the *acquis* produced during the pre-accession period (chapters 11 and 12).[12] Linguistic and cultural diversity also plays a role in the area of criminal justice, where action has been taken at EU level requiring all Member States to provide court interpreting of 'sufficient quality' to all accused persons and suspects (if needed), thus guaranteeing their right to a fair trial (Chapter 13). Looking into the future, all actors participating directly or indirectly in the production, interpretation and application of EU multilingual legislation at EU and national level, insiders and outsiders, old and new Member States, are encouraged to cooperate in shaping the linguistic and cultural processes driving the dynamic development of EU law, taking care at all times to strike a proper balance between unity and diversity.

The book is divided into three parts. Part I lays the groundwork by reflecting on the relationship between law, language and culture in the EU and by introducing

---

8 In this context, see Šarčević (2012: 96–102); also Kjær (2007: 72).

9 According to Lönnroth (2008: 12), former Director-General of the DGT, the task of EU translators is to achieve absolute concordance of all language versions of EU legislation; cf. Kjær (2007: 84–6), who regards this as a 'contradiction in terms', which she discusses in detail in Chapter 6 of this volume.

10 For a detailed analysis of the methods of interpretation used by the CJEU and national courts, see Derlén (2009); on the multilingual and multicultural legal reasoning of judges at the CJEU, see Bengoetxea (2011: 107).

11 See Kühn (2005: 563–82) on the application of EU law in the new Member States in light of the historic enlargement of 2004.

12 On translation procedures and preparations to translate the *acquis* in candidate countries, see Šarčević (2001: 76–91).

the main topics. Emphasis is placed on challenges in EU multilingual lawmaking and the interpretation of EU multilingual legislation and case law at national level. The key role of language in the Europeanization of private law takes centre stage, as does the call for a European legal culture. Legal translation is presented as a tool of comparative legal analysis playing a significant role in the harmonization of European private law.

Part II focuses on translation in the multilingual and multicultural context of EU law. The first two chapters deal with theoretical issues, the last two are practice-oriented. The theoretical discussion is opened with thought-provoking reflections on the paradoxical relationship between language, translation and the autonomy of EU law. While it is generally agreed that a comparative approach is required in EU legal translation, a hypothetical situation depicting the two classic approaches to translation strongly suggests that too much comparative analysis is an unnecessary burden for EU translators and even for lawyer-linguists. In this respect, the insider perspective reminds us that high quality translation in all language versions is a precondition for the proper functioning of EU law and that readability and comprehensibility are also criteria for assessing quality. All translators must deal with new problems arising as a result of the increased use of English as a *lingua franca*, which is an inevitable pragmatic solution that brings not only advantages but also disadvantages.

Part III shifts the focus to concepts, terminology and court interpreting. The stage is set by raising the sensitive issue of the viability of the autonomy of EU concepts, a premise of EU law which is of crucial importance for ensuring uniform interpretation and application Union-wide. Attention is then shifted to the new Member States and problems encountered by candidate countries in their endeavour to create the entire vocabulary of EU law in their national language for the purpose of translating the *acquis*. Following a multilingual approach to EU term formation, the important issue of terminology harmonization is dealt with at the level of the term and the concept. Finally, all Member States are encouraged to cooperate in developing uniform standards for court interpreting in order to ensure successful implementation of Directive 2010/64/EU.

Part I: Law, Language and Culture in the EU

Michele Graziadei opens the discussion in Chapter 2 by calling for a new European legal culture. In retrospect he attributes past failures of legal scholars to 'map the development of a new European legal culture' to the fact that they ignored the multilingual dimension of EU law. In his opinion, multilingual legislation opens the door to an understanding of law that places greater emphasis on the normative forces and communicative practices underlying the development of law across Europe. Commenting on the application of EU multilingual legislation by the CJEU and its effects on citizens, he reminds us that the wording of a text serves only as the starting point for interpretation, which is primarily teleological in nature. While this enables the CJEU to establish a uniform meaning despite linguistic divergences between the authentic language versions, it also leads to legal uncertainty for EU citizens and can even clash with the principle of equal authenticity, which is contrary to the very purpose of multilingual legislation. According to Graziadei, one of the many preconceptions of lawyers about the relationship between law and language is the idea that law is inextricably linked to the language in which it is expressed, thus implying that different languages cannot express the same law. In his view, such preconception is not warranted. Instead, he sees the main reason for divergent interpretations of EU multilingual legislation in the failure to establish uniform concepts and a uniform referential system at EU level. Legal harmonization across Europe cannot succeed unless all those responsible for achieving the uniform application of EU law share a common understanding of EU legislation. To this end, he encourages the ongoing work by the EU legislator, legal scholars and the CJEU to establish a uniform set of common concepts shared Union-wide. Furthermore, the successful 'drafting' of multilingual legislation requires the ability to foresee how the terms used in the different language versions will be interpreted in practice. This underlines the important role of comparative legal linguistic work, which, in his opinion, is essential for the development of legal translation studies and intercultural communication in multilingual Europe. This leads the author to conclude that 'the birth of a new legal culture in multilingual Europe' will be the product, among other things, of a new awareness of 'sophisticated linguistic needs'.

Chapter 3 by Colin Robertson shifts the perspective to that of an 'insider', an EU lawyer-linguist engaged many years in checking and revising draft EU multilingual legislative texts before final adoption. In his analysis of the interfaces of law, language and culture in EU multilingual law, Robertson gives us a close-up view of the dynamics of EU law by explaining how EU multilingual law is made in the EU institutions, with special emphasis on legal and linguistic considerations that come into play during the legal-linguistic review of a text in a single language (vertical dimension) and the alignment of all language versions (horizontal dimension) so as to ensure terminological consistency within a single language and across languages, as well as the 'best possible quality in all language versions and the closest equivalence in message between them'. The author provides a wealth of information on the relationship between EU and national law, the sources of EU concepts, inevitable cultural shifts in meanings that pose a risk to readers who are versed only in the national legal culture, the effects of linguistic borrowing on the national languages as a result of the translation process, and much more. As a long time 'insider' in the EU institutions, there is no doubt in Robertson's mind as to the existence of an EU legal culture: 'The shared culture of the EU is founded on the primary treaty texts. These are negotiated and signed by the Member States. They have a double function since they are rooted in the legal culture and language of international law, but they create the legal system and culture of EU law.' As regards the structure of the chapter, each of the interfaces of law, language and culture is examined from four viewpoints: law, language, policy and action, which the author originally imagined as providing methods for checking and revising legislative texts legal-linguistically but later also used for the purpose of analysing terminology. In addition to scrutinizing the production of EU legislation, Robertson offers insight into the second vital stage in the life of every EU legislative text, that is, its interpretation and application by the courts, thereby providing a transition to the next chapter.

Focusing on the multilingual interpretation of EU legislation and case law, Chapter 4 by Mattias Derlén examines the important role of the CJEU and above all that of the national courts of the Member States, which he regards as the 'key players in the practical application of EU law'. Derlén's two labels 'single text' and 'single meaning' signify opposite approaches to multilingualism in legislation and case law that have left their mark on the multilingual interpretation of EU law by national courts. According to Derlén, legislation follows 'full multilingualism', where all languages are '*de jure* equally authoritative' and all language versions together in dialogue are regarded as expressing a 'single meaning'. On the other hand, CJEU judgments are authentic in one language only. Thus, the multilingual regime of CJEU case law is characterized by the idea of a 'single text', indicating the 'existence of a *de jure* original' that, at least in theory, is 'alone decisive in interpretation'. Drawing on cases decided by national courts in five Member States, he shows that national courts use both of the above approaches when interpreting EU law, however, 'without adhering to the distinction between legislation and case law'. Although the single meaning approach is now required by settled case law and is considered crucial for ensuring the uniform interpretation and application of EU law, it is challenged by the existence of two *de facto* originals: English in legislation and French in case law. Moving beyond the English-dominated drafting of EU legislation, Derlén explains the language regime of CJEU case law, pointing out that CJEU judgments are still drawn up exclusively in French, translated into the language of the case, if it is not French, and then into the other languages. Since French remains the sole working language of the CJEU, it has retained a notable grip on the interpretation of EU case law, despite the fact that, for practical purposes, judgments are authentic only in the language of the case. Today, as Derlén concludes, national courts are caught in a realm of uncertainty, forcing them to come up with innovative methods of dealing with the multilingual character of EU law and the increasing number of official languages. In numerous cases they are blending the two approaches of a single meaning and a single text, as a result of which the 'role of official languages in the interpretation of legislation and CJEU case law is in a state of flux'.

Chapter 5 by Barbara Pozzo introduces the topic of legal translation from the perspective of a comparative lawyer. As the author points out, 'Legal translation has always been considered an important tool for comparative law analysis'. In comparative law, translation is a complex intellectual activity involving several operations at the level of the concept: understanding the 'deep meaning' of the source concept, identifying a corresponding concept in the target legal system and comparing their similarities and differences. Constantly confronted with the conceptual incongruity of different legal systems, comparative lawyers develop a keen awareness of the inherent links between law, language and culture, making them excellent candidates to assume a major role in constructing the new European legal order. According to Pozzo, problems of legal translation take on a new dimension in the multilingual and multicultural context of EU law 'where the aim of secondary legislation is to harmonize rules with a view to guaranteeing equal rights to all EU citizens'. In the area of European private law, comparative lawyers rose to the challenge and set out to create a common European terminology in the Draft Common Frame of Reference (DCFR), which lays down fundamental principles and model rules in contract law and other areas of private law. The author's main interest is the 'new' language of the DCFR. Although drafted in English, this is not the English of the common law but a neutral English 'associated with a classic civil law background'. The definitions in the DCFR take on the important function of making suggestions for the development of a uniform European terminology. However, as Pozzo stresses, the quest for a uniform terminology at European level would be meaningless without a consistent theory of interpretation of multilingual texts. In order to retain their harmonizing role, shared concepts need to be interpreted according to the same hermeneutical principles. In light of the dominant role of English in the harmonization process, in her view, the new challenge for EU translators will be to translate from a hybrid language that has been deculturalized or, as she says, 'is not connected with a given system of values'. This is already the case, for instance, in the Commission's Proposal for a Regulation on a Common European Sales Law (CESL), which is based to a large extent on the DCFR.

Part II: Legal Translation in the EU

Dealing with theoretical aspects of legal translation in the EU, Chapter 6 by Anne Lise Kjær is a thought-provoking discussion on the paradoxical relationship between language, translation and the autonomy of EU law in which she raises the question whether legal translation in the EU is really translation or whether it is something different that needs a new theoretical construction. The point of departure is the basic paradox of equal authenticity and translation: none of the 24 equally authentic language versions has the status of an original text and none is designated as a translation. Thus the traditional definitions of source and target text no longer apply. Similarly, the idea that the meaning of the single instrument is the collective meaning of all the authentic texts taken together is totally foreign to translation studies. Kjær's aim is to explain how it is possible that, from the theoretical point of view, translating EU law is a contradiction in terms, while in practice EU translation really works. The crux of her analysis focuses on another basic paradox that goes to the very heart of EU law, exposing the contradictory relationship between its multilingual and multicultural character and the premise of the autonomy of EU concepts, which, according to the CJEU, are semantically independent from the national legal systems. In this context, Kjær reopens the debate that has engaged comparative law scholars for almost 20 years, raising the question 'whether it is possible to establish a common legal language in Europe across the divergent national legal languages and cultures'. In her view, not only is a common European language emerging as a result of the increasing use of English as a *lingua franca* but also a common European discourse which is used by EU lawyers and judges and is distinct from national discourses. According to Kjær, speech acts by the CJEU declaring concepts to be autonomous 'affect communities of lawyers at both European and national levels, enabling the development of a new unity above and across linguistic and cultural diversities'. As for EU legal translation, it works because it involves the reproduction of hybrid texts in 24 languages. Furthermore, the semantic independence of autonomous concepts is ensured by producing linguistic precedents which become almost binding in the sense that they must be repeated in each language and across languages, thus resulting in horizontal texts which are deemed to have the same meaning.

In Chapter 7, C.J.W. (Jaap) Baaij presents a hypothetical situation in which he applies Schleiermacher's views on the two classic translation strategies in literary translation to the EU context. Focusing on the relationship between EU and national law, Baaij raises the question how much knowledge EU translators and lawyer-linguists need of their national law and culture in order to achieve sufficient legal or linguistic equivalence in translations of EU legislative texts so as to ensure uniform interpretation in the respective Member State(s). In essence, his main aim is to determine 'the burden of legal knowledge and comparative skills' that each approach would hypothetically require of EU translators and lawyer-linguists if the EU would commit to either approach. Baaij opens the debate by introducing the two opposite approaches to translation, which he calls 'familiarization' and 'exteriorization'. He then builds the case for each of the two approaches, applying them analogously to the translation of EU legislation. The familiarization approach, which finds support in translation theories such as functionalism, entails the production of a receiver-oriented target text that 'loosens' syntax and uses terminology familiar to the target legal cultures, with the aim of achieving equivalent legal effects in all language versions. On the contrary, the source-oriented exteriorizing approach advocates reproduction of the source text by following the syntax as closely as possible and using terminology that is foreign to the target legal cultures, with a view to achieving linguistic equivalence across all language versions. In his conclusions Baaij notes that the familiarizing approach would demand a significant burden of legal knowledge and comparative skills, thus requiring additional training on the part of translators and lawyer-linguists. In addition, a complete restructuring of the current institutional arrangements would be required in order to group translators and lawyer-linguists according to national legal systems. Conversely, the exteriorizing approach would require only a 'nominal awareness' of their national law and culture in order to know which national terms not to use. To this end, no additional legal training and skills would be required and no restructuring of the institutional arrangements.

Since a mixed approach is excluded, such rationale tilts the balance decidedly in favour of exteriorization, which is essentially literal translation.

EU law is sometimes described as a law without a common language; however, as Annarita Felici shows in Chapter 8, despite the EU's strong multilingual policy, English has assumed the unofficial role of a *de facto lingua franca*. In light of the growing number of EU official languages, this is an inevitable pragmatic solution, but the question arises whether the advantages of translating from a *lingua franca* outweigh the disadvantages. Examining the nature of English as a *lingua franca* (ELF), in general, and EU legal English, in particular, Felici confirms that the latter is a non-native variety of ELF with features of general English that distinguish it from standard legal English, making it useful as a vehicular language for texts drafted primarily by non-native speakers. Since the first EU texts in English were translations from French, both terminology and drafting style are shaped by the continental legal tradition and Romance language influence. Void of cultural specificity, EU legal English is neutralized to the greatest extent possible, thus enhancing its translatability, while also supporting the goal of establishing a new European culture, which has been dubbed an 'aculture' in translation studies. From a linguistic point of view, the limited inflection of English and its morphological flexibility make it relatively easy to form new terms, sometimes blending different concepts into a single term. At the same time, the generic concepts and indefinite semantics of EU legal English make it a useful 'diplomatic tool' for expressing compromises and ensuring a mix of national interests. On the other hand, the fuzziness and imprecision of English also lead to unwanted ambiguities and consequently to misinterpretations. The text itself is produced by a large number of authors from different cultural and linguistic backgrounds, who often import their own syntax, stylistic features and drafting conventions into the *lingua franca*. In conclusion, Felici regards ELF as 'both a problem and an opportunity for EU legal translation'. Nonetheless, she concludes that 'ELF seems to be the sort of English that best serves the Union's needs'.

Chapter 9 shifts the focus to quality and quality management, but what is quality? According to Ingemar Strandvik, quality manager at the DGT, 'quality is a matter of meeting needs and expectations' (ISO 9000 standard for quality management systems). Thus, as he points out, it is natural for the different actors and stakeholders in EU multilingual lawmaking to have different perceptions of quality. Making a distinction between quality issues inherent in multilingual lawmaking and quality perceptions related to norms, beliefs and values, Strandvik suggests that 'beliefs and values about legislative quality and legal translation determine how the work is organized, how drafting guidelines are applied and, consequently, what the resulting texts actually look like'. As for EU drafting guidelines, he finds a discrepancy between theory and practice. Although Guideline 1 of the *Joint Practical Guide* requires legislation to be 'clear, precise and concise', in practice, legal and linguistic complexity is the rule rather than the exception. This is in sharp contrast to his native Sweden where legal professionals have 'learned to express legal complexity in clear writing without jeopardising legal precision', thus ensuring clarity and predictability, which are at the top of Strandvik's list of quality requirements for legislation, including translations. Citing Koskinen (2008), Strandvik remarks that EU translators are often caught between conflicting norms and beliefs, one of which is fidelity. While fidelity to the source text may be the overriding concern, he encourages translators to be faithful to the receivers by striving to produce texts that will be understood by citizens, administrators and judges of the target language with the aim of promoting uniform application of EU law by national courts. In his opinion, the choices made by translators of multilingual legislation should depend on the text in question and the way it relates to their own language, culture and national legal system. As an example of best practice, Strandvik cites the findings from a case study he carried out on the translation of the Common European Sales Law (CESL), showing how the Commission organized this high profile translation assignment with a view to ensuring the highest quality possible.

Part III: Terms, Concepts and Court Interpreting

In Chapter 10, Jan Engberg tackles the sensitive issue of whether the autonomy of EU concepts formulated in different languages is fact or fiction. A linguist by training, Engberg examines the issue from the perspective of Knowledge Communication, which presumes that knowledge about legal concepts can be exchanged only through language. As Engberg points out, the notion of autonomous EU concepts developed in the case law, dating back to the landmark decisions in *Costa* and *CILFIT*. Since then, it has acquired the role of a 'premise upon which fundamental principles of EU law are built' and is thus central to the notion of EU law as a supranational legal order. At the offset, Engberg investigates the characteristics of the EU concept of consumer in the negative definition in Article 2(2) of Directive 97/7/EC in English, French, German and Danish. The fact that the essential characteristics of the concept differ in the respective language versions sheds doubt on whether this basic concept in the consumer protection *acquis* can be perceived as autonomous. This doubt is further intensified when Engberg shows that these differences are rooted in the traditional conceptualization of the corresponding concepts in the respective national legal systems. In the theoretical part Engberg examines language-carried concepts through two descriptive lenses, which, consciously or unconsciously, correspond to the opposing views taken by legal scholars in the debate initiated in the 1990s on the feasibility of developing a European legal culture. Engberg's first lens, which he refers to as culture, represents the collective dimension of language, according to which 'what one experiences in world is actually *constituted* by language' (Legrand 2008). Seen through this lens, the idea that EU legal concepts expressed in different languages can be perceived as autonomous is inconceivable. The second lens, referred to as interpersonal communication, focuses on the creative power of individual language users to influence the collective through interpersonal communicative actions. Seen through this lens, the autonomy of EU concepts is feasible as part of a learning process, for example, through communicative interaction with university professors. Combining the lenses leads to different conclusions highlighting the need for the EU to shape meanings in the different EU languages and the possibility of developing 'shared culture knowledge'.

Chapter 11 by Susan Šarčević deals with the formation of terms to designate EU legal concepts and institutions as part of the EU multilingual lawmaking process, in general, and by candidate countries for the purpose of translating the *acquis*, in particular. Arguing for a systematic approach to EU term formation, the author attempts to identify some basic principles and propose criteria for creating EU terms which will guarantee effective communication by promoting the uniform interpretation and application of EU law. The stage is set by examining sources of EU concepts and stressing the need to create neutral and transparent terms in the original drafting language which can be easily translated into all languages without unwanted connotations. The process of secondary term formation, which is one of translation, is characterized as a tension between creativity and conformity, in which translators and terminologists are encouraged to satisfy target user expectations by being creative with language, but at the same time are under constant pressure to align terms on the other languages with the aim of achieving conformity across languages, at least visually. Attempting to shed light on the thought process underlying the choice of terms, the author focuses on the linguistic, cultural and legal dimensions of term formation, warning translators and terminologists not to fall into the trap of 'blindly' accepting EU neologisms and internationalisms. In support of her plaidoyer for a multilingual approach to EU term formation, examples are cited from as many languages as is practical, including both the 'old' and 'new' languages. Special emphasis is devoted to problems of new Member States and candidate countries, which are advised to implement best practices of term management in their Herculean endeavour to create the entire vocabulary of EU law in their national language during the pre-accession period. This includes, among others, the standardization of terms, which is a precondition for effective communication in EU law. New Member States are encouraged to establish post-accession coordination between national bodies and the EU institutions, with the aim of reminding EU translators and terminologists of their duty to strike a proper balance between creativity and conformity, thus preventing them from totally submerging in the 'aculture' prevailing inside the EU institutions.

In Chapter 12, Maja Bratanić and Maja Lončar examine the topic of EU terminology harmonization from the perspective of terminology studies and their experiences in terminology projects in Croatia prior to accession. From a theoretical standpoint, the goal in multilingual settings such as EU law is to achieve terminology harmonization and thus terminological consistency within a single language and across languages. However, as the authors show, in reality the harmonization of EU terminology is a myth on both national and EU level. Despite efforts to coordinate the development of EU terminologies at the level of the term and the concept, the entries in IATE, Euramis and *EuroVoc* reveal that inconsistent terminologies continue to be created. This chapter attempts 'to identify the main linguistic and extra-linguistic causes' of terminological inconsistency based on the 'example of the translation of the *acquis* by candidate countries, in this case Croatia, and to provide an overview, albeit not systematic, of various causes, both systemic and pragmatic, contributing to such mismatching'. In the theoretical part a distinction is made between primary and secondary term formation and applied to the multilingual context of EU law. Ideally, in multilingual primary term creation, new concepts are lexicalized simultaneously in more languages, thus excluding the need for translation. In practice, however, multilingual primary term creation takes place in two steps: primary term creation in one or more languages followed by secondary term creation, that is, the lexicalization of existing concepts in the other languages by translation. Theoretically, translating terminology is an onomasiological process that commences at the concept level by first comparing the conceptual systems in question and then finding or creating an equivalent in the target languages for a given source term. As the authors show, this process often becomes semasiologically oriented in practice, especially in the translation of the *acquis* by candidate countries. Although terminological consistency is a condition of legal certainty, translations of the *acquis* are often plagued by terminological inconsistency at both the level of the term and the concept. After explaining several pragmatic reasons for the lack of terminological consistency, the authors identify linguistic sources of disharmonization, citing examples from the Croatian translations of the *acquis* made in the pre-accession period.

Chapter 13 by Martina Bajčić deals with the implementation of the Directive 2010/64/EU on the Right to Interpretation and Translation in Criminal Proceedings of 20 October 2010 in the Member States and its implications for the profession of court interpreters Union-wide. With the goal of providing access to justice across language and culture, the Directive extends the basic right to interpretation (free of charge) to suspects and accused persons who do not understand the language of the proceedings, thus guaranteeing a fair trial in accordance with Article 6 of the European Convention on Human Rights. The Directive requires common minimum rules to be adopted in all Member States; however, as Bajčić points out, these rules must be 'Strasbourg-proof' in the sense that they meet the standards of the ECHR and settled case law of the European Court for Human Rights. The right to interpretation in criminal proceedings is not limited to the trial but includes the investigation, police questioning and other pre-trial activities as well. Moreover, the right is not restricted to court interpreting in the narrow sense but also covers the written translation of 'essential documents'. As regards this and other vague provisions in the Directive, Bajčić cites relevant German transposing provisions as examples of how vague wording can be concretized in the national implementation instruments. Particularly sensitive and challenging is the requirement that the interpretation and translation provided must be of 'sufficient quality' to safeguard the fairness of the proceedings. Satisfying this requirement is crucial not only for the success of the Directive but also provides an opportunity to review and improve the status of court interpreters throughout the EU. According to Bajčić, attempts to make court interpreting more uniform throughout Europe should proceed on two tracks: the educational or institutional and the professional. To this end, she encourages institutions of higher learning to establish specialized training programmes for court interpreters which focus on the development of interdisciplinary competences. At EU level, EULITA (European Legal Interpreters and Translators Association) is taking concrete steps to mobilize national professional associations with the aim of improving the quality of court interpreting throughout Europe. However, as Liese Katschinka, president of EULITA, remarks: 'The EU's ambitious goal of facilitating linguistic support for suspects, accused, witnesses and victims who are not fluent in the language of the court is still far from becoming a reality.'[13]

References

Ajani, G. and Rossi, P. 2006. Multilingualism and the coherence of European private law, in *Multilingualism and the Harmonisation of European Law*, edited by B. Pozzo and V. Jacometti. Alphen aan den Rijn: Kluwer Law International, 79–93.

Arzoz, X. (ed.) 2012. *Bilingual Higher Education in the Legal Context: Group Rights, State Policies and Globalisation*. The Netherlands: Brill/Nijhoff.

Bengoetxea, J. 2011. Multilingual and multicultural legal reasoning: the European Court of Justice, in *Linguistic Diversity and European Democracy*, edited by A.L. Kjær and S. Adamo. Farnham: Ashgate, 97–122.

Dannemann, G. 2012. In search of system neutrality: methodological issues in the drafting of European contract law rules, in *Practice and Theory in Comparative Law*, edited by M. Adams and J. Bonhoff. Cambridge: Cambridge University Press, 96–119.

Dannemann, G., Ferreri S. and Graziadei, M. 2007. Consolidating EC contract law terminology: the contribution of the terminology group, in *Principles of the Existing EC Contract Law (Acquis Principles)*. Contract I, prepared by the Research Group on the Existing EC Private Law (Acquis Group). Munich: Sellier European Law Publishers, xxxiii–xl.

De Mestral, A. 2003. Bisystemic law teaching: the McGill programme and the concept of law in the EU. *Common Market Law Review*, 40, 799–807.

Derlén, M. 2009. *Multilingual Interpretation of European Union Law*. Alphen aan den Rijn: Kluwer Law International, 183–202.

Helleringer, G. and Purnhagen, K. 2013. On the terms, relevance and impact of a European legal culture, in *Towards a European Legal Culture*, edited by G. Helleringer and K. Purnhagen. Oxford: Hart, 3–15.

13 See Katschinka's message at: http://www.aptij.es/img/doc/EULITA-transposition%20expired.pdf.

Hesselink, M. 2013. The new European legal culture: ten years on, in *Towards a European Legal Culture*, edited by G. Helleringer and K. Purnhagen. Oxford: Hart, 17–24.

Kjær, A.L. 2007. Legal translation in the European Union: a research field in need of a new approach, in *Language and the Law: International Outlooks*, edited by K. Kredens and S. Goźdź-Roszkowski. Frankfurt am Main: Peter Lang, 69–95.

Koskinen, K. 2008. *Translating Institutions: An Ethnographic Study of EU Translation*. Manchester: St. Jerome.

Kühn, Z. 2005. The application of European law in the new member states: several early predictions. *German Law Journal*, 6(3), 563–82.

Legrand, P. 2008. Word/world (of primordial issues for comparative legal studies), in *Paradoxes of European Legal Integration*, edited by H. Petersen, A.L. Kjær, H. Krunke and M.R. Madsen. Aldershot: Ashgate, 185–233.

Lönnroth, K.-J. 2008. Efficiency, transparency and openness: translation in the European Union. Speech at the XVIII World Congress of the International Federation of Translators in Shanghai (2008), 1–21. Available at: http://ec.europa.eu/dgs/translation/publications/presentations/speeches/20080801_shanghai_en.pdf.

Perfumi, C. 2013. Constructing a common contract terminology, in *The Transformation of European Private Law: Harmonisation, Consolidation*, edited by J. Devenny and M. Kenny. Cambridge: Cambridge University Press, 130–47.

Pozzo, B. 2012. English as a *lingua franca* in the EU multilingual context, in *The Role of Legal Translation in Legal Harmonization*, edited by C.J.W. Baaij. Alphen aan den Rijn: Kluwer Law International, 183–202.

Robertson, C. 2012. EU legal English: common law, civil law or a new genre? *European Review of Private Law*, 20(5–6), 1215–39.

Simantiras, N. 2013. A common culture in European legal education? A constitutional approach on applied pluralism, in *Towards a European Legal Culture*, edited by G. Helleringer and K. Purnhagen. Oxford: Hart, 223–42.

Smits, J.M. 2007. Legal culture as mental software, or: how to overcome national legal culture? In *Private Law and the Many Cultures of Europe*, edited by T. Wilhelmsson, E. Paunio and A. Pohjolainen. Alphen aan den Rijn: Kluwer Law International, 143–51.

Šarčević, S. 2001. Translation procedures for legal translators, in *Legal Translation: Preparation for Accession to the European Union*, edited by S. Šarčević. Rijeka: Faculty of Law, University of Rijeka, 75–109.

Šarčević, S. 2012. Coping with the challenges of legal translation in harmonization, in *The Role of Legal Translation in Legal Harmonization*, edited by C.J.W. Baaij. Alphen aan den Rijn: Kluwer Law International, 83–107.

PART I:
Law, Language and Culture in the EU

Chapter 2
Law, Language and Multilingualism in Europe: The Call for a New Legal Culture

Michele Graziadei[1]

Introduction

The unique linguistic regime in which European law operates constitutes part of the complex system of lawmaking established by the European Treaties. Until recent years, the problems and opportunities arising within the framework of the EU linguistic regime were not high on the agenda of mainstream scholarly research. Brilliant forward-looking efforts, such as those to map the development of a new European legal culture, still ignored the challenges and consequences of the choice to frame the law in a plurality of languages across the European space.[2] This situation is changing. The Court of Justice of the European Union (CJEU) is regularly confronted with the problem of how to deal with discrepancies among the various language versions of EU legislation. Abundant specialist literature exists on the drafting, interpretation and application of multilingual EU law in the 24 official languages of the European Union, as well as on the challenging translation issues connected to this dynamic. This chapter therefore does not intend to discuss that linguistic regime and the institutional arrangements making it possible, nor does it comment on the state of the art in the related field of translation studies concerning EU law.[3]

The purpose of this chapter is rather to address a point not fully elucidated so far, that is, how the culture of the community of lawyers involved in the application

---

1 The research for this chapter was partly funded by the University of Torino under the agreement with the Compagnia di San Paolo 'Progetti di Ateneo 2011' (project title: 'The Making of a New European Legal Culture: Prevalence of a Single Model, or Cross-Fertilisation of National Legal Traditions?') coordinated by the author of this chapter. The author is indebted to Prof. Susan Šarčević for her helpful comments and suggestions.

2 Scholars who disagree in other respects share at least this observation; see, for example, Kjær (2008: 150) and Glanert (2012: 137).

3 Three contributions in this volume are enlightening in this respect: chapters 3, 6 and 9 by Robertson, Kjær and Strandvik, respectively. One may also profit from several recent publications by the DG for Translation (DGT) in the series *Studies on Translation and Multilingualism*, in particular: Document quality control in public administrations and international organisations (2013), Study on language and translation in international law and EU law (2012), Study on lawmaking in the EU multilingual environment (2010).

of European law in the Member States is changing as a result of efforts to cope with the multilingual dimension of EU law.

My argument is that there is still a tendency in Europe to succumb to general ideas about the relationship between language and the law that obscure the complex nature of the process leading to the application of legal rules. Multilingual legislation displaces theories about the relationship between law and language which rely on those ideas by pushing both lawyers and linguists to understand how (and under which conditions) normative texts drafted in different languages can result in convergent interpretative practices. Multilingual legislation thus opens the way to an understanding of law that invites less unthinking reliance on the normative virtues of texts as such, placing more attention on the normative forces and communicative practices underlying the development of the law across Europe.

Many Languages for a Single Voice

EU citizens can expect to be bound by European legislation available in at least one of their languages. This expectation is based on, if not protected[4] by the current EU linguistic regime establishing that the EU has 24 official languages. According to this regime, EU regulations and other documents of general application must be drafted in all official languages of the EU institutions.[5] Granted, there are EU citizens who do not know any of the official languages in which EU law is enacted, just like there are Italian citizens who are unable to express themselves in Italian or who cannot understand legislation written in Italian. To a certain extent, therefore, the linguistic regime of the law is based on a normative presumption which does not necessarily match the facts.[6] When the tension between norm and facts becomes incompatible with basic human rights standards, the law must accommodate more stringent linguistic regimes tailored to the needs of the individual. In this case, it cannot resort to a fiction which presumes that the EU official languages are understood by EU citizens or non-EU citizens residing in

4 The linguistic regime of EU legislation was probably designed having in mind that the Treaty is binding on the Member States, but the expectation mentioned above in the text is defensible in light of developments of the law under the Treaty. See Case C-161/06, *Skoma-Lux sro* v. *Celní ředitelství Olomouc* [2007] ECR I-10841.

5 According to Article 55(1) TEU, all language versions of the Treaty are authentic. The linguistic regime of EU legislation is set out in Regulation No. 1 determining the languages to be used by the EEC (OJ L 17, 6.10.1958, at 385), as amended (see Art. 342 TFEU). Note, however, that not all official languages of the Member States are EU official languages: Luxembourgish, an official language of Luxembourg since 1984, and Turkish, an official language of Cyprus, are not official languages of the EU.

6 This tension has multiple dimensions which will not be discussed here, such as the claim that the EU commitment to multilingualism is undermined by a tendency to resort to one or more vehicular languages in the production of its norms.

or travelling in the EU. For this reason, Directive 2012/13/EU of 22 May 2012 on the right to information in criminal proceedings provides suspects or accused persons with certain basic information rights that must be guaranteed in criminal proceedings. Those rights include, among others, the right to an interpreter or a translator – free of charge – to get access to essential information concerning the proceedings in a language that he/she understands, and to enable him/her to communicate with a defence lawyer (see Chapter 13 by Bajčić in this volume). Leaving this possibility aside, by opting for 24 official languages, the European Union intends to make its law accessible on equal terms, at least in principle, in all official languages of the Union, as mentioned above.

Nonetheless, by now it is clear that, in cases where the various language versions of the Treaty or secondary legislation diverge, EU citizens have no right to rely on the provision in the language they are consulting, which is usually the language (or one of the languages) of the country of their nationality or residence. The CJEU has repeatedly denied such right in several well-known cases (for details see Baaij 2012: 217–31). Given the initial premise, that is, the equal authenticity of all language versions of instruments of EU law, this outcome is bound to be controversial and difficult to reconcile with the principle of legal certainty (see Graziadei 2014; also Šarčević 2013: 4–11).

Confronted with such case law (and the problems caused by the necessity to draft EU legislation in a growing number of official languages), commentators have addressed these sensitive issues and proposed reforms with a view to providing pragmatic solutions to the problems confronting national courts and litigants under the current linguistic regime of European law.[7] While these proposals are being considered, the cultural presumptions about the relationship between law and language undermined by the case law of the Court, and indeed by the entire linguistic regime of EU law, should not go unnoticed. These presumptions are widely shared across Europe, either consciously or unconsciously, by academics and the legal professions (as well as by members of the public). I will briefly address them in the following paragraphs, challenging conventional wisdom by presenting each in the form of a question.

7 See, for example, Derlén (2011: 157), who argues in favour of establishing French and English as mandatory consultation languages, while preserving the rule of the equal authenticity of all the language versions of EU legislation. A more radical solution is proposed by Schilling (2010: 64), who suggests that there be only one authentic version of every EU enactment. This, however, would turn the clock back to the time in which a single language (Latin) dominated the communicative aspects of the law. For an evaluation of these two proposals (and a third one), see Šarčević (2013: 17–25), who proposes concrete measures for improving the quality of EU multilingual legislation in an attempt to preserve the current linguistic regime. Other scholars acknowledge the need for reform but believe no changes are imminent in the foreseeable future, for example, Bengoetxea (2011: 98–105).

(Legal) Language: A Badge of Cultural Identity?

Today it would be foolish to argue that language is not a badge of cultural identity. The wealth of evidence elevating this point almost to a self-evident truth is impressive. Since antiquity, philosophers maintain that a distinctive trait of mankind is the ability to speak, thus establishing our identity as human beings by the innate ability to communicate through speech. Linguists show that an individual reveals essential information about his/her culture and socio-economic condition as soon as he/she begins to talk. Linguists and psychologists have debated whether and how cultural and cognitive categories are encoded by languages affect the way people think, suggesting that they think and behave differently depending on their language (Everett 2013: 255–72). Political scientists remind us that language policies adopted by States contribute to the formation of a certain collective cultural identity. Lawyers as well may regard language as a hallmark of cultural identity by drawing on a number of poignant observations from the field of law.[8]

Granted, language is now considered a badge of cultural identity, but culture and cultural identity are products of a number of different layers or components, pointing in different directions. Culture is not a cage; cultural differentiation and cross-cultural interactions have been the rule ever since the beginning of mankind. Culture changes over time under the influence of projects for the future and evolving notions of community. *Mutatis mutandis*, the language of the law, a language developed for special purposes, is also a cultural expression characterized by similar features.

For centuries the language of the law of the State in many continental countries was mostly Latin, a language that was understood and used by lawyers, but not necessarily by their clients. Along with Latin, Law French was one of the languages of the law in England, and remained so long after Anglo-Norman French ceased to be spoken by the ruling class of England.

Even today, where different languages are spoken by the population, a vehicular language is sometimes used to frame legislation or decide cases, although the language in question may be spoken or written only by a segment of the population. This can occur despite constitutional provisions providing for the

8 Unfortunately, lawyers may also accept this view when making language policy and deciding legal issues. Mertz (1982) shows how the US Supreme Court and other US courts endorsed a crude 'folk' version of the Whorfian theory (by assuming that languages shape the range of conceptualization of their speakers) in the period between the last quarter of the nineteenth century and the first half of the twentieth century. According to Mertz, these courts held that 'U.S. political concepts were thought to be inextricably entwined with the English language; the concepts could not be understood unless one spoke English'. The same author further notes: '[T]he appearance of a "Whorfian" premise in this folk theory also lends support to the suggestion by cognitive anthropologists that scientific theories are typically systematized adaptations of folk theories.'

equal status of several official languages.[9] As a vehicular language, that language may have distinctive features which distance it from the language spoken by native speakers.[10]

Multilateral treaties and conventions are written in a limited number of languages. Access to the authentic texts of international norms created by agreement is the privilege of those who know those languages in the jurisdictions where such norms are in force. Furthermore, even when the law is drafted in a language known by the people to whom it is addressed, relevant texts of the law may refer to a foreign system of concepts and rules, or even to a plurality of foreign systems of concepts and rules, without fully incorporating the system of values and philosophical notions underlying them. Countries which at first changed their laws by adopting local versions of foreign legal texts, such as Japan, are a telling testimony to this possibility, although such reception results in a high degree of hybridization and complexity of the language of the national law (Kitamura 1993). To a lesser extent, this is also true of the law of several European jurisdictions. Over the centuries, the language of the law in these jurisdictions has been enriched by a variety of loanwords and adaptations across a large number of legal fields, from commercial law to ecclesiastical law and constitutional law. In all contexts, much give and take has occurred across the European space because the peoples of Europe have shared broad socio-economic and cultural elements.[11]

When the CJEU rules against the language version of a provision consulted by one of the litigants in favour of other language versions, which in its opinion spell out the applicable rule, it reiterates the fundamental message that European law is enacted in different languages. The fact that the Court upholds this approach reminds us that the relationship between cultural identity, language and the law is more flexible than it is often considered to be, as I have argued. Actually it is flexible to the point that, under certain circumstances, a citizen may not be able to rely on the provision in question in the language he/she regularly consults. Furthermore, there are also cases where litigants before the Court invoke the rule in a language version *other than* their own.[12] Flexible to what point, one may ask?

9 On the South African situation, see Harms (2012).

10 See Chapter 8 by Felici in this volume; on the peculiar features of the CJEU's 'Court French', see McAuliffe (2011: 97–115).

11 In this sense one can speak of a common legal *discourse* without a common *legal language*; see Kjær (2004: 397). Kjær develops her ideas in Chapter 6 of this volume where she recognizes the increasing use of EU legal English as a *lingua franca* but views the development of a common legal discourse at EU level as the dominant factor making it possible for EU concepts to be perceived as autonomous.

12 See, for example, *Bayerische Hypotheken- und Wechselbank AG* v. *Edgar Dietzinger Environment and consumers*, Case C-45/96 [1998] ECR I-1199. In this case, the Belgian, Finnish, French and German Governments, relying on the English text of the relevant directive, argued that the guarantee obtained by the bank from a consumer was not a contract for the purpose of Directive 85/577 'because the guarantee is not a synallagmatic contract – namely a bilateral agreement involving mutual and reciprocal obligations or

The CJEU has held that an act adopted by an EU institution cannot be enforced against natural and legal persons in a Member State before they have the possibility to access the authentic text of the act in their own language in the Official Journal.[13] In operational terms, this is where the boundary is drawn.

The Message is in the Text: Is it Really?

Learning to read, write and master a specialized language takes a great effort, and such abilities are essential to survive as a lawyer in all modern jurisdictions. Law students spend most of their time reading a variety of legal materials and learning to write legal texts for various purposes. They learn the power of the spoken and written word as a tool to make the law. Sometimes they have the opportunity to reflect on the failure of both as an effective means of changing the law. And yet, the way students are socialized as lawyers leads to very different ways of understanding texts as sources of law, as does the practice of law itself.

One way to reflect on texts as sources of law is to look at them through the lens of the conduit pipe metaphor, which represents language as a sort of universal conduit pipe, conveying messages encoded in a particular language from speaker A to speaker B (see the seminal paper by Reddy (1979)). Unfortunately, languages are a poor means of communication for the purpose of establishing certain practices. Some messages would indeed be extremely difficult to grasp if they were expressed only in words. In his short comic novel *Portuguese Irregular Verbs* (2003: 9), Alexander McCall Smith makes fun of two German professors of philology who are on a tennis court for the first time and decide to play a game, using a tennis rule-book as their only guide to learn the sport. The hilarious results show how language may completely fail to convey a message explaining the organization of complex activities. It is arguable that the organization of such complex tasks as those governed by a variety of normative texts – tasks much more complex than playing tennis – cannot rely entirely on a message entrusted to verbal expression. Indeed, language is often the second best option to provide information even with respect to relatively simple matters such as getting directions. 'Take the third turn

duties – but a unilateral undertaking from the point of view of the guarantor' (Opinion of Advocate General Jacobs delivered on 20 March 1997, Case C-45/96 [1998] ECR I-1199, para.14, summarizing the submissions of the above-mentioned Governments). The UK Government, on the other hand, did not argue that the guarantee was outside the scope of the Doorstep Selling Directive.

13 C-161/06 *Skoma-Lux sro* v. *Celní ředitelství Olomouc* [2007] ECR I-10841; see also Case C-345/06 *Gottfried Heinrich* [2009] ECR I-01659 (part of a regulation that has not been published cannot be enforced against an individual who cannot, by the very nature of things, know what the regulation in question lays down).

on the right, and then the fourth on the left' is less clear than looking at a map![14] Nonetheless, 'as soon as speech, and the use of signs are introduced into any action, the action becomes transformed and organised along entirely new lines' (Vygotsky 1978: 24).[15]

On the other hand, lawyers know (although they may be reluctant to admit it!) that verbal propositions framing normative texts provide at best a linguistic cue to understanding the law as a form of practice. Read the text of any constitution and you will still not be a constitutional lawyer. Normative texts generally regulate only some aspects of a rule-bound practice. They focus on what is salient or patently needs to be settled and can ignore the rest. What remains implicit, nonetheless, may be just as relevant. Comparative lawyers have noticed this, and speak of cryptotypes to refer to tacit knowledge that influences how the law is applied (Sacco 1991: 343, 385; cf. Grossfeld and Eberle 2003). Lawyers are also confronted with misleading normative texts either because they reflect obsolete norms or provide dysfunctional legal regimes which gain little to no support in practice. In medieval England, claimants suing for trespass had to allege that they had been the victim of an injury caused by the defendant *vi et armis*. But quite often this was a fiction: no violence or weapons were necessary for realization of the tort.[16] Legal texts are recorded in linguistic signs standing for concepts and expressing rules that evolve and change over time through usage by professionals and lay persons. Unstructured concepts such as *good faith* are just the tip of the iceberg of a whole world of indeterminate linguistic signs.

The CJEU has rejected the literal approach to interpretation in a wide range of cases, holding that the wording alone often provides little guidance for ascertaining the meaning of the law. In light of the Court's preference for the teleological method of interpretation, it is fair to ask whether it is really worth making the effort to compare the various language versions of EU legislation, given that a functional approach to ascribing meaning to EU texts often prevails (cf. Derlén 2011: 156).

A step in the right direction is to openly acknowledge that EU legislation often contains linguistic signs with no established meaning. Their meaning is created and exists thanks to the activity of lawyers, scholars and judges who compare the different language versions of EU legislation, reflect on the purpose of the

14 Citing this example to illustrate the difficulty of using abstract terms of a language to give directions, Aitchison (1997: 23) concludes that the conduit pipe metaphor of language is misleading.

15 Sacco's work (1991) on cryptotypes and formants shows how similar insights are fundamental to understanding the relationship between law, language and action; see also Sacco (1995).

16 This is not a recent development in the law: Anon. (1304) Y.B. 32 & 33 Edw I, Roll Series, 259, reproduced in Baker and Milsom (1986: 297) . It is not by chance because, as Milsom (1981: xi) noted, 'The life of the common law has been in the unceasing abuse of its elementary ideas.' Of course, the same observation holds for other legal systems as well.

enactment, draw from their knowledge of the law, and collectively take a decision on which norms must be enforced, thus making European law evolve in a more or less uniform direction.

Considered from this perspective, the texts of European provisions are nothing but a focal point for the practice of creating norms, a support prompting individuals to work out meaning which was not there from the very beginning.[17] The structure of these practices determines the meaning eventually ascribed to the text.

This last point helps to clarify how it can happen that a certain provision produces the same regulatory effect, although the provision in question is drafted without using harmonized terminology and defining key concepts. A good example in this respect is provided by Directive 2002/47/EC of 6 June 2002 on financial collateral arrangements. The title and the text of this Directive in English studiously avoid reference to the notion of 'contract', with the exception of a single sentence in the entire text. On the other hand, the French and Italian versions of the Directive speak respectively of *contrats de garantie financière* and *contratti di garanzia finanziaria* to convey what the English version of the Directive calls *collateral arrangements*. The German version of the same Directive uses the term *Finanzsicherheiten*, while other versions of the same provisions, such as the Spanish, favour agreements (*acuerdos*) over financial guarantees. One could hardly think of more variations to designate the same concept. And yet, when consulting the various language versions of the Directive on this point, we find rules on the same type of transactions.[18] The subject is the same because the transactions covered by the Directive correspond to the same set of financial transactions structured by model master agreements drafted by major global market players.[19] On the other hand, other aspects of that instrument, such as reference to the notion of 'reasonableness', are not harmonized and will thus be interpreted in accordance with the national laws of the Member States (Graziadei 2012).

A Change in Language is a Change in the Law?

Lawyers have many preconceptions about the nature of the relationship between law and language. Among them is the idea that law is inextricably linked to the language in which it is expressed. Of course, natural languages *are* different. Even a modest exercise in legal drafting such as consolidating the consumer *acquis*

17 For a fundamental contribution on this aspect from the perspective of legal theory, see Kennedy (1998).

18 One would be tempted to add that, despite all its variations, the facts to which the story refers are still the same, as in Raymond Queneau's *Exercices de style*.

19 See Riles (2011) for a closer look at the practice generated by these agreements in different places.

in English for a European-wide audience poses problems as to what kind of language should be used for this purpose (Dannemann et al. 2007). And yet, the idea that different languages cannot express the same law is not warranted by the general observation that languages are different and that they possess different phonological, graphological, morphological, syntactic, semantic, pragmatic and stylistic structures, as well as socio-cultural backgrounds.[20] As has been rightly noted, this is just the beginning of the story (see Sin 2013: 929–51).

Multilingual uniform legislation could be adduced as *prima facie* evidence against the idea that it is impossible to express the same law in a plurality of languages, were it not for the circumstance that, contrary to the purpose of such legislation to unify the law across national boundaries, there is a good chance that it will lead to divergent decisions by the national courts of the States where it is in force. It is therefore tempting to analyse the failures of multilingual uniform legislation as compelling evidence of the fact that different language versions of the same rule produce conflicting meanings of the (uniform) enactment. Divergent interpretations of uniform texts would thus prove that each language is bound to communicate different meanings, even though the purpose and will is to adopt a common set of rules. As the argument goes, each language ultimately carves up the world in its own way.

Without taking issue with this last general assumption, which was the subject of lively debate among linguists and psychologists in the twentieth century, this is an unsatisfactory way to conceptualize the relationship between the law and its linguistic formulation(s). Uniform legislation produces divergent interpretations when the languages in which it enters into force do not denote the same concepts and express the same rules across national boundaries. Hence, divergent interpretations of uniform legislation do not occur simply because languages have a particular genius of their own, but because of the lack of uniformity at the conceptual level. In other words, the linguistic signs in the different authentic language versions do not always have the same referential meaning. Like legal translations lacking such basis, uniform legislation without a uniform referential system is also bound to fail.[21]

Accordingly, the problematic record of uniform multilingual legislation is not due to the nature of the tool employed to achieve the intended result, that is, sets of

---

20 I share the observations by Pozzo, in Chapter 5 of this volume, on the relationship between language, culture and the law.

21 In her fundamental contribution Šarčević (1997) shows that the lack of harmonization in multilingual EU terminology can be identified as a problem of conceptual discrepancy and must be tackled as such. In the field of computer science and jurisprudence, Sartor et al. (2011) address this problem from the perspective of the different legal ontologies underlying each legal system.

linguistic signs belonging to certain natural languages, but to the failure to use that tool to achieve the same referential meaning, for semantic[22] and syntactic reasons.[23]

A change in the language used to frame the law does not *per se* entail a change in the law; it does only when it involves a change in the referential system. For example, when France abandoned Latin in favour of French to draft its civil code, the change in the linguistic signs used to express the law did not change their referents at first. To take a vivid example of this dynamic and its limited consequences, the term *faute* mentioned in Art. 1382 Code civil has the peculiar meaning(s) highlighted in numerous comparative works,[24] not because it is somehow very French, but because it mirrors the (complex) meaning of the Latin term *culpa* in the *ius commune,* which was eventually rendered in French by the term *faute* (see Graziadei 2010: 126). The law did not change at first simply because a new linguistic sign was introduced; the sign was attributed the same semantic value as *culpa*.

German legal scholars followed a different strategy when they began to draft the law in German. Their commentaries introduced not only a new set of linguistic signs to express the law, but also new referents to sharpen the conceptual system of the law. This was a reaction to what they perceived as an overly unstructured approach to delictual liability. Confronted with the old notion of *culpa*, nineteenth-century German scholars systematically distinguished its various meanings, linking each of them to a different German linguistic sign. Placing greater emphasis on differentiating negligent and intentional wrongdoing, they distinguished these two elements from the objective element of wrongfulness. Eventually § 823 of the German BGB codified all these distinctions, thereby setting new boundaries to delictual liability. The languages of the law in Germany and France could begin to converge once more if both countries would opt for a new common terminology, or if the French would accommodate their language to make room to express more consistently the distinctions of delictual liability known in Germany.[25]

The failure to distinguish between the different layers of language and law when framing the same law in different languages may lead to major errors of perspective. One of these is the belief that the more distant two languages are from the linguistic point of view, the more difficult it is to render the concepts and rules of one legal system in the language of the other system. This is not necessarily true if the two languages in question share the same referential system.

---

22 Think of the possibility of ending up with a translation which does not recognize a foreign term as a false friend: Ferreri (2010); Honnold (1988: 208) warns in general terms against the 'natural tendency to read the international text through the lenses of domestic law'.

23 On this point see Chapter 7 by Baaij in this volume; see also Visconti (2010: 29 ff.).

24 See, for example, Markesinis and Lawson (1982: 185 ff.).

25 On the possibility of moving in this direction, see Borghetti (2008). On the development of French and German as languages of the law, see Šarčević (1997: 29–53).

For example, when the Hong Kong ordinances were first translated into Chinese in preparation for the return of Hong Kong to the People's Republic of China in 1997, a whole new vocabulary had to be created to express the common law concepts in Chinese. Since the new terms were assigned a common law meaning, the Chinese texts derive their meaning from the English source texts, not from Chinese law. As a result, the Chinese expression for *merchantable quality* derives its meaning from the common law concept in the Hong Kong Sale of Goods Act, which, in turn, is modelled on the English Sale of Goods Act (on this point Sin 2013: 939–40; see also Šarčević 1997: 274–5).

The process of creating terms (signs) to designate uniform concepts in different languages requires considerable skill and expertise (however, the same applies to other aspects of the language as well).[26] When choosing terms to designate new concepts or objects (referents) one can either create a new term (neologism) or assign a new meaning to an existing word or phrase. A general feature of word formation is the tendency to use an existing sign to denote a new referent.[27] Different languages, however, may choose different words to denote the same object or referent, depending on how the new association between the sign and referent or object is established. For example, when glasses[28] were invented in Europe, they were called *occhiali* in Italian, *lunettes* in French, *gafas* in Spanish and *Brille* in German. Each of these words evokes a different association linked to the same object. The German word is derived from the name of the crystal that was originally used to make lenses. The French word refers to the shape of glasses, *lunette* being a diminutive of the word *lune* (moon). In Spanish the name is taken from the curved stem that bends behind the ear to hold the lenses in place in front of the eyes. The Italian name for glasses is derived from *occhi*, the word for eyes. The English word was initially associated with the idea of glasses for the eyes (eye-glasses).

When using a term, the associations or connotations it evokes in a particular language should always be taken into account. In the field of law it is particularly important to avoid choosing terms which could evoke connotations having unwanted or negative implications for the development of the law. A lawyer, for example, should not translate *soviet* with *council* because of the political connotations of the first word.[29]

Drafters of multilingual legal instruments, interpreters and translators are constantly confronted with the problem of finding words which are sufficiently neutral so as to avoid unwanted meanings or connotational baggage (see

26 On this point see Chapter 11 by Šarčević and Chapter 12 by Bratanić and Lončar in this volume.

27 See, for instance, the example provided by Case 533/07 *Falco Privatstiftung and Thomas Rabitsch* v. *Gisela Weller-Lindhorst* [2009] ECR I-03327, discussed by Ioriatti Ferrari (2010: 320, note 28).

28 This example is cited in Alinei (2009: 77–8).

29 This example is from Sacco (1992).

Dannemann 2012: 96–9). EU legislation cannot have uniform effects nor can harmonization of national laws be achieved, unless EU multilingual lawmaking is accompanied by the development of a common set of concepts shared by all those involved in its application.

The CJEU is one of the principal agents advancing the quest for a common set of concepts. The Court's decisions disavowing the authority of one or more language versions of a EU normative text are motivated by the necessity to uphold the unity of European law. Such unity cannot be secured if the different language versions of EU legislation are interpreted and applied differently in the Member States. However, the CJEU's insistence on developing autonomous EU legal concepts also shows that determining which concepts constitute the essential building blocks of European law is a problem that can also surface within the semantic field of a single language (see chapters 6 and 10 in this volume by Kjær and Engberg). For this reason linguistic evidence does not *per se* determine the meaning to be assigned to a particular EU legal provision.

Conclusions

Recent scholarly research in law has repeatedly addressed the theme of the birth of a new European legal culture which is gradually developing in a variety of ways at multiple sites. All too often the missing piece in the story is how to build this new legal culture on the multilingual foundations provided by the present linguistic regime of the European Union.

This chapter makes the point that any contribution on law and culture which ignores the multilingual foundations of European law fails to recognize a fundamental aspect of the law in Europe today.[30] Every text enacted by the EU institutions raises the question of how it will be interpreted and applied across national boundaries. Multilingual legislation in Europe cannot produce uniform legal change or legal harmonization across Europe, unless all those responsible for achieving its uniform application share a common understanding of EU legislation. Lack of coherence in the application of European law is very often due to the fact that EU enactments cannot rely on a uniform set of concepts shared across the European space. The work towards building uniform concepts is ongoing. Furthermore, the framing of multilingual legislation requires a more general ability to explore the effects that linguistic signs will have in practice when used to express European law. This requires carrying out linguistic and legal

30 On the other hand, some scholars show a strong awareness of this dimension; see, for example, the contributions in Wilhelmsson, Paunio and Pohjolainen (2007); also Glanert (2014). Moreover, this is the essential message elaborated by Pierre Legrand in his many challenging contributions on law, language and culture, in which he tends to show that there is no way out of the labyrinthine dimension of language (and of a specific culture). See also Kjær's and Engberg's comments in chapters 6 and 10 of this volume.

comparisons which are essential for the development of legal translation studies and for intercultural communication in multilingual Europe.

I began this chapter by insisting on the necessity to focus less on the normative virtues of texts as such, and more on the normative forces grounding the practice of law in Europe. I maintain my premise, however, my conclusion ends on a different note. The birth of a new legal culture in multilingual Europe will be the product of a new awareness of the various ways and means available to a multilingual lawmaker, as well as of sophisticated linguistic needs that must be satisfied to make the law a credible communicative act.

References

Aitchison, J. 1997. *The Language Web: The Power and Problem of Words*. Cambridge: Cambridge University Press.

Alinei, A. 2009. *L'origine delle parole*. Roma: Aracne Editrice.

Baaij, C.J.W. 2012. Fifty years of multilingual interpretation in the European Union, in *The Oxford Handbook of Language and Law*, edited by P. Tiersma and L. Solan. Oxford: Oxford University Press, 217–23.

Baker, J.H. and Milsom, S.F.C. 1986. *Sources of English Legal History: Private Law to 1750*. Cambridge: Cambridge University Press.

Bengoetxea, J. 2011. Multilingual and multicultural legal reasoning: the European Court of Justice, in *Linguistic Diversity and European Democracy*, edited by A.L. Kjær and S. Adamo. Farnham: Ashgate, 97–122.

Borghetti, J.-S. 2008. Les intérêts protégés et l'étendue des préjudices réparables en droit de la responsabilité civile extra-contractuelle, in *Études offertes à Geneviève Viney*. Paris: L.G.D.J., 145–71.

Dannemann, G. 2012. In search of system neutrality: methodological issues in the drafting of European contract law rules, in *Practice and Theory in Comparative Law*, edited by M. Adams and J. Bonhoff. Cambridge: Cambridge University Press, 96–119.

Dannemann, G., Ferreri, S. and Graziadei, M. 2007. Consolidating EC contract law terminology: the contribution of the terminology group, in *Principles of the Existing EC Contract Law (Acquis Principles)*. Contract I, prepared by the Research Group on the Existing EC Private Law (Acquis Group). Munich: Sellier European Law Publishers, xxxiii–xl.

Derlén, M. 2011. In defence of (limited) multilingualism: problems and possibilities of the multilingual interpretation of European Union Law in national courts, in *Linguistic Diversity and European Democracy*, edited by A.L. Kjær and S. Adamo. Farnham: Ashgate, 143–66.

Everett, D. 2013. *Language: The Cultural Tool*. London: Profile Books.

Ferreri, S. (ed.) 2010. *Falsi amici e trappole linguistiche: Termini contrattuali anglofoni e difficoltà di traduzione*. Torino: Giappichelli.

Glanert, S. 2012. Europe, aporetically: a common law without a common discourse. *Erasmus Law Review*, 5(3), 135–50.

Glanert, S. (ed.) 2014. *Comparative Law – Engaging Translation*. Abingdon: Routledge.

Graziadei, M. 2010. Liability for fault in Italian law: the development of legal doctrine from 1865 to the end of the twentieth century, in *The Development and the Making of Legal Doctrine (Comparative Studies in the Development of the Law of Torts in Europe)*, edited by N. Jansen. Cambridge: Cambridge University Press, 126 ff.

Graziadei, M. 2012. Financial collateral arrangements: Directive 2002/47/EC and the many faces of reasonableness. *Uniform Law Review*, 17, 497–506.

Graziadei, M. 2014. Many languages for a single voice: the heteroglossia of EU private law and the evolving legal cultures of Europe, in *Translating the DCFR and Drafting the CESL: A Pragmatic Perspective*, edited by B. Pasa and L. Morra. Munich: Sellier European Law Publishers, 69–83.

Grossfeld, B. and Eberle, E. 2003. Patterns of order in comparative law: discovering and decoding invisible powers. *Texas International Law Journal*, 38, 291–316.

Harms, L.T.C. 2012. Law and language in a multilingual society. *Potchefstroom Electronic Law Journal*, 15(2), 21–31.

Honnold, J. 1988. The Sales Convention in action – uniform international words: uniform application? *Journal of Law and Commerce*, 8, 207–12.

Ioriatti Ferrari, E. 2010. Draft Common Frame of Reference and terminology, in *A Factual Assessment of the Draft Common Frame of Reference*, edited by L. Antoniolli and F. Fiorentini. Munich: Sellier European Law Publishers, 313–34.

Kennedy, D. 1998. *A Critique of Adjudication (fin de siècle)*. Boston: Harvard University Press.

Kitamura, I. 1993. Problems of the translation of law in Japan. *Victoria University of Wellington Law Review*, 23, 1–40.

Kjær, A.L. 2004. A common legal language in Europe, in *Epistemology and Methodology of Comparative Law*, edited by M. Van Hoecke. Oxford: Hart Publishing, 377–98.

Kjær, A.L. 2008. Language as barrier and carrier of European legal integration, in *Paradoxes of European Legal Integration*, edited by H. Petersen, A.L. Kjær, H. Krunke and M.R. Madsen. Aldershot: Ashgate, 149–56.

Markesinis, B. and Lawson, F. 1982. *Tortious Liability for Unintentional Harm in the Common Law and the Civil Law*. Cambridge: Cambridge University Press.

McAuliffe, K. 2011. Hybrid texts and uniform law? The multilingual case law of the Court of Justice of the European Union. *International Journal for the Semiotics of Law*, 24, 97–115.

McCall Smith, A. 2003. *Portuguese Irregular Verbs*. New York: Anchor Books.

Mertz, E. 1982. Language and mind: a Whorfian folk theory in United States language law. Sociolinguistics Working Paper Nr. 93, July. Available at: http://ccat.sas.upenn.edu/~haroldfs/540/theory/mertz1.html [accessed 1 December 2013].

Milsom, S.F.C. 1986. *Historical Foundations of Common Law*. 2nd edition. Cambridge: Cambridge University Press.

Reddy, M.J. 1979. The conduit metaphor: a case of frame conflict in our language about language, in *Metaphor and Thought*, edited by A. Ortony. Cambridge: Cambridge University Press, 284–324.

Riles A. 2011. *Collateral Knowledge: Legal Reasoning in the Global Financial Markets*. Chicago: University of Chicago Press.

Sacco, R. 1991. Legal formants: a dynamic approach to comparative law II. *American Journal of Comparative Law*, 39, 343–401.

Sacco, R. 1992. *Introduzione al diritto comparato comparato*. 5th edition. Torino: Utet.

Sacco, R. 1995. Mute law. *American Journal of Comparative Law*, 43, 455–67.

Sartor, G., Casanovas, P., Biasiotti, M. and Fernández-Barrera, M. (eds) 2011. *Approaches to Legal Ontologies: Theories, Domains, Methodologies*. Dordrecht, Heidelberg, London and New York: Springer.

Schilling, T. 2010. Beyond multilingualism: on different approaches to the handling of diverging language versions of a Community law. *European Law Journal*, 16, 47–66.

Sin, K.K. 2013. Out of the fly-bottle: conceptual confusions in multilingual legislation. *International Journal for the Semiotics of Law*, 26, 927–51.

Šarčević, S. 1997. *New Approach to Legal Translation*. The Hague: Kluwer Law International.

Šarčević, S. 2013. Multilingual lawmaking and (un)certainty in the European Union. *International Journal of Law, Language & Discourse*, 3(1), 1–29.

Visconti, J. 2010. Piccole insidie e grandi danni: connettivi e preposizioni, in *Falsi amici e trappole linguistiche. Termini contrattuali anglofoni e difficoltà di traduzione*, edited by S. Ferreri. Torino: Giappichelli, 29–50.

Vygotsky, L.S. 1978. *Mind in Society: The Development of Higher Psychological Processes*, selected and edited by M. Cole, V. John-Steiner, S. Scribner and E. Souberman. Cambridge, MA: Harvard University Press.

Wilhelmsson, T., Paunio E. and Pohjolainen, A. (eds) 2007. *Private Law and the Many Cultures of Europe*. Alphen a/d Rijn: Kluwer Law International.

Chapter 3
EU Multilingual Law: Interfaces of Law, Language and Culture

Colin Robertson[1]

Introduction

This chapter takes a look at EU multilingual law from perspectives of law, language and culture. The aim is not to examine substantive issues, but instead to reflect on some of the influences which operate on EU law from a viewpoint of interfaces. The law of the European Union is a relatively new phenomenon, as it has been in existence for only 60 years. The idea of states voluntarily agreeing to allow themselves to be constrained by laws and policies created through international institutions over which they have limited control has not been widespread historically. The 'raw materials' in terms of methods and ideas to construct this new system of supranational law must come from somewhere. One can explore the sources of ideas and study the ways in which they have been woven into the ongoing story of European integration, of which EU law forms a major strand. The obvious approach is to study books of history on European integration and the EU. However, there is another approach, which is investigated here, and that is to reflect on some of the underlying processes and mechanisms, seen in essentially functional terms. Here one is looking not so much at who did what and when but rather more at basic methods and techniques, viewed impersonally. It is a technical point of view. In it the particular identities of the players and the particular historical details are placed in the background, to be replaced by attention to structural issues and operational methods and choices. Similarly, it is not a case of analysing how certain theories, in particular economic theories, are applied through EU law, but rather of reflecting on the tools that are used to that end, in particular the tools of law and language. As a living organism EU law is a site of engagement of many influences and selecting the additional viewpoint of 'culture' represents an attempt to consider ways in which competing values and interests that exist within and between Member States come together and are mediated through the process of creating EU legislative texts that receive widespread support. The primary focus of attention here is the EU legal text, and the aim is to reflect on interfaces that act on the text and influence its formal structure, its contents and its language. The primary focus is on legislative rather than court or other legal texts.

1 All comments are purely personal.

The starting point is from the view of a practitioner of law and language engaged over many years in checking and revising draft EU multilingual legislative texts before final adoption, signature and publication. For simplicity, it is called a 'lawyer-linguist' viewpoint. From this perspective, accuracy of legal texts, immediacy of details, urgency of tasks and the need to find solutions to terminology problems within and across languages play a prominent role. For legislative texts, the issues that loom large centre around obtaining agreement by all negotiating partners and working towards texts that comply with the requirements of EU law, EU legislative drafting methods and a high quality of language to achieve the desired legal effects. Each EU legislative text goes through a process of drafting, translation into all EU languages, scrutiny, amendment, and legal-linguistic review and alignment of all language versions. Within this environment, the task of EU lawyer-linguists is to ensure the best possible quality in all language versions and the closest equivalence in message between them. But that is equally the aim for all participants (on quality, see Chapter 9 by Strandvik in this volume).

Each EU legislative act takes the form of a linear text that moves from a beginning to an end, but each part of it is worked on carefully and intensively and bears witness to the impact of a variety of influences. Among these one can cite influences touching on form that relate to the structure and format of the texts. Here there are influences deriving from legal considerations where, for example, there is a need to indicate the treaty provisions that confer the powers to make a subordinate act such as a regulation or directive. But there are also linguistic issues, such as the type of verb to use in different parts of the act: verbs of command, such as *shall*, for the enacting provisions (articles), conditional verbs, such as *should*, for the recitals which explain and justify the contents of the act. Third come influences deriving from the contents of each act, such as the actions or legal effects sought and the policy field(s) under contemplation. All these are set against a background of the interests, needs and cultures within the Member States (and third countries) which generally have the ultimate responsibility to implement the act, transpose its provisions into their national legal systems and generally ensure that the rules are observed.

EU Legislative Texts and Viewpoints

Each EU legislative text is written with the aim of bringing about some action or change to EU law and/or to the laws of the Member States, and because of that function each text becomes a site of engagement and interaction for a multitude of forces and pressures. This potentially turbulent environment is subject to a high level of control and discipline to ensure that the most efficient results can be achieved. The institutions and the staff employed as officials oversee, guide and advise on the processes in that respect. On the one hand there are the methods by which each text is produced, for example through negotiation in accordance with the rules of procedures of the institutions, such as the Council's Rules of

Procedures[2] and in accordance with procedures established by treaty (such as the *ordinary legislative procedure*, referred to in Article 294 TFEU). On the other hand, each text must comply with the terms of the relevant treaty (TEU, TFEU, TEAEC, etc.), which comprise *primary law*,[3] as well as the general rules of law and principles laid down over the years by the Court of Justice of the European Union (see Rosas et al. 2012). Yet there are other influences that operate on each text, for there is the human dimension; the texts are generally drafted within the European Commission which has the monopoly for proposing EU legislation (Article 17 TEU[4]); they are checked and revised by officials, experts and politicians in each Member State, working with administrators and lawyers in the Council of the European Union;[5] they are similarly studied and amended by members of the European Parliament[6] working with their officials; they are checked by other institutions and bodies, as well as by national parliaments in accordance with the type of act and type of procedure.[7] In each case, those involved in studying the text bring to bear their knowledge, experience, language and culture. It is this circumstance that provides the underpinning to the work of the EU institutions and the quality and acceptance of the legislative texts within the Member States. Each text reflects a balance in terms of the interests of the participants and a synthesis in terms of the policy and results sought from the act, expressed through language adapted to a multilingual and multicultural environment.

The shared culture of the EU is founded on the primary treaty texts. These are negotiated and signed by the Member States. They have a double function since they are rooted in the legal culture and language of international law, but they create the legal system and culture of EU law. They confer legal personality on the EU (Article 47 TEU) and so now the EU is clearly distinct from its Member States. It has its own institutions: the European Parliament, European Council, Council, European Commission, Court of Justice of the European Union, European Central Bank and Court of Auditors (Article 13 TEU), as well as other bodies and organs (see Chalmers et al. 2010: 52–89). Each institution and body comprises members drawn from the Member States, whether it be Commissioners, members of the European Parliament or the heads of state and government and their ministerial colleagues who preside and constitute the European Council and the Council

2 Council Decision of 1 December 2009 adopting the Council's Rules of Procedure (2009/937/EU) (OJ 325, 11 Dec. 2009, at 35); see http://eur-lex.europa.eu/LexUriServ/LexUriServ.do?uri=OJ:L:2009:325:0035:0061:en:PDF. All web-based references in this chapter were live and accessed on 12 November 2013.

3 See, *inter alia*, http://europa.eu/legislation_summaries/institutional_affairs/decision making_process/l14530_en.htm.

4 See also http://www.europarl.europa.eu/ftu/pdf/en/FTU_1.3.8.pdf.

5 See http://europa.eu/about-eu/institutions-bodies/council-eu/.

6 See http://europa.eu/about-eu/institutions-bodies/european-parliament/.

7 On the role of national parliaments in EU lawmaking, see http://euromove.blog activ.eu/2013/11/05/what-role-for-national-parliaments-in-eu-law-making/.

of Ministers. In each case the persons involved share in the collective decision-making processes that give rise to EU law and EU policies. In so doing they bring to the table their national interests, culture, experiences and needs.

For the practitioner, involved in the process of preparing, checking and reviewing the draft legislative texts in the different language versions, what matters is that the final text expresses the collective wishes accurately, efficiently and effectively. The lawyer-linguists have the task of checking all language versions while the texts are still in draft (see Guggeis and Robinson 2012: 64–70). This involves reviewing issues of legal form and style, language and terminology, but also that the legal effects of each language version align as far as possible. The texts are frequently complex and efficient working methods have been devised.

In Robertson (2010a) it was suggested that EU legal texts could be reviewed from the perspective of four different viewpoints: law, language, policy and action. Taking each in turn, one is led to reflect on different issues and implications concerning the text and in that way review their efficiency and effectiveness; it forms part of quality control. For example, a 'law view' leads to studying issues that relate to the legal powers, form and structure of the act in terms of EU law, but also the legal policy being followed and legal implications for the Member States when it comes to implementing the act. A 'policy view' leads to a study of the general field in contemplation (agriculture, budget, competition, environment, social policy)[8] and how the new texts fits within the pre-existing arrangements within the area of policy under consideration, as well as other policy areas of EU law since there is invariably interaction between them. A 'language view' leads to checking the structure and layout of the text, the way the sentences are structured, the syntax, spelling and terminology. Since these express also legal and policy ideas there is of course an overlap, but the language viewpoint also leads to considering how the different language versions fit together, interrelate and form a whole single multilingual text. Lastly, there is the 'action view'. This involves asking for each term, phrase, sentence, paragraph and article why it is there and what it is intended to do. Is the meaning clear? Can the reader understand and predict the intended action? To which one can add: does each language version lead to the same legal effects in each provision? The action view provides a test of equivalence of terminology across languages, because if the answer is 'yes', then it provides a degree of confidence in what are frequently highly subtle and complex domains. One should bear in mind that each draft legislative text is a projection into the future; it lays down future legal provisions and every effort is made to ensure as far as possible that the desired results will be understood by readers in the way intended by the authors. The difficulty, however, for the lay-reader is that frequently EU legal texts are primarily written for specialists. This is part of EU culture.

Taking each of these four points of view and reflecting on implications for EU legal texts leads gradually on towards thinking about the influences that lie

8 On EU policies, see http://ec.europa.eu/policies/.

behind each text, as well as the influences that will lie in front of it in the future and govern how it is read, understood and implemented. The EU is a 'dynamic' organization that is constantly responding to new circumstances, pressures and deep-level political balances within the Member States and that is reflected in the constant flow of new texts. This 'dynamic' dimension exists, because the purpose of EU texts is generally to bring about changes within the national law of the Member States. One can see this in the concept of EU 'directive', which is defined in Article 288 TFEU as being 'binding as to the result to be achieved, upon each Member State to which it is addressed, but shall leave to the national authorities the choice of form and methods'. Such acts allow time for transposition into national law.

The relationship between EU law and the law of the Member States may perhaps most simply be described in terms of 'conditionality'. It is a condition of mutual dependence. On the one hand, EU law is dependent on the Member States for its existence, since they created it by treaty. The function of EU law is to regulate national law as regards the matters set out in the treaties in accordance with the secondary legislative (and other) acts made under them. On the other hand, the national law of each Member State has become heavily influenced by, and to that extent dependent on, the law of the EU at supranational level. With agriculture and fisheries the EU has mainly taken over responsibility (Article 38 TFEU),[9] but in other areas the relationship is somewhat different, with the balance varying according to policy field. In the case of environmental policy the national law of the Member States is heavily influenced by EU legislative acts and law.[10] Why enact measures under EU law? With environmental law it is because environmental problems cross borders and the market for goods and products is European. National laws cannot solve problems created in neighbouring countries. It is possible, and normal, to regulate cross-border issues by international agreement, but the texts need to be signed and ratified by each state and that takes time, sometimes a long time, sometimes never. The EU provides an institutional environment, with meeting rooms, secretariats, language and translation facilities for 24 languages (more if needed), established procedures and working methods, and experts on hand to guide and help achieve the desired results within shorter periods of time. This is a functional role.

We see from this set of relationships between adjacent European states that there are three types of context in operation: the national legal systems of Member States, international law governing relations between them, and EU law which functions 'above' (supranational) and 'between' them. We can see this in terms of a 'matrix' (Robertson 2011) and we can use it as a starting point to explore interfaces of law, language and culture in EU multilingual law.

---

9 See also http://ec.europa.eu/policies/agriculture_fisheries_food_en.htm.

10 See the European Environmental Law Network at: http://ec.europa.eu/policies/agriculture_fisheries_food_en.htm.

Interfaces of Law

The viewpoint of law is useful when considering terminology because it leads to thinking about the precise legal context of words and terms. The meaning of legal terms derive from their legal context and are specific to the legal system in which they function, although there tends to be broad overlap between culturally related legal systems, as where civil law systems have shared terms from Roman law and common law systems have shared terminology from English law. However, EU law does not really fit these concepts of legal system, because it starts from entirely different positions, namely the operation of markets, competition and international relations. The function of EU law is not to regulate civil society, its institutions and legal relationships between people (covering matters of status, transfer of property, etc.); rather it is to coordinate methods of economic production and trade as between states and economic operators. In that respect it might be classified under a heading of mercantile law (which also includes law relating to companies and businesses), with a focus on international markets and competition, which is an area generally regarded as different from civil law and common law (Robertson 2012a). A second point is to ask whether EU law can be thought of in terms of being a legal system. To answer that question goes beyond the present scope, but for the present purpose we can take the view that it endeavours to be systematic and to exhibit the features that one expects of a legal system.

It is convenient to consider EU legal language in terms of a separate genre (Robertson 2012a). Such a view is consistent with the legal perception of EU law as being a separate 'legal order' with potential direct effects over national law, as ruled by the Court of Justice on 5 February 1963 in Case 26–62 *van Gend en Loos*.[11] Following the concept of 'matrix', EU law is located between the other two legal orders of national and international law; it has been created from international law through treaties and regulates primarily the national law of the Member States. One can explore the relationships between the legal orders in legal terms, but also in linguistic and cultural terms. Further, one can search for influences and implications at the level of the individual texts, but also within each text at the level of individual terms and their meanings. The practical benefit to be drawn from such an approach derives from emphasizing the need to think carefully in each instance about how every text or term stands in relation to the three legal orders. Within a national legal system, taken on its own, that may not be a major issue since the national rules, concepts and terms generally prevail, but within EU law and draft EU legislative texts, it becomes an issue, because concepts and terms have generally come from somewhere else and also because the EU text is generally intended to have effects within national systems or within international law, all of which comprise different legal and semantic contexts. In practice that means that EU texts and terms come into close relationship with national law

11 Case 26–62 NV *Algemene Transport-en Expeditie Onderneming van Gend & Loos* v. *Netherlands Inland Revenue Administration* [1963] ECR 1.

texts and, therefore, terminology, and they are read side by side by readers who may be versed only in the national legal culture, with a risk of conferring different meanings on terms from the ones intended by the EU drafters. With international law texts, placed alongside EU texts, there is probably less risk as readers generally already have high levels of awareness of cultural shifts in meanings. Reading and understanding legal texts implies being versed in the legal culture within which they have been created; education is an important factor here.

Some EU legal texts derive from international law texts, for example from United Nations resolutions[12] or the World Trade Organization.[13] It is possible that the EU text then becomes a starting point for transposition into the national legal systems, or it may remain at the EU level for direct application if in the form of a regulation (Article 288 TFEU). In such a case, we can see a sort of legal, and linguistic, 'cascade': an international text made, say, by the UN is transposed into the EU legal order by an EU legal act, which in turn is transposed into the law of the Member States. The Member States could have perhaps transposed the UN text directly into their systems, but where the EU has 'competence' it is for the EU to act on their behalf, which in practice means in close consultation with them. On the other hand there may be 'shared' or 'mixed' competence which means that the Member States and the Commission act for the areas they have responsibility; we enter into complex legal territory here. Copyright law is a field where there are legal texts at the international level (Berne Convention for the Protection of Literary and Artistic Works[14]), EU level (Directive 2001/29/EC on the harmonization of certain aspects of copyright and related rights in the information society[15]) and national law level (UK Copyright, Designs and Patents Act 1988[16]). The practical legal, and linguistic, questions concern concepts, terminology and meanings at each level: are they the same? The answers depend on a close analysis of the relevant texts, each in their context. But should an issue arise in a court case involving litigation between opposing parties concerning those texts, then a range of other factors come into play in addition to specifically linguistic ones relating to the text in question: facts, rules of law, legal meanings to be drawn from each text, legal hierarchy between texts and between meanings, choice of law, etc. In such contexts the interfaces can be complex on all levels.

The interplay of factors regarding EU legal texts are possibly at their most intense with respect to two stages in the life of a legal text: first, at its creation; second, at its interpretation, in particular when interpreted by the courts in the context of a dispute. We can take these as two reference points to study interfaces of law, language and culture. If we take first the context of a draft EU legislative text, we start by asking where it is to fit in the system: primary treaty text or secondary

12 See http://www.un.org/en/sc/documents/resolutions/.

13 See http://www.wto.org/.

14 See http://www.wipo.int/portal/en/index.html.

15 OJ L 167, 22 June 2001, at 10.

16 Available at: http://www.legislation.gov.uk/ukpga/1988/48/contents.

or tertiary implementing text? The answer to this question points to aspects of form and structure: a treaty text takes one form, and we can find out what form by looking at past EU treaties. A secondary or tertiary level EU act may be one of several types as laid down by treaty, for example regulation, directive, decision, recommendation or opinion (Article 288 TFEU). For their structure one studies the EU legislative guidance, in particular the *Interinstitutional Agreement of 22 December 1998 on Common Guidelines for the Quality of Drafting of Community Legislation*, the *Joint Practical Guide for Persons involved in the Drafting of European Union Legislation* and the *Manual of Precedents for Acts established within the Council of the European Union*. These texts are all the product of prior discussion and negotiation so that if one wishes to examine the interfaces further, one should refer to the processes by which these guidance texts themselves were constructed. There is a background of national law practice and methods, as also international law methods, in the guidance as to how the EU secondary and tertiary legal acts are to be structured. Similarly as regards the operations that are applied to legal texts, whether it be amendment or consolidation, which in EU jargon is referred to as *codification*,[17] deriving from French concepts of types of codification. In the case of the legal procedure for rectifying material errors in legislative texts, the procedure in Article 79 of the Vienna Convention on the Law of Treaties 1969[18] is adapted to the EU context (*Manual of Precedents for Council Acts*: 163–6).

While the formal structure and the basic requirements of an EU legislative act are essentially laid down in advance for the act, each act implements policy and provides for legal consequences and effects. In this context, there are influences of many kinds that come to be exerted on the text. Most of these relate to the policy contents. The legal dimension consists in ensuring the contents are coherent, systematic, consistent with existing EU law (treaties, other legislative acts, case law, general principles of law, etc.) and that the texts conform to standards of legislative quality.

If we now turn to the interpretation side of the EU legal text, there are two aspects to bear in mind: the first concerns the meaning(s) to be given to each EU multilingual text; the second concerns, in the event of a dispute, the court process that surrounds the interpretation of the text. It is of interest to reflect on this latter aspect because it can have a bearing on how the text is interpreted and therefore on the meanings given to it. We find the matrix of laws is relevant also to the court side. The Court of Justice of the European Union (Court of Justice, General Court and Civil Service Tribunal)[19] is the ultimate arbiter on the meaning of EU legal texts, but all national courts interpret and apply EU texts (on practices of national courts, see Chapter 4 by Derlén in this volume). In that sense every national court

17 See explanation at: http://ec.europa.eu/dgs/legal_service/codifica_en.htm.

18 Available at: http://treaties.un.org/doc/Treaties/1980/01/19800127%2000-52%20AM/Ch_XXIII_01p.pdf.

19 See http://curia.europa.eu/jcms/jcms/Jo2_6999/.

is a 'EU court', for EU law is not like federal law with federal courts to apply it. National courts make references to the Court of Justice pursuant to Article 267 TFEU to clarify the meaning of EU texts where there is doubt or dispute. In such cases generally the parties are persons subject to national law and there is a dimension that relates to national law, perhaps also international law, as well as the provisions relating to EU law. The law on sex discrimination is an example here.[20]

Court cases and procedures can be regarded as coming within the 'law' view, although we could equally classify them in terms of legal policy. They play a role in determining the meaning to be drawn from EU legal texts. An EU legal act may potentially come up for scrutiny and interpretation in any court in any legal order. A range of questions touching on legal interfaces arises: which court has jurisdiction? Which system of law applies to the court's procedure, to questions of evidence and how facts are proved? Which system of law is to be applied by the court to the case? Each party to an action is subject to legal rules governing their status and their rights to pursue or defend an action. Can the issue be resolved without recourse to EU law? Language itself can be a legal issue, as where there are legal rules regarding choice of language. The relationship between legal texts, how they interrelate and which takes precedence are also legal issues. There are also rules, or legal methods, for interpreting texts (for example broad or narrow approaches) and these can vary according to the legal system that is being applied. Thus English statutory interpretation has the *literal rule*, the *golden rule*, the *mischief rule*, the *purposive approach*.[21] For EU interpretation the *teleological approach* is well known (see Derlén 2009: 43–7). An interesting legal analysis of comparative methods of statutory interpretation is presented by Murray (undated). These various factors are not evident 'on the surface' as regards the meaning attached to EU legal acts, but they lie behind in the background like submerged 'icebergs' and can have an indirect influence.

Interfaces of Language

Like the law viewpoint, language is all-embracing since legal texts are linguistic products, thus requiring one to clarify at the outset the range of topics under contemplation. To that end it is proposed to draw a distinction between 'vertical' and 'horizontal' linguistic issues. The former is intended to refer to a single language and all the texts that have been, are being or may in the future be created within that language. The latter, on the other hand, is intended to refer to all the languages taken together in parallel, seen from above, as it were; the image of a line of language 'soldiers' marching in step gives a flavour. Thus one can consider interfaces in terms of the internal dynamics within each language, but also in terms

20 See http://ec.europa.eu/justice/gender-equality/rights/.

21 On statutory interpretation in the UK, see http://www.e-lawresources.co.uk/Statutory-interpretation.php.

of the influences that EU languages have on each other collectively. The EU legal act is typically multilingual, currently extending to 24 languages, not to mention translation into Icelandic and Norwegian, languages of states which are not EU Member States but are parties to the European Economic Area and adopt most of the EU legislation relating to the single market pursuant to the Agreement on the European Economic Area.[22]

The 'vertical' and 'horizontal' viewpoints give rise to different sorts of question and information. With the former, one is looking at the structure and contents of each text from the point of view of the language in question: what are the parts, how is the text structured, how are sentences constructed, do these conform to the standards laid down for the language, are the words correctly spelled, and so forth. However, the viewpoint also considers terminology: is it consistent with higher-ranking texts that govern it? A secondary act cannot change the terms in a treaty but must adhere to the treaty language. Are terms used consistently within domains? Do different terms have the same or different meanings? To that one can add the historical dimension and ask whether terms have changed over time. At the level of the text, the EU legal acts have remained broadly similar over the years, but there have been structural changes, such as the numbering of recitals and introducing them with a single phrase *whereas* once, rather than repeating this for each recital. There has been a tendency for EU legislative acts to become longer and more complex, but that is also a function of the complexity of the issues being addressed. For example Regulation (EU) No 650/2012 relating to succession matters has 83 recitals.[23]

Within each language, interfaces arise between texts though the need to repeat terminology from higher-ranking texts in lower-ranking texts made under them, as well as across texts dealing with similar matters in order to ensure consistency of terminology in texts within the same policy field. A third method involves citing other texts or articles by name or number and incorporating the terms or text in them by reference. Another 'vertical' linguistic dimension touches on the relationship between the form of language, terminology and meanings that occur in EU legal texts and making comparisons with similar forms in national law or international law. In general terms a language is an EU official language and used for EU legal texts if it is listed as such in Regulation No 1 determining the languages to be used by the European Economic Community as amended.[24] However, as with most matters relating to EU law and language, it has come from somewhere else: it is an official language in one or more of the Member States. The national form of the

22 See http://www.efta.int/media/documents/legal-texts/eea/the-eea-agreement/Main%20Text%20of%20the%20Agreement/EEAagreement.pdf.

23 Regulation (EU) No 650/2012 of the European Parliament and of the Council of 4 July 2012 on jurisdiction, applicable law, recognition and enforcement of decisions and acceptance and enforcement of authentic instruments in matters of succession and on the creation of a European Certificate of Succession (OJ L 201, 27 July 2012, at 107E).

24 OJ L 17, 6 October 1958, at 385.

language provides the starting point and a reference standard in terms of grammar, syntax, orthography, etc., as well as for terminology and their meanings. However, EU law has many concepts of its own (names of institutions, legal acts, types of procedure, and specialized domain terms) and these are not always matched by the national language context; so the national language has to be adapted to the EU context, which is something that starts as part of the process of preparing to join the EU as a new member. To this one can add that some languages are used in more than one state (for example, English: UK, Ireland, Malta; French: France, Belgium, Luxembourg; German: Germany, Austria, Belgium; Dutch: Netherlands, Belgium). There can be differences between the forms of language used in the different countries (see, for example, the *Austrian German Glossary*[25]) and so for EU legal texts an internal negotiation over terminology between speakers of the language may arise. A similar situation arises for international legal texts. Thus, one can see that the 'matrix' of national, international and EU legal contexts applies also to language issues. As with law, there is a frontier, this time linguistic, between the systems and that is important for terms and their precise meanings. This observation brings one back to the earlier discussion under the law view on the meanings of legal terms.

If one takes the example of EU English, the original treaty texts and the (at that time) ECSC/EEC/EAEC '*acquis*' were translated into English as the EU texts needed to be available in English. For that purpose the basis was British English, the Queen's English, using terms and expressions found in dictionaries such as the *Oxford English Dictionary*; in a word 'standardized' official English. This concerned spelling, punctuation, syntax, terminology, etc. However, as with other EU languages, the English language had to be adapted to the EU context. That meant (and still means) creating new terms for EU concepts not part of standard English. Many new terms and expressions entered into the English language (*sheepmeat*, *goatmeat*, *acquis*, *comitology*, but also journalese expressions such as *butter-mountains* and *wine-lakes*): but equally some existing terms acquired specialized EU meanings (*codification* in the sense of *consolidation*). The English texts were mainly translated from French, which has provided the principal semantic structure to EU legal texts. Thus it is tempting to see them as calques from that language, although that would be to overstate the relationship. Nonetheless it marks out EU English from standard English legal usage with its roots in different traditions. This is the linguistic frontier that is experienced by each EU language. It has risen imperceptibly and efforts are constantly made to keep the effects to a minimum by paying close attention to the terms used in EU texts and seeking to maintain close proximity with national usage; the use of definitions of terms plays a significant role in rendering differences clearer while at the same time enhancing equivalence across all language versions. EU legal acts are mainly intended to have effects within Member States and to exist alongside national texts and terms. Transposing an EU directive into national law implies replacing

25 Available at: http://german.about.com/od/vocabulary/a/Austrian.htm.

EU terminology with national terminology; it is a form of intra-lingual translation. It arises as a general issue between legal systems that have a common language (see, for example, Robertson (1999) on English and Scottish legal language).

A significant reason for linguistic divergences in EU legal texts can be traced to the horizontal viewpoint that considers influences across and between languages. In the EU context there are many factors at work here. The first, and most evident, is that EU texts tend to be drawn up first in one language and then translated into the other EU languages, so that the base language can have a significant impact on the others in terms of syntax and terminology. Historically French has been the principal EU drafting language; it has 'lost ground' to English over the years for the essentially pragmatic reason that national delegates and experts tend to have better knowledge of English than French and feel more comfortable in it. Nonetheless French remains a reference language of the institutions with English alongside and personal experience has been that the two languages work very closely together as drafting and working languages.

Between EU languages there are functional issues that can be seen from the 'horizontal' viewpoint. For example, the texts in all languages have the same formal structure and layout; recitals and articles have the same numbering; titles and headings match up and the same information is found on the same numbered page in documents bearing the same number but code-marked with ISO signs to indicate language version (not always easy to detect). In a word, the language versions are synchronized and this is called the *synoptic approach* in the *Interinstitutional Style Guide*, which gives linguistic advice on how to write EU texts in every language. The synoptic approach is essential for a multilingual legal system, because if a negotiator or lawyer refers to a particular article or sentence, everyone must be able to find the same reference in his or her language version easily and quickly so as to check it too. The language versions march in step like a row of soldiers, each aiming to convey the same message. It means also that special care is needed over the amount of information inserted in each page, as some languages are more concise and others more verbose; all must fit into the page using the same font size and margins. This is a skilled secretarial task, which involves first creating a 'model' in the base language which is followed by the other languages and adjusted in the event of problems for any of them.

Another linguistic influence on EU texts stems from the translation environment surrounding them. Each text is drafted so as to be translated into the other languages and those other language versions will have the same status in law as 'authentic' so it is important that the initial draft takes account of problems and difficulties encountered by other languages in encoding the information. Usually drafters cannot be aware of these in advance, so that it is generally a case of ensuring that there is an efficient 'feedback loop' to enable a horizontal review of all the language versions taken together. Such an opportunity is structured into the EU legislative procedures via the lawyer-linguists in each institution whose task is to ensure linguistic alignment of all language versions through checking, legal-linguistic revision and meeting with the experts for all languages to review and finalize the base language version together and then finalize each language version (Morgan 1982; Robertson 2010a; Šarčević and Robertson 2013). This is at the final stages of the preparation of the text, but there are also opportunities at earlier stages via observations by delegates and translator feedback to identify terminological difficulties and explore solutions.

A particular dimension of writing for translation[26] concerns the desirability of writing stylistically to facilitate comprehension and translation. Here shorter sentences are desirable. Complex sentences are more difficult to reproduce in every shade of nuance. Terms and concepts specific to particular legal systems are to be avoided where possible; this is mentioned in the *Interinstitutional Guidelines* and the *Joint Practical Guide*. Diplomatic ambiguity (Gallas 2006) is another issue as what functions neatly in a base text for the purposes of a political compromise does not always work so neatly for other languages which have difficulties in reproducing the ambiguity. This is an issue in particular for inflected languages such as Slavic languages where precise relationships must be indicated. The translator may be obliged to 'interpret' the text, which usually entails consulting other language versions and, if possible, consulting the authors. The wider problem with ambiguity is that it can leave the door open to uncertainty and oblige economic actors to litigate to resolve the uncertainty; in the end the courts become involved in settling the issue. It can be a costly business.

When considering the law viewpoint earlier, a distinction was made between the process of text creation and that of interpretation, perhaps involving a court process. One can adopt the same approach with respect to language issues. The main background difference is that whereas Regulation No 1 applies directly to the text creation process, Article 7 provides: 'The languages to be used in the proceedings of the Court of Justice shall be laid down in its rules of procedure.' The Court of Justice has a separate linguistic regime, and there are rules of procedure for the Court of Justice, General Court and Civil Service Tribunal. From the point of view of language and translation, the main difference is that with legislative texts it is possible to select one language as a general drafting language and then arrange for translation into all other languages, in a single step. However, with court cases, the action is generally raised before the Court of Justice in the language of the court of referral for a preliminary hearing, or the language of a/the party(ies) (see the individual rules of court for the permutations) and so it is possible for any language to have the role of language of the case. That implies translation from any language towards all other languages. Practical factors come into play connected with the possible number of language combinations and the limitations on translator services to master them all simultaneously, and so internal methods are adopted such as relay translation through pivot languages (McAuliffe 2010). The Court maintains

26 For practical examples, see http://developer.gnome.org/gdp-style-guide/stable/locale-5.html.en.

'linguistic stability' by translating all cases into French and using that language as the internal working language (see Chapter 4 in this volume).

If we again recall the law viewpoint and the distinction drawn between interpreting a text and the environment of the court process surrounding and leading up to that interpretation, we enter, on the one hand, into the field of multilingual interpretation of EU legal texts (Robertson 2012b; Derlén 2009) and, on the other, into the linguistic permutations of court cases. If there is no difference in the meaning, in terms of legal effects, between language versions, there is no conflict between the texts to be resolved, which is the normal situation. However, should there be a discrepancy, the Court of Justice has developed methods for determining which version(s) are to be treated as most closely expressing the applicable rule. It may be the majority, or a few, or even a single language in exceptional cases,[27] but everything depends on the context, the purpose of the act, the intention of the author(s), the treaty base, applicable principles of law, etc. However, we should note that here we are moving away from what the texts say linguistically, to which version conveys the rule, which is a legal question.

So far, emphasis has been placed on the Court of Justice context, but the references to it for a preliminary interpretation normally start with proceedings before a national court where EU legal texts are being pleaded by one or more parties. In that context there are potentially many linguistic variables: the language of each party, the language of each witness, the language of the court and its proceedings, the language(s) of documents and evidence, the language(s) of the national laws which apply, the language versions of international acts which may or may not exist in the language of the court, and there are also the language versions of EU legal acts. In a purely national case in a monolingual legal system where there are no foreign elements, a single language prevails. It is national language for national legal issues and texts and EU language for EU texts; but parties may seek to argue for 'national' style interpretations of EU texts if it supports their case. We again enter into complex legal territory as the methods and solutions to each possible scenario are covered by rules: rules of private international law (choice of court, choice of applicable law), the rules of procedure of the court, rules on evidence and arrangements for translation and interpretation.[28]

27 See Opinion of Advocate General Stix-Hackl in Case C-265/03 *Igor Simutenkov* v. *Ministerio de Educación y Cultura, Real Federación Española de Fútbol* [2005] ECR I-02579.

28 As regards court interpreting in EU Member States and transposition of Directive 2010/64/EU on the right to interpretation and translation in criminal proceedings, see Chapter 13 by Bajčić in this volume. See also the European Commission website: Justice, the Right to Interpretation and Translation at: http://ec.europa.eu/justice/criminal/criminal-rights/right-translation/index_en.htm.

Interfaces of Culture

We turn now to consider interfaces of culture in EU multilingual law. What is culture? There are various definitions in English as a study of dictionaries reveals, but it is proposed to retain the following from the *Oxford English Dictionary*: 'the ideas, customs, etc. of a society or group (1796, after German Kultur).' This definition is sufficiently wide as to embrace all ideas about law and language and the associated ideas behind our ways of living. From that perspective, everything noted earlier in relation to the law and language viewpoints on EU law and language comes within the scope. However, if one thinks in terms of interfaces of culture, the definition leads one to think in terms of specific societies and groups. Within the EU context that leads one to think about the Member States as entities of culture, but each state itself can be seen in terms of complex sets of groups and societies on larger or smaller scales of consistency. Corporate businesses have their culture, as do government departments, local administrations and families. Most of this has little direct relevance to EU law and language, but some of it does. The question is which and what? Here, leaving aside specific historical details which can be obtained from history books, explanatory reports and *travaux préparatoires*, it is proposed to focus on some structural aspects by means of which cultural influences come to bear on EU legal texts. First, there is the cultural environment created by the EU treaties already touched on for law and language; second, there is the cultural environment of secondary legislative acts, determined in large part by the treaties, but influenced also by the policies being implemented in the individual texts; third, there are the cultures of the Member States and the negotiating parties that are brought to bear on each text under preparation.

One of the policy fields of EU law is entitled 'culture' (Article 167 TFEU; see also Europedia Moussis) and there are EU texts on culture[29] and the annual EU 'Capitals of Culture'.[30] Here the focus mainly centres on social activities such as theatre, art, dance, cinema, and the function of the EU legal texts is generally to encourage sharing, mixing and getting to know each other, so that barriers are made lower and the single 'cultural space' of the EU enhanced through greater understanding. Although these cultural activities stand slightly apart from the EU texts and the EU institutions, they are events in the Member States which the EU seeks to encourage and stimulate.

A fourth approach to the question of interfaces of culture is to take each legal text and reflect on the forces at work on it and, more significantly, what it is seeking to achieve; such effects can also be seen in terms of cultural choices that have been made. In that respect a market economy and competition are 'cultural' choices, but they must fit in and adapt to a large range of policy areas, which have cultural

---

29 See the Europa Agenda for culture at: http://ec.europa.eu/culture/our-policy-development/european-agenda_en.htm.

30 See http://ec.europa.eu/culture/our-programmes-and-actions/capitals/european-capitals-of-culture_en.htm.

orientations that may align or conflict. Each EU legal text has its history and this history is made up of background circumstances, ideas, events, negotiations, hard bargaining, compromises and solutions. To ascertain the cultural influences on a legal text we need to access the working papers and read detailed reports by those involved in making the text. To take an example, in the field of Succession Law, mentioned earlier, the Explanatory Report by Waters on the Convention on the law applicable to succession to the estates of deceased persons, drafted by experts under the auspices of the Hague Conference on Private International Law,[31] sets out the problems encountered, approaches proposed and solutions found in the negotiations for the Convention. However, EU legislative texts are different, as explanatory reports do not form part of the act. The explanatory part of the EU text lies in the recitals. These set out the reasons for the text and introduce particular provisions in the articles. They are part of the legal text. They do not relate the story of how the text was brought about. References to particular issues and problems tend to be expressed in abstract, general and neutral language, so as to enhance impartiality. This is EU legislative technique.

If one wishes to go beyond the surface of a legal text into deeper levels of meaning, implication and cultural influences, then one method is to recall the four viewpoints mentioned at the outset: law, language, policy and action. We have discussed the law and language viewpoints. What about policy and action? These can be seen as 'culture in action'. If a society has a 'business' culture, it favours business-oriented policies that facilitate action by business. Similarly if a society is rural, urban, consumerist, nature-oriented, religion-oriented it will tend to adapt its policies and action towards those ends. The viewpoints of policy and action can be seen as to some extent reflecting the 'cultural values' of the authors of texts. From this perspective, a study of EU treaties and secondary acts over the last half century shows how there has been a gradual shift from an initial emphasis on coal and steel towards wider economic issues, and then later widening to include ancillary fields relating to justice, home affairs, foreign policy, environment, citizenship, currency and banking. These are policy domains, but they reflect culture and the interplay of cultural values between Member States as shaped by specific economic and social needs. The current EU policies are to be found in the TEU, TFEU, TEAEC, etc., and there is a convenient list in the European Commission's website for the European Citizens' Initiative.[32]

Looking at EU legal texts from a 'culture' viewpoint, we can pick up again on the duality between text creation and reading and interpretation in the context of a court process. On the creation side, there is the interplay of values and interests that centre round, and are merged into and 'frozen', in the legislative text. On the reading and interpretation side there is the interplay of values and interests that push and pull the meaning and effects to be given to particular words and phrases. In many cases there is a single authority which applies the text in its own way and

31 See http://www.hcch.net/index_en.php?act=publications.details&pid=2959.

32 See http://ec.europa.eu/citizens-initiative/public/welcome.

thus controls the meanings to be given; for example, the Commission interprets its own rules of procedure on the basis of advice from its legal service. It also gives guidance to Member States regarding the transposition of EU directives into national law. However, once a legislative text has been adopted and enters into force, it leads a 'life of its own' and is used by the economic actors in the Member States and elsewhere. Disagreements can arise and these can lead to court disputes (or arbitration), usually when linked to economic interests and a deep pocket as litigation is costly. The court case is an arena for legal dispute, but also for cultural dispute in terms of ways of thinking, acting, believing. The court provides an arena; the rules of procedure structure the 'game' between the parties; the court decides on the result; the parties lead their evidence and argue their points. They seek to 'pull' the meaning of texts in their favour and 'away' from their opponent in terms of effects and action. Maybe they also give different views as to the policy intentions behind the legal act, especially if that act contained ambiguous wording. These influences also have an impact on EU law and language.

Finally it can be said that a new Member State undergoes a process of cultural adaptation when it accedes to the EU pursuant to Article 49 TEU. This adaption covers all the four viewpoints mentioned: first, the national laws and policies must be adjusted so as to be consistent with existing EU law. (For example, if not already known, a system of value added tax is introduced.) To that end, EU legal acts must be translated and EU concepts reproduced in terminology if the acceding state brings with it a new EU language. Translation of the EU texts in force (the *acquis*) is a huge task and it places heavy emphasis on language and terminology, requiring preparation of detailed glossaries of many newly created terms (see chapters 11 and 12 in this volume). On the other side, EU law needs to be adjusted to take account of the new Member State. This takes place through the treaty of accession when existing EU treaties and many secondary legislative acts are textually amended to include the new state. All this activity is designed to ensure that the policies of the new state become aligned on those of existing EU law. Adjustments to EU law are needed to take account of particularities of the new state and typically these are mentioned also in the accession treaty annexes. In the end it is perhaps the action viewpoint that prevails, so that the results flowing from the EU legal texts will apply to the old and new Member States in a similar way, in accordance with the provisions of the treaties. The process of accession involves a change of culture. It takes time.

At the other end of the scale, a Member State may decide to withdraw from the EU pursuant to Article 50 TEU. The process involves the negotiation of an international agreement to settle the details. However, after years of close legal, linguistic and cultural interaction with EU law and institutions and the other Member States, the effects of close cooperation must surely leave their traces, as with any form of divorce or separation. In the case of Greenland, which left the EEC in 1985, a continuing close relationship remains with Denmark and the EU. Withdrawal from the EU means changing one set of interfaces and replacing them with another set. The precise details of relationships of law, language, policy and action change, but they nonetheless continue. In particular the relationship with EU law and language remains, but with less scope to influence and contribute to its future development. At the same time the cultural richness of the EU is diminished.

Conclusion

This chapter has examined a range of interfaces of law, language and culture in EU multilingual law by invoking four viewpoints of law, language, policy and action. Originally imagined (Robertson 2010a) as providing methods for checking and revising legal texts legal-linguistically, these viewpoints can also be used for the purpose of analysing terminology in texts through enquiring as to function and context for each term. For legal terms, which are abstract and system bound, this can help to clarify the cultural associations that may be attached to them. The analysis can also be combined with a semiotic approach involving seeing terms as signs (Robertson 2010b).

In the course of this chapter emphasis has been placed on two points in the life of texts: the point of creation and the point of reading and interpretation as to meaning and effects. These are the moments of 'engagement' for legal texts. The various influences and interfaces that come to bear when a text is created become 'encoded' in the 'linear' text. At the point of reading, these are 'decoded'; for EU legal texts this is perhaps very often by readers who lack knowledge of the factors that led to the creation of the text. The reader seeks to extract information from the words themselves, drawing on their understanding of law and language so as to obtain a mental picture of the policy context and goals and the precise effects intended. Different mental pictures are possible and these are not infrequently tinged with self-interest. Disagreements arise which lead to litigation in courts. Each court process can be seen as a site of interfaces and these can also have a bearing on the reading of the EU legal text. Within and behind each EU legal text and its interpretation lies an internal 'tension' or 'balance' between the national context with its urgent needs and the EU context, which has been allocated a status above national law. The balances are struck and these also form part of the ongoing EU legal environment and have influences. One can glimpse some of them in the declarations attached at the end of the TEU and TFEU.

Throughout this chapter, emphasis has been placed on the idea that EU law is regarded as a separate legal order and lives alongside two other legal orders, relating to national and international law. These together form a matrix. Each provides its own context; words and terms pass between them, but when they do so they are capable of undergoing a shift in meaning. The matrix is primarily legal, but law influences language.

Everything can be seen in terms of culture, but here the emphasis has been on the way cultural viewpoints manifest themselves in legal texts, and through disputes over the meaning of those texts. Analysing texts in terms of policy and action assists in revealing some of the cultural ideas lying behind, and reflected in, each text. EU law has gradually shifted its policy focus over the years and that can be seen as reflecting a cultural development as well. When a new state joins the EU it must adapt in many different ways to the new context. This change is embodied in an accession treaty and each accession treaty can be thought of as a 'snapshot' of EU law at one instant in time, as it stands on the day of accession. By studying each of the past accession treaties in turn one can obtain a glimpse of the historical interfaces of law, language and culture. But what about the future? It is always uncertain but full of possibilities.

References

Chalmers, D., Davies, G. and Monti, G. 2010. *European Union Law, Cases and Materials*. Cambridge: Cambridge University Press.

Derlén, M. 2009. *Multilingual Interpretation of European Union Law*. Alphen aan den Rijn: Kluwer Law International.

Europedia Moussis. Available at: http://www.europedia.moussis.eu/books/Book_2/4/10/03/?all=1.

Gallas, T. 2006. Understanding EC law as 'diplomatic law' and its language, in *Multilingualism and the Harmonisation of European Law*, edited by B. Pozzo and V. Jacometti. Alphen aan den Rijn: Kluwer Law International, 119–28.

Guggeis, M. and Robinson, W. 2012. 'Co-revision': legal-linguistic revision in the European Union 'co-decision' process, in *The Role of Legal Translation in Legal Harmonization*, edited by C.J.W. Baaij. Alphen aan den Rijn: Kluwer Law International, 51–81.

Interinstitutional Agreement of 22 December 1998 on Common Guidelines for the Quality of Drafting of Community Legislation (OJ C 73, 17 March 1999, at 1).

Interinstitutional Style Guide. 2011. Luxembourg: Publications Office of the European Union. Available at: http://publications.europa.eu/code/en/en-000100.htm.

Joint Practical Guide for persons involved in the drafting of European Union legislation. 2013. Available at: eur-lex.europa.eu/content/pdf/techleg/joint-practical-guide-2013-en.pdf.

Manual of Precedents for Acts established within the Council of the European Union. 2010–2011. Brussels: General Secretariat of the Council of the European Union, Directorate for the Quality of Legislation. Available at: http://ec.europa.eu/translation/documents/council/manual_precedents_acts_en.pdf.

McAuliffe, K. 2010. Language and the institutional dynamics of the Court of Justice of the European Communities: a changing role for lawyer-linguists? in *How Globalizing Professions Deal With National Languages: Studies in Cultural Conflict and Cooperation*, edited by M. Gueldry. Lewiston, Queenstown and Lampeter: The Edwin Mellen Press, 239–63.

Morgan, J.F. 1982. Multilingual legal drafting in the EEC and the work of jurist/linguists. *Multilingua*, 1(2), 109–17.

Murray, Justice John L. Undated. Methods of interpretation: comparative law method. Available at: http://curia.europa.eu/common/dpi/col_murray.pdf.

Oxford English Dictionary. Available at: http://www.oed.com/view/Entry/45746?rskey=HMOQuQ&result=1#eid.

Robertson, C. 1999. Il diritto scozzese e il diritto inglese: due sistemi, una lingua. *Quaderni di Libri e riviste d'Italia, la traduzione, Saggi e documenti*, 43(4), 117–34.

Robertson, C. 2010a. Legal-linguistic revision of EU legislative texts, in *Legal Discourse across Languages and Cultures*, edited by M. Gotti and C. Williams. Bern: Peter Lang, 51–73.

Robertson, C. 2010b. EU law and semiotics. *International Journal for the Semiotics of Law*, 23(2), 145–64.

Robertson, C. 2011. Multilingual legislation in the European Union: EU and national legislative-language styles and terminology. *Research in Language*, 9(1), 51–67. Available at: http://versita.metapress.com/content/g851738257gm73k1.

Robertson, C. 2012a. EU legal English: common law, civil law or a new genre? *European Review of Private Law*, 5–6, 1215–40.

Robertson, C. 2012b. The problem of meaning in multilingual EU legal texts. *International Journal of Law, Language & Discourse*, 2(1), 1–30. Available at: http://www.ijlld.com/2012-index.

Rosas, A., Levits, E. and Bot, Y. (eds) 2012. *The Court of Justice and the Construction of Europe: Analyses and Perspectives on Sixty Years of Case-Law*. Berlin and Heidelberg: T.M.C. Asser Press by Springer.

Šarčević, S. and Robertson, C. 2013. The work of lawyer-linguists in the EU institutions, in *Legal Translation in Context: Professional Issues and Prospects*, edited by A. Borja Albi and F. Prieto Ramos. Bern: Peter Lang, 181–202.

Chapter 4
A Single Text or a Single Meaning: Multilingual Interpretation of EU Legislation and CJEU Case Law in National Courts

Mattias Derlén

Introduction: The Importance of National Courts

In her influential work on legal translation Susan Šarčević (1997: 218) identified diverging interpretations of international provisions in national courts as a serious problem, threating the achievements of the translators. She argued that national courts tend to employ their own methods of interpretation, rarely consulting other language versions of the provision than their own. Drawing on Tabory (1980: 195), Šarčević pointed to the need for a uniform interpretation of international provisions.

Like Šarčević, this chapter emphasizes the importance of national courts in a multilingual legal order, in this case the European Union. While there is no denying that the legislator and the courts of the Union are key players, the practical application of EU law is to a significant degree entrusted to national courts. From a positive perspective national courts contribute to the exploration of the frontiers of EU law, by requesting preliminary rulings and providing the Court of Justice of the European Union (henceforth: the CJEU) with opportunities to interpret and develop Union law. From a negative, or at least realistic, perspective they constitute the limits of the impact of EU law. *De jure*, and in the absence of a Treaty revision, the CJEU has the final say on the meaning of EU law (Schroeder 2004: 181). However, from a *de facto* perspective national courts control the meaning of EU law. For 10 years, between the *Cohn-Bendit* and *Nicolo* cases, directives did not have direct effect in French administrative courts, no matter what the CJEU concluded in its case law (Komarek 2007: 473). Given this significant power the limited attention paid to national courts is difficult to understand.

This chapter examines the attitudes of national courts regarding the multilingual character of EU law. The Union legislator has adopted different approaches to multilingualism regarding, on the one hand, legislation and, on the other hand, case law of the CJEU. The differences are discussed in detail below, but in brief legislation follows full multilingualism, where all languages are *de jure* equally authoritative,[1] while judgments of the CJEU are authentic in only one, original language. These different approaches are here referred to as the ideas of a single meaning or a single text. The term *single text* indicates the existence of a *de jure* original, alone decisive in interpretation. The term *single meaning*, on the other hand, indicates that all languages together in dialogue determine the meaning of a provision. National courts also employ these two different approaches, but with significant deviations and, most importantly, without adhering to the distinction between legislation and case law. Drawing on examples from courts in five Member States, this chapter will demonstrate the existence of a number of approaches to multilingual interpretation of EU law and how the different multilingual regimes of legislation and case law are blending together in national courts.

The Multilingual Character of the Treaties and EU Legislation: A Single Meaning

Separate rules exist in the European Union for primary law (more specifically the basic treaties), secondary law (legislation) and CJEU case law. The treaties, as well as EU legislation, enjoy full multilingualism in the sense that they are equally authentic in all 24 official[2] languages. As concerns the basic treaties, it follows directly from Article 55 of the TEU, Article 358 TFEU and Article 225 of the EURATOM Treaty that they are drawn up in a single original in all 24 languages and are equally authentic in those languages. Consequently, Article 55 TEU and the corresponding articles maintain the illusion that the treaties were simultaneously produced in all 24 official languages, thereby emphasizing their equal authority.

---

1 The terms *authentic* and *authoritative* are used interchangeably in the chapter. According to the 1969 Vienna Convention on the Law of Treaties, an authentic text is final and definitive and an authoritative text is to be used in interpretation of a treaty (see further Hilf (1973: 51–2) and Tabory (1980: 171–2)). However, in the EU context no distinction is made between the terms and the fact that a text is authentic means that it is to be used in interpretation. For example, Article 55 TEU designates the languages as 'equally authentic'. The terms *text* and *version* are also used interchangeably, as EU law does not uphold the distinction made by the Vienna Convention, (see further Derlén (2009: 18–20)).

2 Following the CJEU (see, for example, case C-298/12 *Confédération paysanne* v. *Ministre de l'Alimentation, de l'Agriculture et de la Pêche*, ECLI:EU:C:2013:630, para. 22), I use the term *official languages* for the languages in which primary and secondary law are published, the languages which can serve as language of the case before the Union courts and the languages which can be used to communicate with the Union, all according to the relevant rules. The languages are not official in the sense that they create general rights. In case C-361/01 P *Christina Kik* v. *Office for Harmonisation in the Internal Market (Trade Marks and Designs) (OHIM)* [2003] ECR I- 8283, paras. 81–87, the CJEU concluded that no general principle of equality of languages, reaching beyond the established rules in the Treaty and secondary legislation, existed in the European Union.

When it comes to secondary law, Article 342 TFEU charges the Council, acting with unanimity, with determining the language regime of the Union institutions. This is done by way of Regulation 1/58,[3] recognizing the 24 languages as both official and working languages. The effects of this statement are somewhat more ambiguous than the rules on language in the treaties. As pointed out by Hilpold, the definition of the term *working language* remains open. In practice, a difference is maintained between internal and external working languages. From an external perspective the institutions work in all 24 official languages, by publishing binding legislation in all languages and by guaranteeing the right of citizens to communicate with the institutions in the language of their choice (Hilpold 2010: 699). The publication of legislation in all languages is necessary from the perspective of legal certainty, in particular due to the direct applicability and direct effect of EU provisions (Gundel 2001: 781–2). The right of citizens to communicate with the Union in their mother tongue is a basic right of democracy, as expressly pointed out by the German Federal Constitutional Court in its *Maastricht* decision (Gundel 2001: 782). From an internal perspective the institutions have *de facto* adopted a few working languages to simplify day-to-day activities. Some institutions use a single working language, such as English in the European Central Bank, while other institutions employ several working languages, such as English, French and German in the Commission (Robinson 2005: 4).

If we venture beyond this discussion of internal and external working languages, we encounter the question of legal consequences of the equal standing of the official languages. Neither Article 55 TEU and the corresponding Treaty Articles nor Regulation 1/58 provide any information beyond indicating the equal standing of the languages, explicitly in the Treaty Articles and implicitly in Regulation 1/58 by designating them all as official languages in Article 1. Thus, the Member States left the question of legal consequences of the equal authenticity to the CJEU. The Court had three main options, compatible with the wording of the Treaties and Regulation 1/58 (Derlén 2011: 144–5). First, equal authenticity could justify reliance on a single language in the sense that, for example, Swedish is equally as authoritative as French. Second, it could, following the example set by the application of Article 33.3 of the 1969 Vienna Convention on the Law of Treaties, use a criterion of doubt, justifying reliance on a single language as long as the provision in question is clear and unambiguous. However, the CJEU chose neither of these, opting instead for a third option, according to which the equal authenticity of the official languages requires the use of all languages. In other words, every provision of EU law has a single meaning, and all the languages read together create this meaning. The CJEU often emphasizes that EU legislation cannot be understood in a single language, but only after consulting the other languages. In fact, the Court implies that the languages read together demonstrates the aim of the legislator (Derlén 2011: 158–60) by using the following standard phrase:

3 EEC Council: Regulation No 1 determining the languages to be used by the European Economic Community [1958] OJ 17/385, in its amended form.

> According to settled case-law, the necessity of uniform application and, accordingly, of uniform interpretation of an EU measure makes it impossible to consider one version of the text in isolation, but requires it to be interpreted on the basis of both the real intention of its author and the aim pursued by the latter, in the light, in particular, of the versions in all the other official languages.[4]

Here the use of a single text is clearly rejected and the CJEU finds the purpose of the provision by reading all language versions together.

The emphasis on equal authenticity leads to the existence of so-called translated originals, that is, a translation with neither source nor target text (Pommer 2012: 1248). However, this is obviously only a legal construction; in reality legislation is drafted in one language and then translated into the other official languages. Legislative proposals from the Commission are nowadays drafted primarily in English, with French in an ever more distant second place (Schilling 2011: 1471). In 1993 French was still the dominant source language in the Commission, with 43.5 per cent as compared to 36.4 per cent for English (European Commission 1995: 10). However, in 1997 English moved ahead of French and in the twenty-first century the dominance of English is clear, with 77 per cent of documents being drafted in English in 2010 (European Commission 2012: 10). When the Commission has processed a proposal, it is translated into the other official languages before being sent to the legislative institutions (Robinson 2005: 5).

The Multilingual Character of the Case Law of the Court of Justice: A Single Text (or Two?)

While primary and secondary law follow full multilingualism and the idea of a single meaning, the language regime for CJEU case law is fundamentally different. The language regime of the Court of Justice and the General Court is not regulated by Regulation 1/58, but by the Statute of the Court of Justice of the European Union.[5] According to Article 64 of the Statute, language arrangements at the Court are governed by the Rules of Procedure of the Court of Justice and the Rules of Procedure of the General Court.[6] According to Article 36 of the Rules of Procedure of the Court of Justice, any of the 24 official languages can be used as languages of the case. The notion of the language of the case is multilingual and monolingual at the same time. It is obviously multilingual in the sense that all 24 languages can

4 Case C-298/12 *Confédération paysanne* v. *Ministre de l'Alimentation, de l'Agriculture et de la Pêche*, ECLI:EU:C:2013:630, para. 22, references omitted.

5 This follows from an exception in Article 342 TFEU.

6 This chapter only discusses the Court of Justice. The language regime of the General Court (formerly the Court of First Instance) follows that of the Court of Justice (see further Schübel-Pfister (2004: 76–7)). For an analysis of multilingual interpretation of CJEU case law by the Advocates General see Derlén (2014).

be used before the Court. The Court of Justice has emphasized that all institutions of the Union are cognizant of the official languages 'by virtue of an irrebuttable presumption of law'.[7] Thus, the fact that a defendant had provided documentation to the Court in a language other than the language of the case could not render this information unknown to the Court. The Court has also been generous, extending the number of official languages in the absence of formal recognition. For example, Danish, English and Irish were only included as languages of the case in the Rules of Procedure in December 1974, but the Court recognized the languages immediately following the accession of Denmark, Ireland and the United Kingdom (Usher 1981: 277). However, the language regime of the Court is also monolingual, in the sense that a single language is used for the proceedings. Having only one language of the case simplifies proceedings and reduces costs (Loehr 1998: 52).

Article 37 of the Rules of Procedure handles the determination of the language of the case. In direct actions the applicant will normally choose one of the 24 official languages as the language of the case. When it comes to appeals, the language of the case is the language of the decision of the General Court. Finally, in preliminary ruling proceedings the language of the case will be the language of the national court or tribunal referring the matter to the CJEU. It is obviously practical for the referring court to receive an answer in the language of the national proceedings. Furthermore, this system enables the parties to retain the same counsel before the CJEU as before the national court (Sevón 1997: 537). The fact that the language of the national proceedings carries over to the proceedings before the CJEU also furthers access to justice. Given the limited possibility for individuals to challenge acts by way of direct actions, the institute of preliminary rulings is an important means to achieve protection of the rights of individuals. Consequently, it is essential that the preliminary ruling is accessible for the parties and the national court in the language of the national proceedings (Athanassiou 2006: 21).

The language of the case is used for both the written and oral parts of the proceedings.[8] A fundamental distinction can be made between translation into the language of the case and translation from the language of the case (Usher 1981: 279). The parties are responsible for translation into the language of the case. For documents written in another language a translation into the language of the case must be provided. The Court may reject non-translated documents. However, in the case of lengthy documents the Court may authorize the translation to be limited to an extract.[9] The Members of the Court have greater freedom when it comes to expressing themselves in other languages. For example, following Article 38(8) of the Rules of Procedure, the Opinion of the Advocate General may be presented to

7 Case 1/60 *Acciaieria Ferriera di Roma* v. *High Authority of the European Coal and Steel Community* [1960] ECR English special edition 165, at 169.

8 Article 38 of the Rules of Procedure.

9 Articles 38(2) and 38(3) of the Rules of Procedure.

the Court in any of the 24 official languages.[10] The Registrar arranges translation into the language of the case. The Member States also occupy a special position in the sense that they always have the right to submit observations in their own official language when intervening in cases before the Court or when taking part in preliminary rulings.

The Court is responsible for the translation from the language of the case. The Directorate-General for Translation handles this task. Following Article 40 of the Rules of Procedure, the judgment of the Court is translated into all the official languages of the European Union.

The language of the case plays a pivotal role in the proceedings before the CJEU, as demonstrated above. This is reflected in Article 41 of the Rules of Procedure, which states that '[t]he texts of documents drawn up in the language of the case or, where applicable, in another language authorised pursuant to Articles 37 or 38 of these Rules shall be authentic'. Consequently, the judgment is only legally binding in the language of the case (Schübel-Pfister 2004: 70; McAuliffe 2008: 808; Gallo 2006: 181; Kürten 2004: 84; Usher 1981: 281; Hilpold 2010: 701; Mulders 2008: 47; Due 1999: 78). A single text is decisive, as compared to the full multilingualism of primary law and legislation. The existence of a single original version of the judgment is, according to Gallo (2006: 181), explained by the fact that the parties and the national court bound by the judgment must be able to access it in their own language. I would argue that the need of the parties to be able to understand the judgment necessitates the existence of the judgment in the language of the proceedings; it does not explain why the language of the case is the only authentic version. Rather, the status of the language of the case is presumably due to the need of the parties and the national court to be able to rely on the judgment in their own language, not being forced to consult and compare other language versions. Furthermore, the version is truly the original in the sense that the proceedings have been conducted in this language.

Article 38(8) of the Rules of Procedure could be seen as the foundation for the use of one or more internal working languages (McAuliffe 2012: 203; Schübel-Pfister 2004: 71). However, the CJEU has limited itself to a single working language, French (Due 1999: 77; Sevón 1999: 580; Mancini and Keeling 1995: 398; Gallo 2006: 181; Mulders 2008: 47; Athanassiou 2006: 22; Schübel-Pfister 2004: 71; Kürten 2004: 87; von Danwitz 2008: 778; Hilpold 2010: 701; Oppermann 2001: 2665). The status of working language means that all documents are translated into French and that the judgment is deliberated and drafted in French, regardless of the language of the proceedings (Schübel-Pfister 2004: 71–72; Due 1999: 77; Sevón 1999: 583). However, departures from the exclusive use of French

10 However, the Advocates General do not normally make use of the right to deliver the Opinion in their mother tongue. At least since the expansion of the Union in 2004 the Advocates General deliver their Opinion in one of the pivot languages (English, French, German, Spanish and Italian), normally opting for English or French (see further McAuliffe (2008: 816) and McAuliffe (2012: 208)).

have occurred. According to the literature deliberations sometimes take place in English, but French still dominates (Kürten 2004: 87; Oppermann 2001: 2665). McAuliffe (2008: 816–17) argues that English has been used in the General Court 'in the preparation of reports, drafting of judgments or even intermittently slipping into English in deliberations', but French retains a strong position and the working language regime of the CJEU remains unaffected. The discussion concerning the use of other languages besides French in the Court is not new. Already in 1981 Usher (1981: 281) argued that examples of the use of English and German could be found in the Chambers while French was normally used in the full court.

The use of French as the sole working language of the Court comes with both advantages and disadvantages. An obvious, general advantage of using a single working language is that interpreters are not needed at the deliberation of the Court, enabling the deliberations to remain secret (Schübel-Pfister 2004: 72). Hilpold (2010: 702) observes that the need for secrecy is no argument for the choice of French *per se*, and that the historical reasons for choosing French are no longer valid. According to Hilpold, French was employed as the working language in the absence of English (no English-speaking country being a Member State at the founding of the Community), due to the strong position of France and given the standing of French as the language of diplomacy. The future, however, belongs to English. Hilpold's discussion ties in with a common critique of the use of French; it is anachronistic to keep French as a working language based on the historical developments since the founding of the Union. Given the language skills in the new Member States, French-speaking judges are difficult to come by and English would be a more natural choice (Kürten 2004: 90; Schübel-Pfister 2004: 73). Furthermore, the use of French is a clear disadvantage for judges coming from non-French speaking countries, making it more difficult for them to argue persuasively in deliberations (Oppermann 2001: 2665; Kürten 2004: 89; Mancini and Keeling 1995: 398). The use of French will also affect the style of the judgment, a consequence that can be seen as either positive or negative. On the positive side, it is argued that French provides 'concision and clarity' to the judgment (Mancini and Keeling 1995: 398). On the negative side, it is argued that the judges will subconsciously employ French legal concepts, forgoing relevant legal concepts from other legal systems (Schübel-Pfister 2004: 74). Possible advantages also include efficiency of the internal procedure, avoiding excessive translations and securing a consistent vocabulary (Athanassiou 2006: 22; Mancini and Keeling 1995: 398). Furthermore, it is argued that the use of a single working language promotes a feeling of *esprit de corps* among the judges of the Court (Mancini and Keeling 1995: 398). The disadvantages also include possible limitations of the rules on the language of the case. Knowing that the Court reads, deliberates and drafts in French, the parties have an incentive to use French as the language of the case, forgoing their right to use any official language in the proceedings (Schübel-Pfister 2004: 74). As we will see below, the use of French as the working language in the CJEU has consequences also in national courts.

A Single Text in National Courts: Falling Back on the Original Language(s)

When confronted with the multilingual character of EU law, national courts can choose to fall back on an original, letting a single text be decisive in interpretation. However, this is not a homogenous approach. The examples below demonstrate that what constitutes the 'original' and thereby decisive language varies.

Article 41 of the Rules of Procedure sanctions using a single text when interpreting CJEU case law. National courts sometimes demonstrate awareness of the *de jure* original of CJEU judgments. For example, when the Irish High Court interpreted case C-277/11 *M.M* v. *Minister for Justice*,[11] Mr Justice Hogan observed that only the language of the case (English) was authoritative.[12] Similarly, when the German Federal Administrative Court interpreted case C-342/05 *Commission* v. *Finland*,[13] it referred to Article 31 (now 41) of the Rules of Procedure and concluded that only the Finnish language version was binding. Consequently, the wording of the German version of the judgment was seen as an erroneous translation, to be disregarded.[14]

However, we can also find examples of national courts falling back on the *de facto* original of CJEU judgments, letting the French version guide the interpretation. For example, in the *Telewest* case Lady Justice Arden only consulted the French version of the *Henriksen* case,[15] despite the fact that Danish was the language of the case.[16]

Similarly, when Lord Rodger of Earlsferry interpreted the *Card Protection Plan* case,[17] he found paragraphs 29 and 30 of the English language version (which he referred to as 'the English translation') to be somewhat confusing, due to inconsistent terminology.[18] This uncertainty was removed by having recourse to the French language version, where the terminology was consistent. Thus, the French version was decisive in the interpretation, despite English being the language of the case. Lord Rodger of Earlsferry pointed out that the French version was 'the text drafted by the Court'.[19]

---

11 Case C-277/11 *M. M.* v. *Minister for Justice, Equality and Law Reform, Ireland and Attorney General*, ECLI:EU:C:2012:744.

12 *M.M* v. *Minister for Justice and Law Reform*, Ireland [2013] IEHC 9, para. 17.

13 Case C-342/05 *Commission of the European Communities* v. *Republic of Finland* [2007] ECR I-4713.

14 BVerwG, Beschluss vom 17. 4. 2010 – 9 B 5. 10, paras. 7–9.

15 Case 173/88 *Skatteministeriet* v. *Morten Henriksen* [1989] ECR 2763.

16 *Telewest Communications Plc, Telewest (Publications) Limited* v. *Commissioners of Customs and Excise* [2005] EWCA Civ 102, Court of Appeal, para. 79.

17 Case C-349/96 *Card Protection Plan Ltd (CPP)* v. *Commissioners of Customs & Excise* [1999] ECR I-973.

18 *Customs & Excise Commissioners* v. *College of Estate Management* [2005] UKHL 62, the quote at 77.

19 *College of Estate* at 78.

The *Dansk Handel* case, decided by the Danish Maritime and Commercial Court in 1995, is another example of the importance of the French version of CJEU judgments.[20] During proceedings before the Court the parties sought to acquire a preliminary ruling from the CJEU on the interpretation of the Equal Treatment Directive 76/207. However, the Maritime and Commercial Court denied the request, stating that the matter was *acte éclairé* due to the judgment of the CJEU in the *Hertz* case.[21] In interpreting paragraph 16 of the judgment, the Maritime and Commercial Court started out in the Danish version but also consulted the French version of the judgment. The Danish version spoke of illnesses that '*viser sig*' (demonstrate themselves) after the pregnancy. This could, according to the Court, refer either only to illnesses that demonstrate themselves after the pregnancy or to illnesses that demonstrate themselves both during and after the pregnancy. In holding for the latter the Maritime and Commercial Court appeared to find confirmation in the French wording of paragraph 16, using the more general '*apparaitre*'.[22]

Consequently, national courts can resort to both the *de jure* and the *de facto* original of CJEU judgments. Article 41 of the Rules of Procedure directly supports the former approach, while the latter is obviously inspired by an awareness of the working language of the CJEU.

The picture is more complicated when it comes to interpretation of EU legislation. As demonstrated above the understanding of multilingualism in the sphere of legislation is clearly pluralistic. The basic rules follow a different path as compared to Article 41 of the Rules of Procedure by proclaiming the equal authenticity of all official languages, and the CJEU has taken the position one step further by requiring full multilingualism in the interpretation of EU legislative provisions. However, despite this strong support for the single meaning idea, we can find examples of national courts falling back on an original when interpreting EU legislation. Again, the approach is heterogeneous and the original relied upon varies. Three different attitudes can be identified. The first, and most obvious, approach concentrates on the drafting language and elevates this *de facto* original to something closer to a *de jure* original. The recent *Assange* case from the Supreme Court of the United Kingdom is an illustrative example.[23] The Supreme Court had to interpret the term *judicial authority* in the 2002/584/JHA Framework Decision on the European Arrest Warrant and decide if a prosecutor constituted such an authority. As part of this discussion Lord Phillips, following the guidance of an English textbook on legislation, turned to the natural meaning of the words. He consulted the natural meaning of both the English *judicial authority* and the

20 Case 361/1995 *HK som mandatar for Helle Elisabeth Larsson mod Dansk Handel & Service som mandatar for Fotex Supermarked A/S*, UfR 1996.111H.

21 Case C-179/88 *Handels- og Kontorfunktionaerernes Forbund i Danmark* v. *Dansk Arbejdsgiverforening* [1990] ECR I-3979.

22 *Dansk Handel* at 112.

23 *Assange* v. *Swedish Prosecution Authority* [2012] UKSC 22.

French *autorité judiciaire*. When explaining the use of the French version of the Framework Decision, Lord Phillips demonstrated a realistic attitude regarding the EU drafting process. He acknowledged that, as regards the final version of the Decision, the same weight had to be given to the English and French versions. He then added: 'It is, however, a fact that the French draft was prepared before the English and that, in draft, in the event of conflict, the meaning of the English version had to give way to the meaning of the French.'[24] In other words, as the English version was a translation from the French version, the meaning of the Framework Decision was already established by the French version. He found that the terms bore somewhat different meanings and that the context supported the French meaning rather than the English, finally concluding that the prosecutor constituted a 'judicial authority'.

Many similar examples can be found where national courts demonstrate awareness of the *de facto* original of a legislative provision. In these situations the courts frequently refer to the domestic language version as a translation and/or designate another language version as the original or authoritative version. For example, in the *BASF* case the Danish Environmental Board of Appeal described the Danish version of Directive 78/631 as a translation and proceeded to consult the English version of the Directive.[25] Similarly, when the Court of Appeal for Administrative Matters in Baden-Württemberg interpreted Council Regulation 259/93 concerning the supervision and control of shipments of waste, it was reluctant to rely on the German language version. The Court stated that the German version was only a translation of the original text, drafted in French.[26] In the *Cato* case the English Court of Appeal interpreted the English version of Directive 83/515 in light of the French version when deciding on a decommissioning grant for fishing boats. Lord Justice Stocker referred twice to the French version as the original, and Lord Justice Purchas lamented the wording of the English version as it opened up for another, erroneous interpretation.[27]

Lord Grantchester demonstrates a second, more innovative, attitude towards the original text in the *Barkworth* case.[28] The case concerned exemption for medical care from value added tax and the interpretation of Article 13.A.1.c of the Sixth VAT Directive 77/388. Lord Grantchester found the English version unhelpful and the interpretation was instead guided by the French version. He

24 *Assange*, para. 16.

25 Case nr. 71–103 *om klassifikation og mærkningskrav i forbindelse med godkendelse af Fennosan B 100 som slimicid i papirproduktion, indeholdende aktivstoffet dazomet*, decided by the Environmental Board of Appeal, 9 March 1998.

26 VGH Baden-Württemberg 1999-03-23, 10 S 3242/98, reported in *Umwelt- und Planungsrecht* 1999/7, 276–8.

27 *James Joseph Cato* v. *Minister of Agriculture, Fisheries and Food*, Court of Appeal [1989] 3 CMLR 513, at 539–40 and 537–8.

28 *Barkworth* v. *Commissioners of Customs and Excise*, Value Added Tax Tribunal London [1987] 3 CMLR 507.

explicitly observed that French was the working language of the CJEU. Thus, we here see a crossover between the interpretation of case law and the interpretation of legislation. The fact that CJEU judgments are deliberated in French creates a spillover effect, justifying the use of the French version of a legislative provision.

Finally, another approach to the notion of originals is demonstrated by the *Rxworks* v. *Hunter* case from the Chancery Division of the English High Court of Justice. When interpreting the Trade Marks Directive 89/104, the court consulted the 'languages of the Member States of the Community at the time the Directive was adopted in December 1988', that is, the Danish, Dutch, French, German, Greek, Italian, Portuguese and Spanish versions.[29] This attitude does not concentrate on the actual drafting language, but takes a historical perspective. The official languages at the time of adoption of the legislation in question are regarded as originals, while later languages are seen as translations. This attitude might seem exotic, and it clearly deviates from the approach of the CJEU, but the Advocates General have used it at least once. In the *Henriksen* case Advocate General Jacobs made reference to 'the six versions of the Directive authentic at the time of its adoption' when interpreting the Sixth VAT Directive.[30]

A Single Meaning in National Courts: Meaning Constructed by Dialogue

The single meaning approach follows an opposite trajectory as compared to the single text approach discussed above. Rather than identifying an original the court will follow the CJEU by emphasizing the equal authenticity of the language versions and how all the languages create meaning together.

When it comes to interpretation of legislation, we can find many examples of national courts subscribing to the single meaning idea. However, there is a theoretical and a practical aspect of the single meaning doctrine. The equal authenticity of the language versions and the absence of an original constitute the theoretical aspects of the single meaning doctrine, while the use of all language versions in interpretation is the practical side of the doctrine. The CJEU advocates both sides of the doctrine, while national courts tend to be more limited (but with different degrees of ambition) when it comes to the practical application of the single meaning doctrine.

In the recent *X* v. *Mid Sussex Citizens Advice Bureau* case the Supreme Court of the United Kingdom emphasized the equal authority of the language versions of Council Directive 2000/78/EC.[31] Lord Mance found the interpretation of the directive to fulfil the requirements for *acte clair*, as established in the *CILFIT*

29 *Rxworks Limited* v. *Hunter (t/a Connect Computers)*, Chancery Division [2008] E.C.C. 15, at 255.

30 Opinion of Advocate General Jacobs in case 173/88 *Skatteministeriet* v. *Morten Henriksen* [1989] ECR 2763, delivered 17 May 1989, para. 14.

31 *X* v. *Mid Sussex Citizens Advice Bureau and another* [2012] UKSC 59.

case.[32] He observed that the different and equally authoritative language versions of the directive did not cast doubt on the correct interpretation, but reinforced it. However, it is worth noting that he spoke only of the 'language versions to which the Court was referred', that is, the French, Dutch, Spanish and German versions.[33]

Similarly, when the Financial Court in Munich interpreted Council Regulation 754/76 on the customs treatment applicable to goods returned to the customs territory of the Community, it consulted the English and French language versions in addition to the German version.[34] The court underlined that all language versions were equally authoritative, which could be seen as excluding an interpretation based on a single language in isolation. The German version was not unclear or ambiguous *per se*, the English and French language versions were consulted only as confirmation. This indicates an adherence to the single meaning idea; the meaning of a EU provision simply cannot be accessed from a single language. However, while acknowledging the equal authority of all languages, the German court only examined two of them. In other words, the meaning of a EU provision cannot be understood based on a single language, but it is not necessary to examine all, or even a majority, of the languages to determine the meaning. According to the German court, it is sufficient to examine one or two other languages, as they are equally as authoritative as the other languages.

In some cases the use of other languages in national courts is governed more by practical concerns than ideas on the consequences of multilingualism. For example, in the *Smokeless Fuels* v. *Commissioners of Inland Revenue* case, Mr Justice Warner consulted the English and French versions of Directive 73/79. By way of explanation he stated:[35]

> At this point I should mention that, being aware that the texts of an EEC directive or other instrument in all the official languages of the Community are equally authentic, and knowing from experience that it is in general unwise, if one can avoid it, to look at the text of such an instrument in one language only, I asked counsel to refer me also to the French text of the directive, which they did.

Warner acknowledged the equal authority of the different language versions but also emphasized the practical aspects of multilingual interpretation. Knowing that a single text might lead the interpreter astray, he found it necessary to seek the common meaning. However, he apparently found it sufficient to consult the French

32 Case 283/81 *Srl CILFIT and Lanificio di Gavardo SpA* v. *Ministry of Health* [1982] ECR 3415, paras. 16–20.

33 *X* v. *Mid Sussex Citizens Advice Bureau*, paras. 47–48 and 31–33, the quote at para. 48.

34 FG München 1980-01-23, III 234/77 Z, reported in *Entscheidungen der Finanzgerichte* 1980, vol. 7, 348–9.

35 *National Smokeless Fuels Limited* v. *Commissioners of Inland Revenue*, Chancery Division [1986] 3 CMLR 227, quote at 237.

version. In other words, understanding based on a single text is discouraged but contrasting two or three languages is regarded as satisfactory in order to determine the common meaning.

A very interesting development can be observed regarding the single meaning idea and the interpretation of CJEU case law. As demonstrated above, the Rules of Procedure clearly identify an original of CJEU judgments: the judgment in the language of the case. An alternative, *de facto* original (French) is competing with this *de jure* original, but the idea of a single text is clear. However, in spite of this we can find examples of national courts adopting the single meaning idea even when interpreting CJEU case law.

The most striking example of this is the *Laval* case. The *Laval* case concerned the freedom to provide services within the European Union and originated in a dispute between a number of Swedish trade unions and the Latvian company Laval concerning the duty of the latter to sign the relevant collective agreement for the building sector. The Swedish Labour Court requested a preliminary ruling and the CJEU responded in December 2007.[36] The Labour Court delivered its final ruling in the case in December 2009.[37] It was to decide on the liability of the trade unions for damages caused by the collective action taken against Laval. However, difficulties ensued when the Labour Court tried to interpret the preliminary ruling obtained from Luxembourg. The Court of Justice clearly stated that the collective action taken against Laval violated European Union law. However, the Labour Court found that this was not sufficient in order for the trade unions to be liable to pay damages. It was also necessary that Laval could rely on what is now Article 56 TFEU against the trade unions; in other words Article 56 had to be granted so-called horizontal direct effect. Laval argued that the CJEU had granted such horizontal direct effect in its preliminary ruling, while the trade unions claimed that Article 56 could only be used against a Member State. The preliminary ruling should, according to the trade unions, be understood as saying that the violation of EU law had been committed by Sweden. Swedish law granted the trade unions the right to take collective action in the case at hand. This constituted a violation of European Union law. Thus, from the perspective of the trade unions, the CJEU did not strike down the actions of the trade unions but the Swedish legislation permitting these actions.

The Labour Court observed that the Swedish language version of the preliminary ruling appeared to favour the interpretation suggested by the trade unions. In the Swedish version the Court, at paragraph 111, concluded that EU law prevented trade unions from 'being able to take collective actions' ('*ges möjlighet att genom fackliga stridsåtgärder*') as in the case at hand. This implied that the Swedish legislation was at fault, not the trade unions themselves. The

36 Case C-341/05 *Laval un Partneri Ltd* v. *Svenska Byggnadsarbetareförbundet, Svenska Byggnadsarbetareförbundets avdelning 1, Byggettan and Svenska Elektrikerförbundet* [2007] ECR I-11767.

37 AD 2009 nr 89.

French and German language versions of the ruling used similar wordings and thus reinforced the interpretation suggested by the Swedish version. However, the English and Danish versions did not include any similar phrases. These versions stated that EU law is 'to be interpreted as precluding a trade union' from taking the relevant collective action ('*skal fortolkes således, at de er til hinder for, at en fagforening* ...'). In the light of the English and Danish versions, the Labour Court rejected the interpretation advocated by the trade unions. The *Laval* judgment should be interpreted as granting horizontal direct effect to Article 56 TFEU.

The Labour Court clearly adopts a single meaning approach in its interpretation of the CJEU judgment. It discusses the Swedish, French, German, English and Danish versions of paragraph 111 of the judgment. The meaning suggested by the Swedish, French and German versions is rejected due to the clear wording of the English and Danish versions. The Labour Court does not even mention that Swedish, as the language of the case, is the only *de jure* authentic language version of the judgment. Furthermore, the court does not mention that French, as the working and drafting language of the CJEU, is the *de facto* original. The *de jure* and *de facto* originals are put aside due to the wording of two translations, English and Danish. The Labour Court adopts the same kind of single meaning reasoning as it would for interpretation of legislation. This exotic approach provoked a strong reaction from the trade unions. Arguing that the reasoning of the Labour Court, including the use of the 'wrong' language version of the judgment, was obviously incorrect, the trade unions sought extraordinary relief from the Swedish Supreme Court, without success.[38]

The Swedish Revenue Board adopted a similar approach in an earlier case concerning VAT for the rental of parking space in garages, involving the interpretation of the above-mentioned *Henriksen* case from the CJEU.[39] The Revenue Board took its point of departure in paragraph 15 of the English version of the judgment, where the CJEU concluded that the letting of sites for parking was excluded from value added tax if the letting was closely linked to the letting of immovable property used for a different, tax exempt, purpose, 'so that the two lettings constitute a single economic transaction'. The CJEU continued in paragraph 16 to say '[t]hat is so, on the one hand, if the parking place and the immovable property to be used for another purpose are part of a single complex and, on the other, if both properties are let to the tenant by the same landlord'. The Revenue Board found the English version to be unclear as to whether the two conditions described in paragraph 16 were alternative or cumulative. In this situation the Board turned to the German and Danish versions of the judgment, both of which made it clear that the conditions were cumulative. This interpretation was confirmed by the aim of the system of taxation.

Two features of the judgment are of particular interest. First, it is noticeable that the Revenue Board took the English version of the judgment as its point

38 NJA 2010 N 30.

39 RÅ 2003 ref 80.

of departure, not the Danish version (which would have been formally correct as it was the language of the case). Second, when the English version proved ambiguous, the German and Danish versions were consulted. Thus, the French version was not consulted. Instead, in addition to the Danish original the Revenue Board consulted two versions that are neither *de jure* nor *de facto* originals: the English and German language versions.

Some national examples of the single meaning doctrine are very ambitious when it comes to multilingual interpretation. The judgment of the German Federal Administrative Court in April 2010, which included an interpretation of *Commission* v. *Finland*, may serve as an illustration.[40] One of the questions posed to the Federal Administrative Court related to paragraph 29 of the *Commission* v. *Finland* case, concerning when derogations could be granted from the strict protection for animal species listed in Council Directive 92/43/EEC. In English, the first sentence of paragraph 29 states: 'None the less, the grant of such derogations remains possible by way of exception where it is duly established that they are not such as to worsen the unfavourable conservation status of those populations or to prevent their restoration at a favourable conservation status.' The Federal Administrative Court observed that the German version of paragraph 29 was misleading in two ways, first in that it indicated that the two criteria (not worsen the unfavourable conservation status and not prevent their restoration) were alternative, not cumulative, and second in that it required the fulfilment of a third criterion, the presence of exceptional circumstances. The Court turned to the Finnish version of the judgment and emphasized that this was the authentic version according to what was then Article 31 of the Rules of Procedure of the Court of Justice. According to the Finnish version it was clear that 'exceptional circumstances' was not an independent criterion and that the other two criteria were cumulative, not alternative. Furthermore, this interpretation was confirmed by the English, French, Spanish, Italian, Portuguese and Greek language versions of the judgment. Only the Dutch and German versions deviated, and the Federal Administrative Court concluded that the German version suffered from a translation error.

The judgment of the Federal Administrative Court constitutes an interesting mix between the single meaning and the single text approaches. On the one hand the German court is perfectly aware of the language regime of the CJEU and the existence of a *de jure* original. Furthermore, the language of the case is authoritative, guiding the interpretation and rejecting the meaning suggested by the German version of *Commission* v. *Finland*. On the other hand, the English version appeared to be the starting point for the court, and it still felt the need to examine seven other versions of the judgment to confirm the interpretation of the Finnish version. Even when acknowledging the language of the case as the original and authoritative version, the single meaning idea is very much alive.

40 BVerwG 9 B 5. 10, decided 17 April 2010 and case C-342/05 *Commission of the European Communities* v. *Republic of Finland* [2007] ECR I-4713.

Conclusions: Competing Ideologies

EU law is multilingual but the meaning and consequences of multilingualism vary, both *de jure* and *de facto*. The Member States have implemented different language regimes for legislation and CJEU case law. Full multilingualism prevails regarding primary law and legislation, providing for equal authority of every official language. According to the CJEU, legislation simply cannot be understood in a single language. When it comes to the case law of the CJEU, the Member States opted for a more limited form of multilingualism. All 24 official languages can be used before the Court, but the final judgment is only authentic in the language of the case. Consequently, already from a *de jure* perspective we can identify two distinctly different approaches, here referred to as the single meaning and the single text ideas.

The distinctive language regimes reflect opposing views regarding how the sources of law are to be used. The equal value of all official language versions of legislation follows from fundamental ideas of legal certainty and the equal standing of the Member States (Gundel 2001: 780–81). From the perspective of the CJEU the equal authority and single meaning idea is also crucial in order to ensure the uniform interpretation and application of EU law. The absence of full multilingualism for case law indicates a limited view of adjudication, where judgments include the application of legislation to a particular set of circumstances but do not necessarily constitute an independent source of law. Arnull (1993: 265–6) has argued that even the CJEU itself hesitated for a long time to regard its previous judgments as an independent source of law, explaining the lack of a coherent citation methodology. If CJEU judgments are primarily of interest to the parties of the dispute and the referring national court, the single text idea makes sense. The language of the case is the authoritative language, which reflects the proceedings before the CJEU and enables the referring national court to rely on the judgment in its own language. The problem is that this view is too restrictive and ignores the great importance of case law in the EU system. While the original idea might have been to restrict the role played by the CJEU, the Luxembourg court quickly escaped the chains. Today, case law is a crucial component of EU law, sometimes even regarded as the most important source of law (Schermers and Waelbroeck 2001: 133; Stone Sweet and McCown 2003: 113). Seen in that light the single text idea is not an obvious choice. In a system where CJEU judgments are arguably used more like case law in a common law system (Derlén, Lindholm, Rosvall and Mirshahvalad 2013), the fundamental ideas underpinning the language regime of legislation could be regarded as relevant.

However, the *de jure* perspective is only the first part of the discussion. The picture becomes more complex if we move beyond the rules on multilingualism. *De facto* originals exist in the single meaning domain, in the sense that the provisions were drafted in a single language and then translated into the remaining languages. Furthermore, an alternative, *de facto* original is available in the single text domain, due to the use of French as the internal working language of the

CJEU. This creates a situation of competing ideologies and competing originals. The official ideology regarding legislation is the single meaning idea, but this is challenged by the well-known existence of a drafting language. Similarly, the language of the case is challenged by French for the position as the original and thereby authoritative version of CJEU judgments.

National courts find themselves in the middle of this field of uncertainty. As demonstrated above, national courts use a wide variety of approaches to multilingualism, partly reflecting the existing alternatives, partly fusing them together. The general uncertainty is reflected in the behaviour of the courts of the Member States. The various approaches adopted are not only dissimilar but fundamentally distinctive, and even the notion of what constitutes the original varies. As to the last issue, some innovative choices are made, beyond the more obvious alternatives. This includes letting the working language of the CJEU decide the decisive language in interpretation of legislation and treating the official languages when the legislation was adopted as originals.

Most interestingly, we can observe a spillover effect both between case law and legislation and between legislation and case law, blurring the line between the language regimes. The *Barkworth* case discussed above is the most obvious example of the direct influence of case law on the interpretation of legislation. Since the CJEU deliberates in French and presumably consults EU legislation in French, it is reasonable for national courts to concentrate on the French wording of legislation as well. The development in drafting the last 10 years has severely reduced the importance of French in favour of English, but the use of French in the CJEU may enable French to hold on to the perceived position of legislative original for some time yet. However, the language regime of case law has arguably also an indirect influence. By explicitly recognizing a single original, it has opened the door for the same attitude when engaging with legislation. Conversely, the strong message of the CJEU regarding the single meaning idea has apparently spilled over from the legislative domain to the area of case law. Whether this is due to uncertainty regarding the language regime of case law, arguably less well known in the Member States than its legislative counterpart, or a more fundamental acceptance of the single meaning idea, where a single language can never be the base for understanding EU law, is difficult to know. Some examples, such as the Swedish cases *Laval* and *RÅ 2003 ref 80* discussed above, contain no explicit references to the language regime of case law and the special position of the language of the case, enabling both interpretations. Other cases, such as the judgment of the German Federal Administrative Court discussed above, expressly recognize the standing of the language of the case but still find it valuable to consult other language versions, indicating general support for the single meaning idea.

In conclusion, the role of the official languages in the interpretation of legislation and CJEU case law is in a state of flux. Formally, the areas are profoundly different, as expressed by the ideas of a single meaning and a single text. From the perspective of national courts the meaning of the ideas and the dividing line between them are starting to blur. The basic uncertainty, created by the existence of different language regimes for legislation and case law, is amplified by the multitude of techniques employed by national courts engaging in multilingual interpretation. This makes it difficult for parties to a dispute to anticipate which language or languages will be decisive in interpretation. Furthermore, while a move to the single meaning doctrine in the area of case law is reasonable, given the development of case law as a source of law, the reliance on language versions that are pure translations is questionable. Languages that are not the language of the case or French have not received any special attention from the CJEU, and their value as an indication of the intention of the Court is therefore limited. The controversy following the *Laval* judgment discussed above illustrates the potential problems. If the development towards a unified approach to multilingual interpretation is to continue, it will have to be accompanied by changes in the drafting and translation process.

References

Arnull, A. 1993. Owning up to fallibility: precedent and the Court of Justice. *Common Market Law Review*, 30, 247–66.

Athanassiou, P. 2006. *The Application of Multilingualism in the European Union Context*. Legal Working Paper Series of the European Central Bank, No. 2, March 2006.

Danwitz, T. von 2008. Funktionsbedingungen der Rechtsprechung des Europäischen Gerichthofes. *Europarecht*, 769–85.

Derlén, M. 2009. *Multilingual Interpretation of European Union Law*. Alphen aan den Rijn: Kluwer Law International.

Derlén, M. 2011. In defence of (limited) multilingualism: problems and possibilities of the multilingual interpretation of European Union law in national courts, in *Linguistic Diversity and European Democracy*, edited by A.L. Kjær and S. Adamo. Farnham: Ashgate, 143–66.

Derlén, M. 2014. Multilingual interpretation of CJEU case law: rule and reality. *European Law Review*, 39, 295–315.

Derlén, M., Lindholm, J., Rosvall, M. and Mirshahvalad, A. 2013. Coherence out of chaos: mapping European Union law by running randomly through the maze of CJEU case law. *Europarättslig tidskrift*, 517–35.

Due, O. 1999. Understanding the reasoning of the Court of Justice, in *Mélanges en hommage à Fernand Schockweiler*, edited by G.C. Rodríguez Iglesias, O. Due, R. Schintgen and C. Elsen. Baden-Baden: Nomos Verlagsgesellschaft, 73–85.

European Commission. 1995. *A Multilingual Community at Work*. Luxembourg: Office for Official Publications of the European Communities.

European Commission. 2012. *Translation and Multilingualism*. Luxembourg: Publications Office of the European Union.

Gallo, G. 2006. Organisation and features of translation activities at the Court of Justice of the European Communities, in *Multilingualism and the Harmonisation of European Law*, edited by B. Pozzo and V. Jacometti. Alphen aan den Rijn: Kluwer Law International, 179–95.

Gundel, J. 2001. Zur Sprachenregelung bei den E.G.-Agenturen – Abschied auf Raten von der Regel der 'Allsprachigkeit' der Gemeinschaft im Verkehr mit dem Bürger? Anmerkung zum Urteil des EuG von 12.7.2001, Christina Kik/ Harmonisierungsamt für den Binnenmarkt, Rs. T-120/99. *Europarecht*, 776–83.

Hilf, M. 1973. *Die Auslegung mehrsprachiger Verträge – Eine Untersuchung zum Völkerrecht und zum Staatsrecht der Bundesrepublik Deutschland*. Berlin, Heidelberg and New York: Springer-Verlag.

Hilpold, P. 2010. Die europäische Sprachenpolitik – Babel nach Maβ. *Europarecht*, 695–711.

Komarek, J. 2007. In the court(s) we trust? On the need for hierarchy and differentiation in the preliminary ruling procedure. *European Law Review*, 32(4), 467–91.

Kürten, M.A. 2004. *Die Bedeutung der deutschen Sprache im Recht der Europäischen Union – Eine Untersuchung der aktuellen sowie zukünftig möglichen Bedeutung der deutschen Sprache in der EU*. Berlin: Duncker & Humblot.

Loehr, K. 1998. *Mehrsprachigkeitsprobleme in der Europäischen Union – Eine empirische und theoretische Analyse aus sprachwissenschaftlicher Perspektive*. Frankfurt am Main: Peter Lang.

Mancini, G.F. and Keeling, D.T. 1995. Language, culture and politics in the life of the European Court of Justice. *Columbia Journal of European Law*, 1, 397–413.

McAuliffe, K. 2008. Enlargement at the European Court of Justice: law, language and translation. *European Law Journal*, 14, 806–18.

McAuliffe, K. 2012. Language and law in the European Union: the multilingual jurisprudence of the ECJ, in *The Oxford Handbook of Language and the Law*, edited by P.M. Tiersma and L.M. Solan. Oxford: Oxford University Press, 200–216.

Mulders, L. 2008. Translation at the Court of Justice of the European Communities, in *The Coherence of EU Law*, edited by S. Prechal and B. van Roermund. Oxford: Oxford University Press, 45–59.

Oppermann, T. 2001. Reform der EU-Sprachenregelung? *Neue Juristische Wochenschrift*, 2663–8.

Pommer, S.E. 2012. Interpreting multilingual EU law: what role for legal translation? *European Review of Private Law*, 5&6, 1241–54.

Robinson, W. 2005. How the European Commission drafts legislation in 20 languages. *Clarity*, 53, 4–10.

Schermers, H.G. and Waelbroeck, D.F. 2001. *Judicial Protection in the European Union*. 6th edition. The Hague: Kluwer.

Schilling, T. 2011. Multilingualism and multijuralism: Assets of EU legislation and adjudication? *German Law Journal*, 12, 1460–91.

Schroeder, W. 2004. Die Auslegung des EU-Rechts. *Juristische Schulung*, 180–86.

Schübel-Pfister, I. 2004. *Sprache und Gemeinschaftsrecht – Die Auslegung der mehrsprachig verbindlichen Rechtstexte durch den Europäischen Gerichtshof*. Berlin: Duncker & Humblot.

Sevón, L. 1997. Languages in the Court of Justice of the European Communities. *Rivista di Diritto Europeo*, 533–46.

Sevón, L. 1999. Experiencing the Court of Justice of the European Communities, in *Mélanges en hommage à Fernand Schockweiler*, edited by G.C. Rodríguez Iglesias, O. Due, R. Schintgen and C. Elsen. Baden-Baden: Nomos Verlagsgesellschaft, 577–92.

Stone Sweet, A. and McCown, M. 2003. Discretion and precedent in European law, in *Judicial Discretion in European Perspective*, edited by O. Wiklund. Stockholm: Norstedts Juridik, 84–115.

Šarčević, S. 1997. *New Approach to Legal Translation*. The Hague: Kluwer Law International.

Tabory, M. 1980. *Multilingualism in International Law and Institutions*. Alphen aan den Rijn: Sijthoff & Noordhoff.

Usher, J.A. 1981. Language and the European Court of Justice. *The International Contract – Law & Finance Review*, 2, 277–85.

Chapter 5
Comparative Law and the New Frontiers of Legal Translation

Barbara Pozzo

The Task of Comparative Law Analysis

Comparative lawyers are genetically predestined to deal with legal translation issues.[1] The information they seek about foreign legal systems is embedded in the language that the legal system under analysis uses to express its legal rules.[2] That is why legal translation has always been considered an important tool for comparative law analysis.[3]

Traditionally, problems of legal translation arise from the need to transpose concepts from one language into another in the course of comparative law analysis, with the aim of gaining knowledge, seeking divergences and convergences, unveiling traps and concrete difficulties in finding divergences and convergences in legal concepts.

In comparative law, every operation of legal translation implies a complex intellectual work that should be aimed at understanding the 'deep' meaning of what we want to translate and at identifying a possible correspondence in the target language (Durieux 1992: 95). It is far from being a mere technical issue because law and language are profoundly culture bound. That is why translating always implies an interpretation issue (Ioriatti Ferrari 2008), while the mere juxtaposition of legal concepts in the different languages should be avoided, as it could only reach a very superficial result (Legrand 1996: 234).

From this perspective, legal translation needs to guard against the opposite dangers of unfaithfulness to the source culture and unintelligibility of the target text. Something will certainly get *lost*, but comparative lawyers may also *find* something in this translation process (Pozzo 2011: 149).

---

1 In Italy Rodolfo Sacco is the founder of an important school on legal translation issues (see Sacco 1987: 845 ff.; 1994: 475; 2011; Sacco and Castellani 1999).

2 Gerber (2005: 41) and Kitamura (1995: 862).

3 The importance of legal translation for comparative law discourse is shown by the fact that the International Academy of Comparative Law dedicated sessions to this issue at conferences in 1986 and 1998. The proceedings of the first conference at Sydney are published in (1987) 28(4) *Cahiers de Droit*, Faculté de droit de l'Université Laval; the proceedings of the second conference at Bristol in Jayme (1999).

Technical Problems of Legal Translation

Comparative lawyers need to translate legal concepts that are technical, on the one hand, and cultural bound, on the other (Terral 2004: 876). Thus it has been suggested that the teaching of a foreign legal terminology could be a way of teaching comparative law (Bergmans 1987: 89).

In the process of translating, one concern is to identify the various meanings which are expressed by the same word or term (Gu 2006), as even within a single language, each word, phrase or sentence does not have a unitary meaning (Boyd White 1990).

Legal Concepts and the Stratification of Different Meanings

Legal concepts – within a particular legal system – are the result of the stratification of different meanings which have been developed over the course of time.[4] Identifying these meanings is the condition precedent to any translating operation. An example might serve to illustrate the problem better than a wordy exposition.[5] Can the term *Eigentum* be translated by *propriété*, *property* or *proprietà*? For lay persons they mean '*almost the same thing*', as Umberto Eco (2003) would have it.

However, a jurist would first determine the subject-matter of the translation and note that *Eigentum* has a different meaning in the context of the German Civil Code (*Bürgerliches Gesetzbuch*, BGB) and consequently in relations between private parties, than in a constitutional context, where the same term can be found in Article 14 of the *Grundgesetz*.

The definition of the ownership regime under §903 BGB is indeed subject to the limitations imposed by §90 of the same BGB, which provides that '*Sachen im Sinne des Gesetzes sind nur körperliche Dinge*' (Things in the eyes of the law are only corporeals). 'Goods' in the legal sense, as far as the private law property regime is concerned, consist solely of corporeal things, therefore excluding, in this context, any reference to immaterial property. Therefore, the property paradigm in Germany has never offered any scope for providing protection to intellectual property, something which occurs in other national contexts where the scope of application of the notion is broader.

Shifting to the German constitutional context, *Eigentum* under Article 14 of the current German Constitution[6] has always been interpreted by the courts as including patents and copyrights. On the basis of the assumption of 'functional equivalence' between the law on property and other legal fields, the German Constitutional Court, the *Bundesverfassungsgericht*,[7] has further broadened the

4 For this perspective see A. Gambaro in Candian et al. (1992: 3).

5 This example is from Candian et al. (1992: 316 ff.).

6 Art. 14 of the German Constitution (*Grundgesetz*) is taken from Art. 153 of the Weimar Constitution.

7 The leading case is published in *BVerfGE* 4, 240; see Sendler (1971: 20).

constitutional concept of ownership to also include *some* public rights (*subjektive öffentliche Rechte*), where these are of equivalent status to the position of owner (Nicolaysen 1966).

Therefore, even within the German legal system itself, *Eigentum* is not always *Eigentum*, and translating it by using *property*, *propriété* or *proprietà* could have problematic aspects, depending on the relevant context and with the further warning that this divergence in meaning, when applied to private law contexts and constitutional ones, may not exist at all or it may have a different dimension in Swiss or Austrian law, where the term *Eigentum* is also used.

Legal Concepts and their Demarcation Function

Furthermore, when translating legal concepts, we have to remember that their demarcation function may differ depending on the legal system being considered as the reference context. For instance, as regards the notion of contract, considerable differences exist in the various European legal systems, which cannot be explained merely on the basis of the common law/civil law antithesis.

Just to frame the issue, we should perhaps remind ourselves that marriage is a *contrat* for the French, while it is not as far as the Germans, Italians and English are concerned. Similarly, donation is contractual for Germans and Italians, but not for the English. Trusts are common law instruments governed by the law of property; however, if any effects of this institution are transposed into civil law jurisdictions, recourse must be made to mechanisms which for all purposes are part of the law of contracts.

Bearing all this in mind, can we translate *contratto* as *Vertrag*, *contract*, or *contrat*? Since the demarcation function of the notion of contract varies according to each individual reference context, the problem arises how to inform the translator of the risk of using a literal translation which fails to emphasize the limitations and lines of demarcation of the concept being translated.

Problem of Immanent Values

Our immediate perception of legal rules is that they seem inseparable from their written form. However, when speaking about legal languages and legal translation, it is important to remember that written language is only one of the possible forms of expression and manifestation of the law. From an historical point of view, the law has not always been laid down entirely in written form (Sacco 1995: 783; 1999).

In the Western legal tradition we are accustomed to thinking about language in terms of writing, and we are trained to lay down laws primarily in written terms. From this perspective, only written law is considered authoritative (Grossfeld and Eberle 2003: 306). In other legal traditions, such as in China (see Cao 2004: 161) or in African legal systems (see Allott 1967: 63), this perception might be different, as the unwritten character of customary rules could prevail in the practice of law.

Furthermore, legal rules, whether oral or written, might be profoundly influenced by invisible structural patterns that need to be unveiled prior to translation (Grossfeld and Eberle 2003: 297). Generally speaking, one might say that the task of understanding the culture in which legal rules are rooted is implied in every translation process; however, in some cases the cultural element could be of major importance.

In order to uncover the invisible patterns and ascertain the immanent values of a legal system, the comparative lawyer needs to understand the deep links between law and culture.[8] Let us take a few examples to illustrate the cultural embeddedness of legal concepts: would it be possible to understand the concept of *private property* in China, without keeping in mind the values of the socialist ideology in which it is embedded? (on this topic, see Chen 2010: 983). Or would it be possible to understand legislation on the remarriage of widows in India, without knowing the values that Hindu traditional law attaches to the word *widow* itself? (see Carroll 1983).

New Frontiers of Legal Translation

The problem of legal translation gains a new dimension in the context of European multilingualism. EU legislation is necessarily multilingual since EU official texts must be published in all official languages. This often leads to complex and significant translation problems.

Although proposals have been made to reduce the number of official languages, the choice of multilingualism in the European Union does not seem to be questioned, even in the light of the accession of new Member States, which has significantly increased the number of official languages, now 24 with the accession of Croatia on 1 July 2013.[9] At an operative level, it has often been underlined that translating into and from each official language is no longer manageable, as nowadays it is necessary to navigate among more than 500 possible language combinations.

Nonetheless, in our age where pluralism, the protection of minorities and the rediscovery of regional and minority cultures are central interests of the political class and public opinion, introducing restrictions in the number of official languages does not seem to be a plausible solution, despite the mounting translation problems (Jacometti 2009: 4).

8 On the interaction between law and culture cf. Gordon (1984), Krygier (1986) and Abel (1978).

9 Prior to the enlargement of 2004 the official languages were English, French, German, Dutch, Swedish, Danish, Portuguese, Italian, Spanish, Greek and Finnish. On 1 May 2004 nine new languages were added: Estonian, Lithuanian, Latvian, Slovene, Polish, Hungarian, Czech, Slovak and Maltese. Thereafter, Irish was recognized as the twenty-first official language; in 2007 Bulgarian and Romanian were added, and in 2013 Croatian.

Looking at past experience, we see that multilingualism in Europe has created numerous challenges to the traditional attitudes towards legal translation (Salmi-Tolonen 2004: 1167). This is particularly true in regard to the role of legal translation in the EU lawmaking process where the aim of secondary legislation is to harmonize rules with a view to guaranteeing equal rights to all EU citizens.

Difficulties in Achieving Harmonization

At European level there is no uniform legal terminology, created and shaped by a common European legal culture that pre-exists the EU legal text. Consequently, when EU directives use legal terms without defining their content, the legal terminology used to transpose directives into national law will be interpreted according to the respective national background, creating insurmountable difficulties in achieving harmonized results.

Similar problems arise in cases where EU drafters deliberately opt for a technical definition.[10] An example is easily supplied by the Directive 2004/35/EC of the European Parliament and of the Council of 21 April 2004 on environmental liability with regard to the prevention and remedying of environmental damage.[11] According to the definition in Article 2 of the Directive, *damage* means 'a measurable adverse change in a natural resource or measurable impairment of a natural resource service which may occur directly or indirectly'. Failing to supply the interpreter with unequivocal criteria, the definition lends itself to diverse interpretations in the various national contexts, thereby undermining the very process of harmonization which the Directive aims to achieve.

A further observation concerns the problem of lack of consistency and coherency in the use of terminology within the same language version, or when translated from one language into another. Council Directive 85/577 of 20 December 1985 on the protection of consumers in relation to contracts negotiated away from business premises provides an important example in this regard.

Article 4 of the Directive, in the Italian language version, governs the right of cancellation (*diritto di rescindere*) of the contract by the consumer, not the right of withdrawal (*recesso*).[12] The French version provides that the consumer has the 'right to resile from the effects of the contract' (*son droit de résilier le contrat*), using the terms *résilier* and *renoncer* as if they were equivalent, even though they are not. The former refers to the possibility of cancelling or withdrawing from a

---

10 For these problems, see generally Jacometti (2009: 4).

11 OJ, 30.4.2004, L 143/56.

12 The common remedy of *recesso* is set out in Art. 1373 of the Italian Civil Code, which provides: 'If one of the parties has been given the power to withdraw from the contract, such power can be exercised as long as there has been no commencement of performance. In contracts for continuous or periodic performance, such power can also be subsequently exercised, but the withdrawal has no effect as to performance already made or in course.'

contract which is defective, while the latter concerns the possibility of renouncing an intention, as in the case when someone renounces or gives up a right to take legal action. The German version uses the term *Widerruf*, which was generally used in the BGB, at least before the 2002 reform of the law of obligations, to indicate the revocation of a unilateral act, for example, an offer, certainly not a contract. However, the term *Rücktritt* is also used in the German version of the Directive itself, as if it were synonymous. The English version uses the following expressions without differentiation: *to assess the obligations arising under the contract*, *right of cancellation*, *right to renounce the effects of his undertaking*, *right of renunciation*.

Searching for Solutions

The complexity of the situation that characterizes drafting, translating and interpreting EU legal texts led the European institutions to undertake some efforts to rationalize the situation. These joint efforts resulted in the publication of the *Joint Practical Guide of the European Parliament, the Council and the Commission for persons involved in the drafting of legislation within the Community institutions*, which was updated and renamed in 2013.[13]

According to the 'General Principles' of the *Joint Practical Guide*, legislative acts must be drafted in clear, simple and precise language (Principle 1.1.), thus ensuring that the law is accessible and comprehensible to all in order to guarantee the equality of citizens before the law (Principle 1.2.).

The drafter should attempt to express the legislative intention in simple terms, using everyday language to the extent possible (Principle 1.4.1.). The favoured solution appears to be to opt for language which is as simple, common and therefore as non-technical as possible. Chapter 5 of the *Joint Practical Guide* reminds drafters to keep the multilingual nature of EU legislation in mind throughout the drafting process leading to enactment. Principle 5.2. requires the original text to be particularly simple and to avoid terms which are too closely linked to national legal systems (Principle 5.3.2.).

These guidelines will certainly have an important impact on the creation of a body of European private law, where the technical nature of legal language appears to conflict to some extent with the desired vagueness and non-technicality of the terms used. Nevertheless, in order to find new solutions, it is necessary to go beyond the mere question of translation and to create a common terminology in 24 languages, while developing a consistent theory of interpretation of multilingual texts to maintain harmonized results at EU level and national level as well.

---

13 The 2nd edition of the *Joint Practical Guide of the European Parliament, the Council and the Commission for persons involved in the drafting of European Union legislation* is available at: eur-lex.europa.eu/content/pdf/techleg/joint-practical-guide-2013-en.pdf.

The Need to Create a Common Terminology in 24 Languages

The problems relating to the terminology used in EU law have been at the centre of the Commission's attention over the past decade, particularly in the field of contract law. Since its Action Plan of 12 February 2003,[14] the Commission has highlighted, among other problems plaguing the *acquis*, the use of abstract terms in directives which were not defined at all or were too broadly defined, as well as the problem of incoherence within European contract law.

As part of its Action Plan, the Commission financed a Union-wide academic project to elaborate a Common Frame of Reference (CFR)[15] with a view to providing best solutions in terms of common terminology and rules by defining fundamental concepts and abstract terms such as *contract* or *damage* and laying down rules that apply, for example, in the case of non-performance of contracts. The final Draft Common Frame of Reference (DCFR) (von Bar, Clive and Schulte-Nölke 2009)[16] was finally approved and published with a dual purpose in 2009. First, it was intended to serve as a tool for improving the *acquis* by providing clear definitions of legal terms, fundamental principles and coherent model rules of contract law which draw on the existing *acquis* and best solutions found in the legal systems of the Member States. Second, it was said that the DCFR could serve as the basis for an optional instrument on European Contract Law (see Marchetti 2012: 1265–76). Indeed, the *Proposal for a Common European Sales Law* (CESL), published by the Commission in 2011 in the form of a regulation,[17] aims at introducing an optional regime with a uniform set of contract rules for the cross-border sale of goods between businesses and consumers.

For our purpose, we are not interested in the substance of the DCFR but rather its language, which, in turn, has influenced the language and style of the CESL.[18] Although the DCFR was drafted in English, 'this' English is different from the one that expresses the concepts of the common law. In the context of the DCFR, English becomes a neutral or descriptive language associated with a classic civil law background. As such, it no longer transposes common law concepts (nor those of another specific legal order, historically given), but rather those of an emerging

14 Communication of the Commission to the European Parliament and the Council – *A More Coherent European Contract Law, An Action Plan*, Brussels, 12.2.2003, COM(2003) 68 final.

15 Communication from the Commission to the European Parliament and the Council, *European Contract Law and the revision of the acquis: the way forward*, Brussels, 11.10.2004, COM(2004) 651 final.

16 Available at: ec.europa.eu/justice/policies/civil/docs/dcfr_outline_edition_en.pdf.

17 COM(2011) 635 final, Proposal for a Regulation of the European Parliament and of the Council on a Common European Sales Law. The CESL is based largely on the DCFR and the 'Feasibility Study' completed in May 2011 and available at: http://ec.europa.eu/justice/contract/files/feasibility_study_final.pdf.

18 See Chapter 9 in this volume, in particular, the case study carried out by Strandvik on the translation of the CESL by the Commission's Directorate-General for Translation.

legal order, the European legal system, which is greatly influenced by the various cultural and legal backgrounds of the Member States.

Since the emerging European legal order is also multilingual, the drafters made painstaking efforts to create a neutral language void of legalese and technicalities that could be 'readily translated without carrying unwanted baggage with it' (Introduction to the DCFR, von Bar, Clive and Schulte-Nölke 2009: 29). For this reason, terms such as *recission*, *tort* and *delict* are avoided and replaced by descriptive paraphrases. For instance, torts (delicts) are described as 'non-contractual liability arising out of damage caused to another'. The injured party is referred to as 'a person who has suffered legally relevant damage' and the tortfeasor as 'a person who caused the damage' (VI.-1:01). For greater concision, neologisms have been created whenever possible, some of which are descriptive, others literal translations. For example, the rule on *force majeure* is called *event beyond control* (VI.-5:302), the German *Rücktritt* is *unilateral withdrawal*, and *Rechtsgeschäft* is *juridical act* (II.-1:101). Latin phrases are also avoided. For instance, instead of using the usual Latin term *negotiorum gestio*, the civilian institution *Geschäftsführung ohne Auftrag* is called *benevolent intervention in another's affairs* (Book V).

A British assessment of the language of the DCFR confirms that the drafters have generally managed 'to express its rules in terminology which is comprehensible in English but which is not too tied to the technical concepts of English law itself'. Despite the neutral, descriptive language of the DCFR, the assessment notes that 'some significant problems of terminology' remain, which 'will become apparent in the translation of the CFR into all the official languages of the EU' (Whittaker 2008: 10).

In this context it is also important to mention the important role of the definitions in the DCFR, which have the function of suggestions for the development of a European uniform terminology, that is, uniform concepts. In addition to the definitions in the text of the model rules, a list of terms and definitions is published in Annex I, which is considered to be an integral part of the DCFR. The substance of the definitions is derived partly from the *acquis*, but predominantly from the model rules. Therefore, when some scholars suggested that the terminology list could do the job of establishing uniform concepts, the view prevailed that the definitions cannot be separated from the model rules. In other words, the definitions are essential for the model rules, and the model rules for the definitions (Introduction to the DCFR, von Bar, Clive and Schulte-Nölke 2009: 17).

The quest for a uniform terminology at European level would be meaningless if – at the same time – European lawyers could not count on a consistent theory of interpretation of multilingual texts. In fact, once shared concepts are achieved at supranational level, in order to retain their harmonizing role, they also need to be interpreted according to the same hermeneutical principles.

A Consistent Theory of Interpretation of Multilingual Texts

From a historical point of view, we have important examples of how different interpretations of the same text can lead to divergent results over the course of time. For example, when the French Civil Code entered into force in Belgium in the nineteenth century, there was no need for translation. However, it is well known that the same provisions gave rise to quite divergent interpretations in their application by the courts in the two systems (Pozzo 2006: 16).

In this context, the Court of Justice of the European Union (CJEU) plays a major role, given its institutional tasks. According to Article 19 of the Treaty on European Union (TEU), the CJEU has the task of ensuring that, in the interpretation and application of the Treaty, the law is observed. The main instrument for achieving this objective is the competence granted to the Court by the founding Treaties to make preliminary rulings. In this sense, Article 19 TEU provides that the CJEU shall have jurisdiction to give preliminary rulings on the interpretation of the Treaties and the validity of acts adopted by the institutions of the Union.

Over the past decades the Court has developed various interpretation criteria with a view to ensuring uniform application of EU law in deference to the Treaty's objectives (see Derlén 2009). First of all, the Court developed the concept of a new legal order, working out its proper concepts in the *Van Gend en Loos* judgment[19] of 1963. Here the Court made it clear that the language used by the institutions is different from and independent of the national languages, including their legal languages. As Ioriatti points out (2009), the terms used in Brussels to express the new reality are responses to needs of the Union which often arise at the same time as the concepts themselves.

Today this new reality must be expressed and interpreted in 24 different languages in order to achieve the same overall results. In this context we need to recall that all EU texts of primary and secondary law are equally authentic and that this presupposes that all versions have the same meaning and therefore convey the same rules and statements. However, as has been emphasized in comparative law research (Gambaro 2007), this simple presumption is contradicted by evidence that discrepancies exist between the different versions.

In multilingual jurisdictions the interpreter is required to examine more than one authoritative language version. This means that, in the case of equally authentic texts, none of the language versions is dominant for the purpose of interpretation. This principle of *literal interpretation* is settled by CJEU case law,[20] which makes it clear that one language version of an EU legal text cannot *per se* be considered superior. For the sake of achieving the uniform application of EU law, the interpreter is required to take account of the other language versions as well.

---

19 Case 26/62 *Van Gend en Loos* v. *Nederlandse Belastingadministratie* [1963] ECR 1.

20 Case 02.04.1998, C-296/95; Case 20.11.2003, C-152/01.

Beyond such a pronouncement, the decision of the Court poses a problem which is difficult to manage in practical terms in that it requires the interpreter to have a mastery of a vast number of official languages (cf. Ajani and Rossi 2006: 79). In these circumstances, the interpreter must search for the intention of the legislator. This exercise does not have much in common with intention in a psychological sense (Gambaro 2007), but requires attributing a sense to the rules which conforms with the purpose assigned to them.

This teleological criterion seems to prevail in the case law especially since the *CILFIT* case[21] where the Court laid down three main principles for the interpretation of Community (today EU) law. First, in the interpretation of Community law the multilingual nature of the rules must be taken into account, thus requiring a comparison of all authentic language versions. Second, the Court observed that, even in the case of full concordance of the language versions, Community law uses a specific terminology that is proper to its own purposes and that legal concepts do not necessarily have the same meaning in Community law and national laws. Finally, every provision of Community law must be placed in its context and interpreted in the light of the provisions of this body of law, of its purpose and its state of evolution.

After the *CILFIT* case the Court developed two strands of interpretation to be used whenever doubt arises concerning the interpretation of a provision by virtue of its multilingual nature. The first strand supports a purely literal interpretation criterion, the second the principle of purposive interpretation. There are, however, cases in which the Court used a joint application of the two interpretative criteria.

Despite the increasing number of official languages, the Court has in some cases[22] staunchly maintained a rule of interpretation based on a mere comparison of the different language versions. This is mostly the case where a single language version differs from all the others, thus making it easy for the Court to choose 'the' solution which does not raise further problems of interpretation.

The fact that the Court did not make reference to the purpose of the legislation to be interpreted suggests that the problem is resolved by the mere juxtaposition of the different linguistic versions.[23] In terms of interpretation, therefore, the literal

21 Case 283/81, Judgment of the Court of 6 October 1982, *Srl CILFIT and Lanificio di Gavardo SpA* v. *Ministry of Health*. Reference for a preliminary ruling: Corte suprema di Cassazione – Italy. For a discussion of the case law, see Pozzo (2008: 383–431).

22 See, for example, Case 144/86, Judgment of the Court of 8 December 1987, *Gubisch Maschinenfabrik AG* v. *Giulio Palumbo*. Reference for a preliminary ruling: Corte suprema di Cassazione – Italy; Case 114/86, Judgment of the Court of 27 September 1988, *United Kingdom of Great Britain and Northern Ireland* v. *Commission of the European Communities*; Case 357/87, Judgment of the Court of 5 October 1988, *Firma Schmid* v. *Hauptzollamt Stuttgart-West*. Reference for a preliminary ruling: Finanzgericht Baden-Württemberg – Germany.

23 In the Case *Gubisch Maschinenfabrik AG* v. *Giulio Palumbo*, the judges simply stated (under 14) that the German version had to be 'construed in the same manner as the other language versions'. In the Case *United Kingdom of Great Britain and Northern Ireland*

criterion plays an important role in most simple cases where the doubt vanishes on the basis of a mere comparison of the wording of the different language versions.

In other cases the Court makes specific reference to 'the majority of the language versions' to achieve its interpretative goal.[24] In another group of cases, the Court commences by applying the literal rule of interpretation and if a mere comparison does not prove sufficient to reconcile the multilingual divergences, it then applies the teleological approach by analysing the purpose of the legislation in question.

When measuring the differences in the various language versions, the Court also refers to *systematic evaluations*, adopting inconsistent terminology referring sometimes to the 'system',[25] at other times to the notion of 'systematic'[26] or even to the 'system function and the purpose of the legislation'.[27]

Altogether, the examination of the CJEU case law reveals that there is still no coherent theory regarding the interpretation of EU multilingual texts which could offer a safe ride for reconciling divergent language versions.

Certain linguistic divergences can be the result of translation mistakes due to the technicality of EU law, time pressures and the large daily workload of the lawyer-linguists and translators of the EU institutions. However, more profound differences in meaning are caused by the difficulty of finding equivalent

---

v. *Commission of the European Communities*, the Commission submitted (under 3) that, 'in accordance with the established case-law of the Court, the need for a uniform interpretation of Community legislation requires that this version [i.e. the English version] should not be considered in isolation and that where doubt arises it should be interpreted and applied in the light of the other language versions'. In case *Firma Schmid* v. *Hauptzollamt Stuttgart-West*, the Court draws the solution (under 8 and 9) from the 'comparison of the different language versions', interpreting the imprecise definition contained in the German version in the light of the provisions of the other official languages.

24 As in case C-228/94, Judgment of the Court of 11 July 1996, *Stanley Charles Atkins* v. *Wrekin District Council and Department of Transport*. Reference for a preliminary ruling: High Court of Justice, Queen's Bench Division – United Kingdom, under 30: 'That interpretation is borne out by the fact that, *in most language versions* of the Directive, the singular is expressly used in Article 1 in stating that the purpose of the Directive is the progressive implementation of the principle of equal treatment for men and women in the field of social security and other elements of social protection provided for in Article 3.'

25 Case 135/83, Judgment of the Court of 7 February 1985, *H.B.M. Abels* v. *The Administrative Board of the Bedrijfsvereniging voor de Metaalindustrie en de Electrotechnische Industrie*. Reference for a preliminary ruling: Raad van Beroep Zwolle – Netherlands.

26 Case 136/80, Judgment of the Court (First Chamber) of 17 September 1981, *Hudig en Pieters BV* v. *Minister van Landbouw en Visserij*. Reference for a preliminary ruling: College van Beroep voor het Bedrijfsleven – Netherlands.

27 Case 449/93, Judgment of the Court (First Chamber) of 7 December 1995, *Rockfon A/S* v. *Specialarbejderforbundet i Danmark*. Reference for a preliminary ruling: Østre Landsret – Denmark.

concepts in the different traditions that have developed in the various European reference contexts.

The Court strives to reconcile the meanings and not just the different language versions with the ultimate aim of developing uniform concepts and values of EU law. It is the task of European legal doctrine to assist the Court in its difficult role of defining EU concepts and constructing a truly *European* system.

A New Logic for Translating

Despite the EU's dedication to multilingualism, the increasing use of English to construct the new European legal order will present new challenges for EU legal translation in the future. First of all, the main problem will no longer be one of merely transferring a legal concept from a legal language which reflects the values, mentality and architecture of a given legal culture into another. In light of the role of English in the current phase of the harmonization process, the new problem will be to translate from a hybrid language, which is not connected with a given system of values, into all other languages (see Chapter 8 by Felici in this volume).

Second, we will have to bear in mind that we are looking for equivalence not between two languages, but across 24 different languages: that is the very reason why a *common frame of reference* was necessary. If we forget that, we will be defeated from the very beginning.

Third, in the translation from standardized English into the other official languages, if there is no equivalent in the target language, it will be necessary either to create 'new' terms (neologisms), concepts and principles, or to use 'old' terms and concepts in a new way, thus leading to dangerous co-existence at national level (see Chapter 11 by Šarčević in this volume).

New problems will arise. In fact we would be blind to think that, once introduced, these neologisms will be interpreted and applied in a uniform manner without suitable tools to guarantee this result. In other words, the use of neologisms in the various official languages will have to be placed under constant monitoring in order to maintain equivalence. That is neither absurd nor impossible. A similar approach has been taken in francophone parts of Canada, where legal terminology has been standardized in more than one language, albeit only in French and English.[28]

In a recent practical inquiry carried out on the Italian legal language (see Pozzo and Bambi 2012), it was possible to demonstrate how various sectors of the law (private law, procedural law, criminal law, criminal procedure) are reacting with different speeds and with different approaches to the language of the European lawmaking process. This phenomenon has created important problems of internal inconsistency of the language resulting in cases where the *same* term is used with *different* meanings.

28 On the interesting experience of Quebec, see Kasirer (2003: 481–501) and Coté (2002: 7–19).

Conclusions

The new terminology of the DCFR has been created at European level to facilitate the harmonization of private law with a view to achieving a standardized terminology. A huge effort has been invested in the project (see Marchetti 2012: 1265–76). Although no prescriptive standardization has been achieved, the results are very valuable. The new English terminology will have to be tested in relation to all other languages, in the context of a 'circular' and not purely 'bilateral' logic, always bearing in mind the aim of such legislation.

Comparative law experience in bijuridical and bilingual systems such as Quebec's has shown that, without constant monitoring of the standardized terminologies in various languages, the 'equivalent' terms will diverge in the long run. That is why, without a specific 'European' theory of interpretation and a specific 'European' education based on comparative law research, even if we achieve a standardized terminology in English, it may become difficult to cope with the challenges of translating it into the many EU official languages.

References

Abel, R.L. 1978. Comparative law and social theory. *American Journal of Comparative Law*, 26, 219.

Ajani, G. and Rossi, P. 2006. Multilingualism and the coherence of European private law, in *Multilingualism and the Harmonisation of European Law*, edited by B. Pozzo and V. Jacometti. Alphen aan den Rijn: Kluwer Law International, 79–93.

Allott, A. 1967. Law in the new Africa. *African Affairs*, 66(262), 55–63.

Bar, C. von, Clive E. and Schulte-Nölke H. (eds) 2009. *Principles, Definitions and Model Rules of European Private Law – Draft Common Frame of Reference (DCFR)*. Munich: Sellier – European Law Publishers.

Bergmans, B. 1987. L'enseignement d'une terminologie juridique étrangère comme mode d'approche du droit comparé: l'exemple de l'allemand. *Revue internationale de droit comparé*, 39(1), 89–110.

Boyd White, J. 1990. *Justice as Translation: An Essay in Cultural and Legal Criticism*. Chicago: University of Chicago Press.

Candian, A., Gambaro, A. and Pozzo, B. 1992. *Property-Propriété-Eigentum*. Padova: Cedam.

Cao, D. 2004. *Chinese Law: A Language Perspective*. Aldershot: Ashgate.

Carroll, L. 1983. Law, custom and statutory social reform: the Hindu Widow's Remarriage Act of 1856. *The Indian Economic and Social History Review*, 20(4), 363–88.

Chen, L. 2010. Private property with Chinese characteristics: a critical analysis of the Chinese Property Law of 2007. *European Review of Private Law*, 18, 983–1004.

Coté, P. 2002. L'interprétation des textes législatifs bilingues au Canada, in *L'interprétation des textes juridique rédigés dans plus d'une langue*. Torino: L'Harmattan Italia, 7–19.

Derlén, M. 2009. *Multilingual Interpretation of European Union Law*. Alphen aan den Rijn: Kluwer Law International.

Durieux, C. 1992. La terminologie en traduction technique: apports et limites. *Terminologie et Traduction*, 2, 95–103.

Eco, U. 2003. *Dire quasi la stessa cosa – Esperienze di traduzione*. Milano: Bompiani.

Gambaro, A. 2007. Interpretation of multilingual legislative texts. *Electronic Journal of Comparative Law*, 11(3). Available at: http://www.ejcl.org/113/article113-4.pdf.

Gerber, D.J. 2005. Authority heuristics: language and trans-system knowledge, in *Ordinary Language and Legal Language*, edited by B. Pozzo. Milan: Giuffrè, 41–59.

Gordon, R.W. 1984. Critical legal histories. *Stanford Law Review*, 36, 57.

Grossfeld, B. and Eberle, E.J. 2003. Patterns of order in comparative law: discovering and decoding invisible powers. *Texas International Law Journal*, 38, 291–316.

Gu, S. 2006. *The Boundaries of Meaning and the Formation of Law: Legal Concepts and Reasoning in the English, Arabic, and Chinese Traditions*. Montreal: McGill-Queen's University Press.

Ioriatti, E. 2009. Linguistic precedent and nomadic meanings in EC private law. *Revista General de Derecho Público Comparado*, 6. Available at: http://www.iustel.com/v2/revistas/detalle_revista.asp?id=14.

Ioriatti Ferrari, E. (ed.) 2008. *Interpretazione e traduzione del diritto*. Atti del Convegno tenuto a Trento presso la Facoltà di Giurisprudenza on 30 November 2007, Padova: Cedam.

Jacometti, V. 2009. European multilingualism between minimum harmonisation and 'a-technical' terminology. *Revista General de Derecho Público Comparado*, 6. Available at: http://www.iustel.com/v2/revistas/detalle_revista.asp?id=14.

Jayme, E. (ed.) 1999. *Langue et droit*. Bruxelles: Bruylant.

Kasirer, N. 2003. Legal education as *métissage*. *Tulane Law Review*, 78, 481–501.

Kitamura, I. 1995. Brèves réflexions sur la méthode de comparaison franco-japonaise. *Revue internationale de droit comparé*, 47, 861–9.

Krygier, M. 1986. Law as tradition. *Law and Philosophy*, 5, 237.

Legrand, P. 1996. How to compare now. *Legal Studies*, 16, 232–42.

Marchetti, C. 2012. Legal categories and legal terms in the path towards a European private law: the experiment of the DCFR. *European Review of Private Law*, 5–6, 1265–76.

Nicolaysen, G. 1966. Eigentumsgarantie und Vermögenswerte subjektive öffentliche Rechte, in *Hamburger Festschrift für Friedrich Schack*, edited by H.P. Ipsen. Berlin: Metzner, 107–23.

Pozzo, B. 2006. Multilingualism, legal terminology and the problems of harmonising European private law, in *Multilingualism and the Harmonisation of European Law,* edited by B. Pozzo and V. Jacometti. Alphen aan den Rijn: Kluwer Law International, 3–19.

Pozzo, B. 2008. L'interpretazione della Corte del Lussemburgo del testo multilingue: una rassegna giurisprudenziale, in *Europa e Linguaggi giuridici*, edited by B. Pozzo and M. Timoteo. Milan: Giuffrè Editore, 383–433.

Pozzo, B. 2011. Lost and found in translation, in *Les frontières avancées du savoir du juriste: L'anthropologie juridique et la traductologie juridique / The Advanced Frontiers of Legal Science: Legal Anthropology and Translation Studies in Law*, edited by R. Sacco, Actes du Colloque ISAIDAT, Turin, 25–28 April 2007. Bruxelles: Bruylant, 141–54.

Pozzo, B. and Bambi, F. 2012. *L'Italiano giuridico che cambia.* Firenze: Accademia della Crusca (Academy of the Italian Language).

Sacco, R. 1987. La traduction juridique – un point de vue italien. *Les Cahiers de droit*, 28(4), 845–59.

Sacco, R. 1994. La traduzione giuridica, in *Il linguaggio del diritto*, edited by U. Scarpelli and P. Di Lucia. Milano: Giuffrè.

Sacco, R. 1995. Le droit muet. *Revue trimestrelle du droit civil*, 94, 783–96.

Sacco, R. 1999. *Le fonti non scritte e l'interpretazione*. Turin: Utet.

Sacco, R. (ed.) 2011. *Les frontières avancées du savoir du jurist: L'anthropologie juridique et la traductologie juridique / The Advanced Frontiers of Legal Science: Legal Anthropology and Translation Studies in Law*, Actes du Colloque ISAIDAT, Turin, 25–28 April 2007. Brussels: Bruylant.

Sacco, R. and Castellani, L. (eds) 1999. *Les multiples langues du droit européen uniforme*. Turin: L'Harmattan.

Salmi-Tolonen, T. 2004. Legal linguistic knowledge and creating and interpreting law in a multilingual context. *Brooklyn Journal of International Law*, 29, 1167–91.

Sendler, H. 1971. Die Konkretisierung einer modernen Eigentumsverfassung durch Richterspruch. *Die öffentliche Verwaltung*, 16 ff.

Terral, F. 2004. L'empreinte culturelle des termes juridiques. *Meta*, 49(4), 876–90.

Whittaker, S. 2008. *The Draft Common Frame of Reference: An Assessment.* Assessment commissioned by the Ministry of Justice, UK.

PART II:
Legal Translation in the EU

Chapter 6
Theoretical Aspects of Legal Translation in the EU: The Paradoxical Relationship between Language, Translation and the Autonomy of EU Law

Anne Lise Kjær

Introduction

The purpose of this chapter is to discuss the issue whether what we call translation in the EU is translation at all, or whether we are witnessing something different for which a proper theoretical concept has yet to be developed. What we know is that EU texts are drawn up in 24 parallel language versions, none of which has the legal status of an original text, and none of which is designated as a translation. Taken together, they are equally important sources of EU law (Kjær 2007). In spite of this paradoxical relationship between the multiple language versions and uniform EU law, we can see that EU law functions and is followed in real life activities in the Member States and that the multilingual rules make sense both inside and outside the confines of the EU institutions. But in theoretical terms we cannot explain why.

EU Law and the Practical and Theoretical Challenges of Multilingualism

One of the greatest challenges of EU law is its multilingualism. It would not function in accordance with the principle of equal authenticity of all official languages without a specialized staff of translators working hard on translating EU legislation so that all generally applicable EU acts are available in all official languages on the date of their entry into force or taking effect. Each time a new country has been accepted for membership of the EU, a cornerstone of the process leading to accession is the translation of the *acquis communautaire* into the national language chosen by that country to be an EU official language. It has even been established in the case law of the Court of Justice of the European Union (CJEU) that EU legislation does not bind citizens and businesses of new Member

States unless it has been translated into their own language and published in the Official Journal of the European Union.[1]

Even though EU law must be translated into the languages of the Member States, EU legislation does not derive its meaning from national law, but from EU law. EU law is defined in the case law of the CJEU as an autonomous legal system which is semantically independent from the national legal systems.[2] Thus, even if the legislative process of the EU institutions requires translation, the formulation of legislative texts in the 24 official languages is not translation *senso strictu* because source text meaning and target text meaning coincide. Theoretically, it is co-drafting, but practically it is not; not only is co-drafting unmanageable in multilingual EU law, but most of the 24 language versions are *de facto* produced as translations, sometimes long after the adoption of the legislative acts.

In my opinion, translation in the EU should be studied as a distinct field of research which deserves to be defined as a translation type *sui generis*. Long-standing conceptions of what legal translation is and entails need to be reconsidered in order to truly reflect the practice of multilingual text production and the supranational nature of EU law. EU translation cannot be accurately described unless it is investigated in relation to the legal and institutional context in which it is embedded. Of special relevance is the autonomy of EU law which is defined by the CJEU and interpreted without reference to the national legal languages of the Member States (cf. Chapter 10 by Engberg in this volume).[3]

In theory and practice legal translation has always been performed by people with a combined knowledge of law and language in general and comparative law and translation in particular. Accordingly, among the main contributors to the state of the art in the field of EU translation are researchers who confess to an interdisciplinary research methodology.[4] Although knowledge of comparative law and language is a necessary condition for performing, evaluating and describing EU legal translation, it is not sufficient to adequately explain the interplay of law, language and translation in the making of EU law. One might even ask whether comparative law and translation theories are the most relevant theories to apply.

---

1 In C-Case C-161/06 *Skoma-Lux sro* v. *Celní ředitelství Olomouc*; for a comment on the judgment, see Bobek (2011).

2 For the first time in Case 6/64 *Costa* v. *ENEL* [1964] ECR 1203.

3 For an introduction to the theory of judicial lawmaking in the EU, see, for example, Barents (2004) and Stone Sweet (2004).

4 See, for example, *Šarčević* (1997, 2012), Baaij (2012), Bobek (2011), Burr and Gréciano (2003), Derlén (2011), McAuliffe (2009), Müller and Burr (2004), Pozzo and Jacometti (2006), Paunio (2013), Prechal and van Roermund (2008) and Kjær (2007).

Paradoxes of Law, Language and Translation in Autonomous EU Law

The title of this chapter (Theoretical Aspects of Legal Translation in the EU) allows me to stick to the ideal world of academia – where one can safely argue for whatever theory one finds fit – without having to bother with the everyday problems and challenges of legal translation. For my purpose, I am trying to shape reflections on the fundamentals of the role of language in law that may help us understand why EU translation works in practice – while in theory translating EU law seems to be a contradiction in terms. This reflection should also motivate us to become more precise when describing theoretically what is happening in translation practice. If we accept that the activity called legal translation in the EU is not translation in the strict sense of the word, we need to propose a new concept which can capture the activity more accurately. The notions of 'hybrid texts' (Trosborg 1997; Snell-Hornby 2001; Schäffner and Adab 2001a), 'linguistic precedent' (McAuliffe 2009 and Mulders 2008) and 'text reproduction' (Kjær 2007) cover aspects of the paradoxes of EU translation. However, we still need to explain why 'hybrid texts' and 'reproduced texts' can be understood and assigned a coherent meaning outside the narrow institutional environment in which they were produced. 'Hybrid texts' are 'produced as original texts in a specific cultural space, which is often in itself an intersection of different cultures' (Schäffner and Adab 2001b). 'Reproduced texts' are not based on the semantics of a source text, but on 'linguistic precedent', that is, the surface level of the wording of prior texts and parallel texts. Regardless of whether meaning is believed to be the intention of the text producer, as contained in the text itself or contingent on the recipient's application of the text, it is a theoretical challenge to explain why such texts can be meaningful.

For the purpose of such a reflection I have formulated the following paradoxes concerning the relationship between law and language and between multilingual law, translation and autonomous EU law. They are meant to puzzle the readers and call for theoretical reactions rather than practical solutions:

> Law and text:
> law is not a matter of text,
> but law cannot be separated from the texts in which law is practised.
>
> Language and legal interpretation:
> legal interpretation is not a matter of uncovering the meaning of words,
> but without words there would be no interpretation and nothing to interpret.
>
> Multilingual law and translation:
> multilingual law is not a matter of translation,
> but multilingual rules cannot be formulated without translation.

Multilingual law and interpretation:
multilingual legislation is phrased in multiple language versions,
but when interpreted the language versions represent only one legal text.

Multilingual EU law and autonomous concepts:
EU legislation is phrased in 24 language versions,
but concepts used in EU legislation are autonomous concepts of EU law and must be understood independently from the languages in which they are phrased.

These paradoxes (which are not paradoxes in a strictly logical sense of the word) are a kind of shorthand for describing the complicated relationship, indeed interdependency of law and language, which I believe is the reason why lawyers and linguists alike are so attracted to the field of law and language.

I will not treat the paradoxes in detail. They indicate the framework of assumptions upon which I base the analysis in the following. I will start by presenting the theory of autonomous concepts which has been introduced and developed by the two common European Courts, the CJEU and the European Court of Human Rights (ECtHR). On the basis of this, I will then turn to the more fundamental intricacies of the relationship between multilingual law, legal translation and autonomous concepts. This implies in particular a return to the question that has engaged comparative law scholars for approximately 20 years, namely, whether it is possible to establish a common legal language in Europe across the divergent national legal languages and cultures; or in other words, whether in the light of increasing legal and political integration at the European level, national legal systems are converging – or not.[5]

Multilingual Law and Autonomous Concepts

The common European Courts, the CJEU and the ECtHR, have both developed a theory of autonomous concepts, that is, concepts that 'enjoy a status of semantic independence' from the meaning that the same concepts possess in domestic law (Letsas 2007: 42–3).

The ECtHR has explicitly characterized eight concepts used in the European Convention on Human Rights as autonomous in this sense. 'Civil rights and obligations' and 'criminal charge' in Art. 6 § 1 are the best-known examples because they form the very basis of delimitating the correct application of one of the core rights of the Convention, namely, the right to a fair trial (Brems 2001: 394–5).

5 Cf. the work of Pierre Legrand who has been a dominant participant in a rather heated academic debate, esp. Legrand (1996).

In the case law of the CJEU, the list of autonomous concepts is not final, as the body of EU legislation is huge and in a constant process of being changed and extended. Key examples are concepts that govern the freedom of movement, for example, the Treaty concepts of EU competition law, 'undertakings' and 'affect trade', the concept of 'worker' in EU labour law, many concepts used in EU tax law, for example, 'residence', and concepts used in the Council Regulation on jurisdiction and the recognition and enforcement of judgments in civil and commercial matters[6] such as 'domicile'.

The overall interpretive ambition of the two Courts is the same. According to the ECtHR, concepts of the European Convention on Human Rights must be interpreted 'in the context of the Convention'. This requirement is expressly stated by the Court in its decision in *Chassagnou*, para. 11: 'The question is not so much whether in French law ACCAs[7] are private associations, public or para-public associations, or mixed associations, but whether they are associations for the purposes of Article 11 of the Convention.'

Unless a provision of EU law makes 'express reference to the law of the Member States',[8] it follows from the notion of EU law as an independent legal order that the semantics of EU legislation cannot be derived from national law; this was established in the case law of the CJEU for the first time in the Court's judgment in *Costa* v. *ENEL*:

> any attempt to explain the contents and nature of Community law on the basis of national law [...] precludes Community law from being conceptualised as an intrinsic unity, thus depriving it of its Community character and challenging its raison d'etre. (Case 6/64 *Costa* v. *ENEL* [1964] ECR 1203)

The EU conception of autonomy is also expressed by the Court of Justice in the famous *CILFIT* judgment that establishes 'the characteristic features of Community law and the particular difficulties to which its interpretation gives rise'.[9] Here the Court defines its own style of interpretation, explicating an interpretive turn in the history of international law, with less weight on the texts of EU law and their wording and more focus on its dynamic development and the fulfilment of the EU's general objectives. The features sum up to a description of EU law as a self-referential, evolutionary legal system with its own terminology and concepts and a general warning to the national interpreters that they should not trust the texts of EU law in their own language.[10]

---

6 Council Regulation (EC) No 44/2001 of 22 December 2000.

7 ACCA is the short form of *Association communale de chasse agréée* in French.

8 Opinion of Advocate General Trstenjak, delivered on 11 May 2010 in Case C-467/08 *Sociedad General de Autores y Editores (SGAE)* v. *Padawan S.L.*, para. 61.

9 Case 283/81 *CILFIT* [1982] ECR, 03415.

10 Elsewhere I have analysed in detail the consequences of the *CILFIT* criteria for the semantics of Community law (when understood literally they imply that EU law is

The meaning of autonomous concepts is constructed by the European Courts above or beyond the differences that characterize similar concepts in the domestic legal orders. Autonomous meanings are even stated without prior comparison of corresponding national concepts; and divergent terminology in the individual language versions of EU legislation (24) and the European Convention on Human Rights (English and French) is treated as merely textual differences of no importance for the European content of the concepts.

But if conceptual and linguistic difference is believed to be irrelevant for the meaning of European law, why even bother comparing and translating? My claim is that whether one takes the theory of autonomous concepts at face value, or rejects it as judicial 'spin', comparative law and legal translation are challenged by the very fact that the protagonists of a common European law actually believe in autonomous concepts and speak and act according to their belief. The very existence of a widespread belief in autonomous concepts should give rise to the disciplinary self-reflection that I have called for: in the light of the increasing autonomization of EU law, scholars of translation studies and comparative law need to reconsider their (our) disciplines and the assumptions underlying law, language and translation.

Multilingual Law, Autonomous Concepts and a Common Legal Language in Europe

In order to sustain the above claim I will return to a debate among comparative law scholars in the first decade of the millennium concerning the possibility of developing a common European language across national differences. In Kjær (2004) I suggested that one should distinguish between the creation of a common European *language* and the development of a common European *discourse* in order to shed light on the role played by the diversity of languages and legal cultures in European legal integration.

My suggestion has been criticized for not defining clearly the notion of a common discourse and for not explaining convincingly how European lawyers may cross the barriers of divergent languages and escape their own language, life world and prejudgment (Glanert 2011). I will therefore take this opportunity to reconsider my distinction between language and discourse and elaborate on it in the light of the theory of autonomous concepts.

Some would say that the introduction of autonomous concepts by the European Courts is an egg of Columbus: simply circumventing the burden of comparing and translating between legal languages and cultures by claiming semantic independence and autonomy of the concepts used in European law. Could it not

non-sensical (Kjær 2010)). From a translational and comparative perspective, the *CILFIT* criteria are equally misleading. Comparison of the language versions is compulsory, but absurd as the meaning of the concepts is identical across language versions.

be said that the invention of autonomous concepts is a shortcut to the creation of a common European law and language? And do autonomous concepts not ultimately put an end to linguistic and cultural diversity and hence to translation in the strict sense of the word?

As stated more or less explicitly by the two European Courts, there is no need to compare national legal concepts or be concerned about differences between the wording of the texts of Human Rights law and EU law. All that really matters is what the Courts make of the texts in their own interpretive history. What counts is prospective meaning-*making* rather than retrospective meaning-*identification*.

This cannot be the end of the story. Stating autonomy may flag the Courts' deliberate attempt to circumvent the legal, linguistic, cultural, historical and socio-political diversity of the Member States. But, surely the simple statement of autonomy does not mark the end of that diversity. To believe that interpreters can free themselves from their individual and culturally embedded background knowledge and beliefs, their *Hintergrundsannahmen* (Habermas) and *Vorverständnis* (Gadamer), seems naïve.

However, claiming autonomy may indeed mark the beginning of the rise of a new unity above and across diversities because the claim is a speech act that affects the communities of lawyers at both European and national levels. From a macro perspective, the development of such a unity may be studied without reference to the diversity of languages and cultures in Europe because broader socio-legal and political processes are the object of study. But from a micro perspective that focuses on the communicative actions materializing the development, language and culture cannot be ignored. On the contrary, at the micro level of analysis the communicative processes and hence the use of language and translation is the core interest.

Any communicative action is conducted in language; thus the total sum of communicative actions that establish European lawyers' discourse on law entails the use of language and, due to the linguistic diversity characteristic of the European continent, often requires translation across languages. These are trivial observations. The important extra distinction to be made is between speech communities and discourse communities.[11] As long as communicative actions are conducted first and foremost among lawyers belonging to the same monolingual legal system within the confines of a nation state, then speech community (those speaking the same language) and discourse community (those speaking about

11 The distinction between speech community and discourse community on which I base my argument stems from Swales (1990). He defines speech communities as communities that share linguistic forms, cultural concepts, and rules of production and interpretation of speech. They are socio-linguistic groupings whose communicative needs are socialization or group solidarity. Discourse communities are socio-rhetorical groupings whose communicative behaviour is dominated by functional determinants. Discourse communities are communities of people who link up in order to pursue objectives and common goals (1990: 21–32).

the same things) coincide. When lawyers' communicative actions increasingly transgress languages, speech communities and discourse communities are no longer identical. In such circumstances, this makes it possible to establish a common European legal discourse distinct from the national discourses on law: not only the topics of discourse, but increasingly also the content of discourse are converging across speech communities.

Multilingual Law, Autonomous Concepts and a Common Legal Discourse in Europe

Autonomy of European law requires the cooperation of national lawyers. If they are not convinced by the interpretations of the European Courts and interpret so-called autonomous concepts differently, or if they are unable to free themselves from their national legal backgrounds and continue interpreting concepts in accordance with their domestic legal orders, autonomy simply does not arise. In other words, even if autonomy entails independency from national law, autonomy does not exist independently from the lawyers and judges who have to apply the autonomous concepts in their national legal systems.

But we know that national legal actors actually do cooperate with the European institutions and Courts. This has been established in research on European legal integration.[12] Therefore, from the point of view of comparative law and translation studies, it is important to ask what will happen to the mutually divergent national languages and cultures of law when independency and autonomy of a common European law are presumed by an increasing number of European lawyers; when they accept the European Courts as legitimate interpreters of a supranational and transnational European law and involve themselves in an increasingly self-referential European legal discourse with lawyers from other European countries; and when communicating about law and speaking the law are no longer conducted in divergent national legal languages, but in a Europeanized legal language with no reference to the domestic laws of the Member States. Will the national languages and cultures disappear and be replaced by a common European standard? And does the change in the framework conditions of European law – with supra- and transnational lawmaking gradually replacing national law – mark the end of legal translation and comparative law in Europe?

In the academic debate on the convergence and divergence of European legal systems of the past decades, I maintain a middle position. I do so, because in my opinion both sides are right to some extent; however, they fail to account for the limits of their argument. On one hand, those who take convergence for granted implicitly base their argument on the assumption that language is an instrument that you can use to your liking for whatever purposes and content you think fit. On the other hand, those who argue that convergence is not possible

12 See, for example, the early work by Alter (1998) and Stone Sweet (2004).

due to insurmountable linguistic and cultural barriers, overlook what I find to be a key characteristic of language, namely that 'language has its true being only in dialogue, in *coming to an understanding*' (Gadamer 2004: 443).

I find it hard to deny that a change in the languages and cultures of European law is in fact taking place, and I believe that this is happening first and foremost because the very speech act performed by the European Courts claiming autonomy and independency of European law brings about that change. Those who can argue convincingly for a claim and have the power and legitimacy to do so can make us believe and act accordingly, until others in power argue convincingly for something else. In Hans Christian Andersen's fairy tale, the swindlers convinced the emperor, his court and his subjects that he had clothes on, and they believed so as long as everybody else expressed the same belief. Nobody wanted to say that they could not see the fabric, because in doing so they would reveal themselves as unfit for their office or unusually stupid. Had it not been for the small child who looked at the emperor at the procession and said, 'But he hasn't got anything on', they would probably still cling to the discursively established reality of the emperor's silken clothes.

Even though Hans Christian Andersen's tale is primarily about vanity and pretence, it also shows how reality is established in the discourse of a group and how the individual group member's beliefs are shaped by what other members say.

The definition of legal language that has been taken for granted in comparative law and translation theory for the past centuries has been repeated so often among lawyers and translators and disseminated so widely that we believe it to describe an objective fact, namely, that national legal languages are individually unique entities that owe their meaning solely to the national legal cultures in which they are used. In some versions of comparative law and translation theory (Legrand 2005; Glanert 2011) the singularity of legal languages is accounted for with reference to the philosophy of Quine (1960) (indeterminacy of translation), the deconstruction theory of Derrida (1985) (the necessity and impossibility of translation), Heidegger's hermeneutics ('There is no translation at all in which the words of one language could or should cover the words of another language ….' (Heidegger 1984: 75)) and the anthropological theory of linguistic relativity (the Sapir/Whorf thesis) (see, for example, Gumperz and Levinson 1996). But the success of legal communication and legal translation in Europe indicates that the concept of distinctness and untranslatability of legal languages is imagined rather than real.

Our understanding of legal languages and cultures cannot be separated from the way we have constructed them in discourse; elsewhere (Kjær and Palsbro 2008) I (we) demonstrated how the concept of legal culture is applied by Danish lawyers to frame Danish law either as uniquely different from other legal systems (and incompatible with foreign ideas stemming from the common European legal systems) or as historically embedded in European law and therefore not only compatible but also deeply intertwined with it. Within the philosophy of Searle, legal languages consist of institutional facts which are established in speech acts

(Status Function Declarations) (Searle 1995, 2010). Language used in speech acts contributes to changing and shaping the reality that language users take for granted, and importantly, it also influences the way people act and how they communicate about reality. What matters is not whether what is said is true, but whether what is said makes sense to those who engage in a conversation.[13]

But if the conception of a barrier between languages is the product of a discourse that has focused more on the differences between languages instead of their similarities, this barrier may not pose an insurmountable obstacle for lawyers who want to understand each other across linguistic differences (see likewise Glenn 2010: 45–6). Understanding may not be achieved easily, and European legal actors belonging to different speech communities will need to compensate for their lack of a common language. However, I submit, this is exactly what they can do and do.

Multilingual Law and Understanding across Languages

In *Logic and Conversation* Grice (1975) has coined the notion of a 'cooperative principle' which is a useful analytical tool to be applied to all communication, talk and text, also in the legal sphere, both within and across speech communities and cultures.

He bases the principle on the assumption that people who communicate generally want their conversation to be successful and the purposes they pursue as speakers and writers, listeners and readers to be fulfilled. Regardless of the ultimate goal, the core condition for the success of any exchange is that the parties make meaningful contributions to the conversation in the context of their exchange. In the words of Grice (1975: 45):

> Our talk exchanges do not normally consist of a succession of disconnected remarks, and would not be rational if they did.

According to the cooperative principle, participants in a conversation expect that each will make a 'contribution such as is required at the stage at which it occurs, by the accepted purpose or direction of the talk exchange in which you are engaged' (Grice 1975: 45). The principle goes both ways: speakers (generally) observe the cooperative principle, and listeners (generally) assume that speakers are observing it. The principle is expressed in four categories that echo Kant's categories: Quality, Quantity, Relevance and Manner. Grice names them conversation maxims and phrases them as rules to be followed by the speaker if he or she wants to

13 On the whole, I subscribe to the theory of meaning formulated by Wittgenstein in *Philosophische Untersuchungen*: 'Die Bedeutung eines Wortes ist sein Gebrauch in der Sprache' (the meaning of a word is its use in language (1984: 43)).

cooperate with the addressee. The maxim of quantity is especially relevant for communication across differences:[14]

> Maxim of Quantity:
>
> Make your contribution as informative as is required (for the current purposes of the exchange).
> Do not make your contribution more informative than is required.

What makes understanding difficult is distance and difference in knowledge background and outlook. Distance and difference are often created by language barriers, but can just as well be caused by cultural, social and epistemological barriers.

It is easier to achieve understanding in speech than in writing. In speech the communicators are present together. In terms of time and space, there is no distance between them. They can see and hear each other and respond to each other's non-linguistic behaviour (gestures, facial expressions, audible peculiarities, tone of voice). Their communication is mutual; it is an exchange of views. They can assert, ask, explain and give feedback. The addressee of the spoken text is always clearly defined, and the speaker can constantly adapt what he says to the needs expressed by the listener. Any distance between them (in the abstract sense of the word, caused by different experience, background knowledge and worldviews) can be dealt with much easier when the actors are in direct contact. They can, as described by Habermas, negotiate a common understanding of the 'objective, social and subjective world' that they are talking about.[15]

The interplay of distance in space and knowledge explains the results of a recent study on the judges at the ECtHR (Arold 2007). Starting from the debate on convergence and divergence of law, Arold assumed in advance that the individual judges' legal, vocational, historical and other experiences would have an impact on their voting behaviour. Her hypothesis was not confirmed; the diversity in the background knowledge of the judges is no hindrance to convergence inside the Court.

The judges at the ECtHR form an independent discourse community. In this self-contained community, autonomous concepts can be introduced, shaped and developed with full mutual understanding because there is no distance between the judges. Not even mentally, as they (in Arold's words) share 'mentalités that

14 The other maxims are: Maxim of Quality – try to make your contribution one that is true; Maxim of Relation – be relevant; Maxim of Manner – be perspicuous.

15 'Allein das kommunikative Handlungsmodell setzt Sprache als ein Medium unverkürzter Verständigung voraus, wobei sich Sprecher und Hörer aus dem Horizont ihrer vorinterpretierten Lebenswelt gleichzeitig auf etwas in der objektiven, sozialen und subjektiven Welt beziehen, um gemeinsame Situationsbestimmungen auszuhandeln' (Habermas 1987: 142).

promote convergence through pushing specific ideals and fostering homogeneity' (2007: 305).

However, in all cases where people want to communicate across linguistic differences, the success of communication depends primarily on their ability to manoeuvre the language barrier. In theories of multilingualism, language crossing is generally considered to be achieved in one of the following ways (cf. Edwards 1995: 39–52):

By speakers learning more than one language
By the use of a *lingua franca*;
By the use of a Creole language;
By the insertion of translators and interpreters.

In European legal communication, all strategies are used. The insertion of translators and interpreters is formalized and extensively used; I shall deal with that in the next section. Individual multilingualism is recommended in EU language policies, and Member States are encouraged to take steps to ensure that all citizens learn two foreign languages at school. Communication in a *lingua franca* is widespread with international English being the absolutely dominant medium, both in formal and informal settings of the EU, among formal and informal networks and in both negotiation and drafting processes (see Chapter 8 by Felici, this volume). Even at the CJEU English is used in the corridors although French is the drafting language. The hybrid texts of EU legislation may be characterized as a kind of Creole language; I will return to the creolization of EU texts in my discussion of EU translation below.

Each strategy constitutes a medium through which communicators can address each other across the barrier of their different languages.

In terms of Quantity in Grice's sense, it is generally acknowledged that more information is needed if the addressee is to understand the message of the speaker across languages and cultures. The speaker will have to *explain* the meaning that is implied by what is said and would be recognizable for an addressee speaking the same language. This is not an easy task and is possible only if the speaker (or the mediator) *knows* what the foreign language user does *not* know about the *background knowledge* of the speaker. But understanding is made possible because communicators cooperate on coming to an understanding, directly in a *lingua franca* (international English) or through translators and interpreters. Even if their life worlds are worlds apart (pun intended!), the cooperation principle that governs any sincere conversation makes interlocutors stay in touch until they have arrived at a common understanding. The result of their efforts may not be perfect understanding, but sufficient mutual understanding for the purposes of their exchange.

Multilingual Law, EU Translation and Autonomous Concepts

When we now turn to translation as mediation between languages and apply Edward's understanding of multilingualism and Grice's cooperation principle to EU translation, we realize that there is an inherent conflict between the idea of mediation and delivering the necessary quantity of information on one hand, and the equality of languages in the EU on the other. One core element of translation in its most fundamental form is that it involves a clear direction. The translator translates from one language into another. He or she translates the content of a source text in L1 into a target text in L2, and if necessary and relevant for the target language reader, equips it with extra information and adaptations to the target language context.

But translation in the EU does not fulfil these basic criteria of translation as an activity of knowledge transfer from one speech community to another and mediation across languages in Edward's sense. First, the dominant use of English as a *lingua franca* in negotiations and as a drafting language in the legislative process, which is documented in several reports of the Directorate-General of Translation, makes the *de facto* original text a hybrid text as defined by Schäffner and Adab (2001a, 2001b). International English is a medium of understanding with no anchor in a specific, clearly defined speech community. Therefore, translation from the hybridized – to a certain extent even creolized[16] – English into the other EU languages is a misleading concept.

Second, with 24 equally authentic languages there is *de jure* no original text; this was established long ago in the case law of the CJEU.[17] In legal terms the language versions are all sources of EU law. This means, on one hand, that the content of EU legislation cannot be derived from a single text, the meaning of which is then transferred to the other languages. On the other hand, an interpretation of EU law must be based on a comparison of all language versions (see Chapter 4 by Derlén, this volume).[18]

Both aspects of the EU multilingual regime have absurd consequences from the point of view of translation studies and comparative law: translation and comparison of EU legislation have no direction (see Kjær 2007). But how does one translate without a source text? And how does one compare texts when none of the texts expresses the meaning to be compared, how does one compare without a standard of comparison?

---

16 Euro-English is not a creole language in the strict sense of the term (a pidgin which has developed into a native language), but it resembles creoles because it is a functional language that to a certain extent is simplified in order to fulfil its function as a drafting language in the multilingual environment of the EU legal system.

17 Prominently in the *CILFIT* judgment: 'Community legislation is drafted in several languages and the different language versions are all equally authentic' (para. 18).

18 *CILFIT* judgment (para. 18): 'An interpretation of a provision of Community law thus involves a comparison of the different language versions.'

Two strategies have been invented in the EU system itself to cope with these absurdities: in the production of translations linguistic precedents become almost binding (McAuliffe 2009; Mulders 2008); in the interpretation of the texts the Court's reference to the semantic independence or autonomy of the concepts applied sweeps away all speculation (Letsas 2007).

How does one as a translator ensure semantic independence? Publicly accessible guidelines for translators in the EU are of little help. The profile of an EU Commission translator is described in traditional terms, focusing on source and target language knowledge and correctness of translation. A translator must possess:

> a capacity to understand texts in the source language and to render them correctly in the target language, using a style and register appropriate to the purpose of the text.[19]

The *Manual of Precedents of Acts established within the Council of the European Union*[20] is more precise. In the section on 'Indications for Drafting, Use of Precedents' the recommendation to drafters reads as follows:

> Acts are frequently drawn up, in whole or in part, on the basis of earlier or similar acts. This is so where provisions which are no longer in force … are to be extended or updated or where provisions similar to those applicable in other sectors are to be adopted (horizontal texts).
>
> There is no need to repeat previous or similar formulations word for word. Any improvements which seem appropriate may be made and errors should be corrected. Changes which are not absolutely necessary should, however, be avoided so that the persons to whom or institutions to which the provisions in question are addressed are not given the false impression that material differences exist between the old and new texts.

Even if these rules are addressed to drafters they apply *mutatis mutandis* to translators as well. The repetition of wording that has been used in previous provisions or in horizontal texts – linguistic precedent – should be followed in order not to give the addressees the false impression that changes in wording mean changes in substance. Translation (and drafting) is to a considerable degree based on text reproduction (Kjær 2007).

---

19 Quoted from the website of the DGT of the European Commission at: http://ec.europa.eu/dgs/translation/workwithus/staff/profile/index_en.htm (last updated 15 April 2013).

20 Version of 9 July 2010 (English revision, 19 April 2011).

Conclusion

The paradoxical relationship between language, translation and the autonomy of EU law mirrors the *sui generis* nature of the European legal order. It is a challenge to practitioners of legal translation and calls for reflection on the part of translation scholars. But it also preoccupies constitutional law researchers who struggle with the same seemingly contradictory forces of unity and diversity, interplay with national law, and independence from national law.

In my opinion, the real challenge in European law is not translation in the narrow sense of the word, but translation in a broader sociological sense, namely, the transfer of the legal knowledge which is produced and developed by the interaction of lawyers and judges in the European institutions and at the European Courts as participants of discourse communities at the supranational level of EU law. At central level the actors may well agree on the 'semantics' of the emerging European law and declare its 'semantic independence' from domestic law. But what happens to the semantics of autonomous concepts of European legal concepts and conceptions when they leave the confines of the international discourse community? Meaning does not reside in the texts of law, but will always depend on the application of the text by the interpreter.

Stating autonomy does not automatically result in autonomy. This may be true, but stating autonomy of European legal concepts marks a shift in the legal discourse of European lawyers, also at national level, and discourse can in fact change what people believe is real. When European concepts are constructed as autonomous, people will increasingly treat them as such.

References

Adab, B. 2001a. The idea of the hybrid text in translation: contact as conflict. *Across Languages and Cultures*, 2(2), 167–80.

Alter, K. 1998. Explaining national court acceptance of European Court jurisprudence: a critical evaluation of theories of legal integration, in *The European Courts and National Courts: Doctrine and Jurisprudence*, edited by A.-M. Slaughter, A. Stone Sweet and J.H. Weiler. Oxford: Hart, ch. 8.

Arold, N.-L. 2007. The European Court of Human Rights as an example of convergence. *Nordic Journal of International Law*, 76, 305–22.

Baaij, C.J.W. (ed.) 2012. *The Role of Legal Translation in Legal Harmonization*. Alphen an den Rijn:Kluwer Law International.

Barents, R. 2004. *The Autonomy of Community Law*. The Hague: Kluwer Law International.

Bobek, M. 2011. The multilingualism of the European Union law in the national courts: beyond the textbooks, in *Linguistic Diversity and European Democracy*, edited by A.L. Kjær and S. Adamo. Farnham: Ashgate, 123–42.

Brems, E. 2001. *Human Rights: Universality and Diversity*. The Hague: Kluwer Law International.

Burr, I. and Gréciano, G. (eds) 2003. *Europa: Sprache und Recht / La construction européenne: aspects linguistiques et juridiques*. Baden-Baden: Nomos (Schriften des Zentrum für Europäische Integrationsforschung Bd. 52).

Derlén, M. 2011. In defence of (limited) multilingualism: problems and possibilities of the multilingual interpretation of European Union law in national courts, in *Linguistic Diversity and European Democracy*, edited by A.L. Kjær and S. Adamo. Farnham: Ashgate, 143–66.

Derrida, J. (1985). Des Tours de Babel, reprint translated by J.F. Graham. New York: Cornell University Press, 165–208.

Edwards, J. 1995. *Multilingualism*. London: Penguin.

Gadamer, H.-G. 2004. *Truth and Method*, 2nd revised edition, originally published 1975. New York: Continuum. Translated from German: *Wahrheit und Methode. Grundzüge einer philosophischen Hermeneutik*, originally published 1960. Tübingen: Mohr.

Glanert, S. 2011. *De la traductabilité du droit*. Paris: Dalloz.

Glenn, H.P. 2010. *Legal Traditions of the World*, 4th edition. Oxford: Oxford University Press.

Grice, H.P. 1975. Logic and conversation, in *Syntax and Semantics: Speech Acts*, vol. 3, edited by P. Cole and J.L. Morgan. New York: Academic, 41–58.

Groth, M. 1997. *Heidegger's Philosophy of Translation. PhD Thesis, Fordham University.* Paper AAI9730092.

Gumperz, J. and Levinson, S. (eds) 1996. *Rethinking Linguistic Relativity*. Cambridge: Cambridge University Press.

Habermas, J. 1987. *Theorie des kommunikativen Handelns*, Band I. Frankfurt am Main: Suhrkamp.

Heidegger, M. 1984. *Hölderlin's Hymne 'Der Ister'*, edited by W. Biemel, Gesamtausgabe 53. Frankfurt am Main: Klostermann.

Kjær, A.L. 2004. A common legal language in Europe? in *Epistemology and Methodology of Comparative Law*, edited by M. van Hoecke. Oxford: Hart, 377–98.

Kjær, A.L. 2007. Legal translation in the European Union: a research field in need of a new approach, in *Language and the Law: International Outlooks*, edited by K. Kredens and S. Goźdź-Roszkowski. Frankfurt am Main: Peter Lang, 69–95.

Kjær, A.L. 2010. Nonsense: the *CILFIT* criteria revisited – from the perspective of legal linguistics, in *Europe: The New Legal Realism: Essays in Honour of Hjalte Rasmussen*, edited by H. Koch, K. Hagel-Sørensen, U. Haltern and J.H. Weiler. Copenhagen: Djøf.

Kjær, A.L. and Palsbro, L. 2008. National identity and law in the context of European integration: the case of Denmark. *Discourse & Society*, 19, 599–627.

Legrand, P. 1996. European legal systems are not converging. *The International and Comparative Law Quarterly*, 45(1), 52–81.

Legrand, P. 2005. Issues in the translatability of law, in *Nation, Language, and the Ethics of Translation*, edited by S. Bermann and M. Wood. Princeton and Oxford: Princeton University Press.

Letsas, G. 2007. *A Theory of Interpretation of the European Convention on Human Rights*. Oxford: Oxford University Press.

McAuliffe, K. 2009. Translation at the Court of Justice of the European Communities, in *Translation Issues in Language and Law*, edited by F. Olsen, A. Lorz and D. Stein. Houndmills and New York: Palgrave Macmillan, 99–115.

Mulders, L. 2008. Translation at the Court of Justice of the European Communities, in *The Coherence of EU Law: The Search for Unity in Divergent Concepts*, edited by S. Prechal and B. van Roermund. Oxford: Oxford University Press, 45–58.

Müller, F. and Burr, I. (eds) 2004. *Rechtssprache Europas: Reflexion der Praxis von Sprache und Mehrsprachigkeit im supranationalen Recht*. Berlin: Duncker & Humblot.

Paunio, E. 2013. *Legal Certainty in Multilingual EU Law: Language, Discourse and Reasoning at the European Court of Justice*. Farnham: Ashgate.

Pozzo, B. and Jacometti, V. (eds) 2006. *Multilingualism and the Harmonisation of European Law*. Alphen aan den Rijn: Kluwer Law International.

Prechal, S. and Roermund, B. van (eds) (2008). *The Coherence of EU Law: The Search for Unity in Divergent Concepts*. Oxford: Oxford University Press.

Quine, W.v.O. 1960. *Word and Object*. Cambridge, MA: MIT Press.

Schäffner, C. and Adab, B. 2001b. Conclusion: the idea of the hybrid text in translation revisited. *Across Languages and Cultures*, 2(2), 277–302.

Searle, J. 1995. *The Construction of Social Reality*. New York: The Free Press.

Searle, J. 2010. *Making the Social World: The Structure of Human Civilization*. Oxford: Oxford University Press.

Snell-Hornby, M. 2001. The space 'in-between': what is a hybrid text? *Languages and Cultures* 2(2), 207–216.

Stone Sweet, A. 2004. *The Judicial Construction of Europe*. Oxford: Oxford University Press.

Swales, J. 1990. *Genre Analysis: English in Academic and Research Settings*. Cambridge: Cambridge University Press.

Šarčević, S. 1997. *New Approach to Legal Translation*. The Hague: Kluwer Law International.

Šarčević, S. 2012. Coping with the challenges of legal translation in harmonization, in *The Role of Legal Translation in Legal Harmonization*, edited by C.J.W. Baaij. Alphen an den Rijn: Kluwer Law International, 83–107.

Trosborg, A. 1997. Translating hybrid political texts, in *Text Typology and Translation*, edited by A. Trosborg. Amsterdam and Philadelphia: Benjamins, 145–58.

Wittgenstein, L. 1984 [1953]. Philosophische Untersuchungen, in *Werkausgabe in 8 Bänden*. Frankfurt am Main: Suhrkamp.

Chapter 7
EU Translation and the Burden of Legal Knowledge

C.J.W. (Jaap) Baaij

EU Translation: Striking a Balance

Achieving uniform interpretation and application of EU law requires 'absolute concordance' of the 24 equally authentic language versions of EU legislation.[1] Translators and lawyer-linguists in the EU legislative institutions are responsible for ensuring that the expression of the law in the original draft text finds its equivalent in the other EU languages. This chapter deals with the question whether and to what extent translators and lawyer-linguists of the EU legislative institutions need to obtain sophisticated knowledge of the regulatory system, culture and history of the EU Member States, and what skills are required to compare such legal and meta-legal data.

Determining the extent of legal knowledge required by EU translators and lawyer-linguists for the translation and revision in the EU legislative procedure, that is, 'EU translation', depends on what equivalence between language versions actually entails. In general terms, one might describe equivalence as a relation of identity, correspondence or likeness between an original or 'source' text and the translation or 'target' text. Equivalence in EU translation specifically entails a relation of correspondence between the original draft text, generally the English language version,[2] and the translations in the other 23 language versions. However, that does not tell us *what* counts as translation equivalence or *when* language versions can be said to be in absolute concordance. The overall *modus operandi* of drafting and translation practices in the EU institutions seems to pursue two notions of equivalence that are potentially at tension with each other. That is to say, EU translators and subsequently lawyer-linguists need to strike a delicate balance between, on the one hand, ensuring linguistic equivalence by using methods of literal translation and, on the other hand, safeguarding readability by taking some liberty to divert from the syntax and wording of the original draft text. In principle each translation must be a faithful and accurate rendering of the original, even if that

1 Paraphrasing Lönroth (2008).

2 Court of Auditors, Special Report No. 9/2006 concerning translation expenditure incurred by the Commission, the Parliament and the Council. OJ C284, 21 November 2006, 1–39; Guggeis and Robinson (2012: 65–6).

would result in reproducing linguistic imperfections or substantive inconsistencies (Strandvik 2012: 33; Wagner et al. 2002: 47–58). Indeed, the case law of the Court of Justice of the European Union (CJEU) shows that both diverging syntactic or grammatical structures and a lack of matching nouns and verbs may create legal problems.[3] The Court's case law further indicates that, in order to realize uniform interpretation and application of EU law, language versions should generally use legal terms that denote the same autonomous EU legal concepts,[4] hence, use a legal language which is specific to the EU legal system.[5]

On the other hand, in order to preserve readability or comprehensibility of EU legislative texts, Principles 1.1. and 1.2. of the *Joint Practical Guide* state that the drafts of legislative acts should be unambiguous and easy to understand so as to avoid uncertainty in the mind of the reader. After all, the EU institutions cannot be considered transparent and accountable if they do not guarantee *every* citizen *equal* access to the law without language barriers.[6] As Phillipson (2003: 126) argues, language versions that follow the exact same sentence structure may strain syntax. This, in turn, would conflict with requirements of clear writing. Further, translating legal terms literally could potentially lead to words that look the same on the surface but connote different legal concepts in the various national legal systems. This could lead to diverging interpretations.[7] Legal terms in EU legislation that are too disconnected from existing expressions at the national level might not be understood, as Dannemann et al. (2010: 77) and Onufrio (2007: 6) argue.

Producing language versions that are fully clear to their respective readers but also sufficiently similar linguistically requires a mix of translation methods that aim to satisfy two potentially divergent objectives. These two objectives resemble a classic dichotomy in translation theory, most famously explicated by Friedrich

3 As to syntactic discrepancies, see, for example, Case C-56/06 *Euro Tex Textilverwertung GmbH* v. *Hauptzollamt Duisburg* [2007] ECR I-04859, para. 16; on the diverging literal meaning of legal terms, see, for example, Case C-29/91 *Dr. Sophie Redmond Stichting* v. *Hendrikus Bartol and others* [1992] ECR I-3189, para. 10.

4 On the autonomy of EU legal concepts, see chapters 6 and 10 by Kjær and Engberg in this volume.

5 In the field of consumer contract law, see Communication from the Commission to the European Parliament and the Council, A More Coherent European Contract Law. An Action Plan, COM(2003) 68 final, 12 February 2003, at 35.

6 Communication of the Commission, A New Framework Strategy for Multilingualism, COM(2005) 596 final, 22 November 2005, at 12; European Union, Many Tongues, One Family. Languages in the European Union (2004), at 17, available at: http://www.euic.hr/images/article/File/publikacije/Many%20tongues,%20one%20family.pdf.

7 See indirectly the reasoning by the European Commission in Communication from the Commission to the Council and the European Parliament on European Contract Law, COM (2001) 398 final, 11 July 2001, 10–11 and Communication from the Commission to the European Parliament and the Council, A More Coherent European Contract Law. An Action Plan, COM(2003) 68 final, 12 February 2003, 8–9.

Schleiermacher (2004) in the field of literary translation.[8] In his view, a poem, for instance, can be translated in two basic ways: the translator either 'brings' the writer to the reader or the reader to the writer. Along the lines of the former approach, the translator adapts the original to produce a translation that will appear natural and familiar to the reader. The alternative method entails reproducing the textual features of the foreign language of the original as closely as possible so as to convey to the reader that he is dealing with a translation of a text foreign to his culture. Venuti (1995: 24) labels the former approach 'domestication' and the latter 'foreignization'. However, since this chapter applies this distinction analogously, it uses instead the terms 'familiarization' and 'exteriorization' respectively, applying them to the context of EU translation. Familiarizing EU translation entails adapting each language version and using legal language that is familiar to the legal culture of the Member State or States applying the particular version. Alternatively, exteriorization requires both the original and the translations to use terminology not used by the respective Member States, thus conveying that the law expressed by the language versions is exterior to their national legal cultures.

Schleiermacher cautioned that the two ways of conducting literary translation should not be combined. Since both approaches point in opposite directions, he reasoned that translators should commit to either one or the other in order to achieve reliable results (Schleiermacher 2004: 49). This chapter takes a corresponding position regarding familiarization and exteriorization in EU translation. That is to say, if the EU institutions are committed to drafting language versions that are clear and fully comprehensible in the receiving Member States, preserving syntactic correspondence and using legal terms unfamiliar in the national legal context will be counterproductive. Conversely, if they aim for maximum textual correspondence and wish to avoid diverging national connotations of legal terms, it is not helpful to attune the respective language versions to the national legal cultures of the Member States that will apply them.

This chapter does not intend to use Schleiermacher's dichotomy to describe the current practice of EU translation. Instead, it brings into play the qualitative distinction between familiarization and exteriorization with the aim of demonstrating the burden of legal knowledge and comparative skills that each approach would hypothetically require of EU translators and lawyer-linguists, if the EU would commit to one or the other approach. It demonstrates that striking the balance in favour of exteriorization over familiarization is less demanding on current translation and revision practices in the EU legislative procedure.

8 I previously applied Schleiermacher's dichotomy to legal translation for the purpose of comparative legal research in Baaij (2014).

'Familiarization' versus 'Exteriorization'

If the EU would only take a familiarizing approach to EU translation, equivalence between the language versions of EU legislation would entail more than mere linguistic equivalence. In translation theories based on a pragmatic conception of language, such as functionalism, language is primarily a tool to communicate information between interlocutors about extra-linguistic reality. As Varó and Hughes (2002: 230) and Šarčević (1997: 48, 234) demonstrate, legal translation based on this pragmatic conception of language places at least as much attention on the communicative context as on semantics and syntax. Here, the consistency of textual features such as grammar, syntax and terminology is only one of many relevant factors. From this point of view, legal translation is not the exact reproduction of a text but an act in multilingual legal discourse, facilitating unhindered legal discourse across different languages and legal cultures (Chromá 2004: 47; Varó and Hughes 2002: 179). Along these lines, equivalence between the language versions of EU legislation would aim exclusively at consistency in the ways the different language versions are applied in practice. According to Šarčević (1997: 48, 73, 234–5), Garzone (2000: 5) and Varó and Hughes (2002: 178–80), EU translators and lawyer-linguists should strive to ensure equivalence of 'legal effects' of all language versions, that is, equivalence of the actual legal consequences in the various legal systems of the EU Member States. The pragmatic conception of language dictates that the *same* text may have diverging effects on different audiences, depending on the readerships' situational context, culture or other unique circumstances of reception (Šarčević 1997: 17). Conversely, applying this view to EU translation suggests that *different* language versions of EU legislation may produce the same legal consequences if each version is drafted differently, in keeping with the linguistic needs and cultural expectations of the target receiver. This implies that EU translators and lawyer-linguists should loosen the syntactic correspondence with the source text and, whenever necessary, adapt the terminology, using legal terms that are understood and generate the same legal effects or outcomes in the different national legal systems (Šarčević 1997: 71–2, 226; De Groot 1996: 158; 2006: 425). The objective of this approach is to choose terminology that creates *legally* equivalent legal concepts, not necessarily *linguistically* equivalent legal concepts. Paraphrasing Dannemann et al. (2010: 80–81), EU translators and lawyer-linguists then convey 'the message from Brussels' better than merely the 'closest literal match of terminology'.

On the contrary, if the EU institutions would commit to an exteriorizing approach to EU translation, EU translators and lawyer-linguists should refrain from choosing terms that are familiar in the target national legal cultures. Dannemann et al. (2010: 77) and Onufrio (2007: 6–7) agree with principles 5.2. and 5.3.2. of the *Joint Practical Guide*, which suggest that terms too closely linked to national legal systems may lead to specific local connotations and thus thwart an autonomous interpretation of EU law. Exteriorizing EU translation would help solve this problem. Parallel to Schleiermacher's preference for 'bringing the reader to the writer', it would help alert the reader to the need to interpret each language version in a context extraneous to domestic law, namely that of the EU's purportedly autonomous legal language. After all, the uniform interpretation and application of EU legislation is promoted by creating a distinctly European legal language that is equally 'foreign' to all national legal languages of the Member States.

A reasonable response to this proposal would be to criticize the exteriorizing approach for potentially hindering clear communication of the 'message from Brussels'. However, emphasizing the transmission of a purportedly intact message from one interlocutor to another belongs to a pragmatic understanding of language. Hence, this response overlooks the fact that exteriorizing EU translation is not derived from or validated by a *communicative* understanding of language to begin with. Instead, it finds support in a *constitutive* notion of language in the hermeneutic tradition, according to which language 'shapes' the very world in which we live. Acknowledging this creative power of language, Schleiermacher (2004: 56–7) maintains that we must acknowledge that our entire knowledge has come to us through language. According to this view, different languages create different realities. Consequently, there is simply no way to transcend languages and freely transfer information between them. In fact, attempting to do so creates the misleading illusion of 'transparent language' in the sense that language is capable of capturing the essence of extra-linguistic subject matter.[9] Applying the constitutive notion of language to EU translation, it follows that the only way to incorporate EU legal language into a national legal culture is by contrasting it with the existing national legal language, thus revealing the inherent contrast between them. An EU translator can achieve this effect by recording the foreignness or extraneous nature of EU law in the language of a particular national legal culture, for example, by creating legal terms that are new to the Member States (cf. Dannemann et al. 2010: 77 and Cao 2007: 55, 57). For this purpose, EU translators or lawyer-linguists may use neologisms. These new terms could be either 'legal neologisms', that is to say, existing ordinary words that do not belong to the Member State's legal language, or 'neologisms proper', words that are new even to its general language (see Chapter 11 by Šarčević in this volume). The use of neologisms makes the reader aware that the underlying legal concepts are exterior to his or her national legal system.

The Positive Role of Legal Knowledge in Familiarization

As argued above, for better results, EU institutions should commit to either a familiarizing or an exteriorizing approach to multilingual legislative drafting,

9 Schleiermacher (2004: 48) and Venuti (2004: 326) make this point in the field of literary translation, although it should be pointed out that their argument is normative, not practical, and concerns oppressive ethnocentrism in literary translation (for example, Venuti 1995: 20; 2004: 19).

rather than combining both. This chapter examines the feasibility of EU translation if the EU Institutions would select either one or the other approach. It does so by comparing the type and extent of legal knowledge that each would require of EU translators and lawyer-linguists. As to the familiarizing approach, some scholars maintain that EU translators and lawyer-linguists should take greater account of the specific cultural, linguistic and legal backgrounds of the target receivers (for example, Dannemann et al. 2010: 75; Šarčević 2012: 89–93; Garzone 2000: 5–6). To this end, both EU translators and lawyer-linguists would need knowledge of the national legal system of the Member State where each language version will be applied (cf. De Groot 1996: 13, 14; Chromá 2004: 48; Varó and Hughes 2002: 23; Cao 2007: 55; Lindroos-Hovinheimo 2007: 375). Especially lawyer-linguists would need to be proficient in this respect, since they are responsible for ensuring equivalence of the legal scope and consistency with existing EU law (Guggeis and Robinson 2012: 61–3). They would need to be familiar with the unique history and culture of the national legal systems, as well as possess advanced comparative skills to assess the equivalence of the legal effects produced by the different language versions in the respective legal systems. Two aspects of familiarizing EU translation support this conclusion.

First, familiarization in EU translation would require lawyer-linguists to anticipate the readership's linguistic needs and specific cultural and legal expectations when choosing the most appropriate terminology (cf. Šarčević 1997: 2, 12, 18; Cao 2007: 10). Talking about legal translation in general, Chromá (2004: 48) and Onufrio (2007: 3–4) argue that, to truly understand the legal vocabulary of both the source and target legal systems, one must be proficient in the languages of these legal systems and possess in-depth knowledge and understanding of how each system deals with the legal issue at hand. According to Šarčević (1997: 72, 229), when searching for legal equivalents, translators should proceed as if they were solving a legal problem, attempting to predict how the courts are likely to interpret and apply the particular language version in cases brought before them (Šarčević 1997: 72, 129, 229, 246). This entails identifying the nature of the issue at hand and, like a judge, ascertaining how *that* issue is dealt with in the target legal system (Šarčević 1997: 235–6).

Second, a familiarizing approach to the translation of EU legislation would require a comparison of the effects of both the source and target texts on their respective readerships. After all, from a pragmatic viewpoint, the uniform interpretation and application of EU law cannot be achieved unless all language versions are legally equivalent. In legal translation studies, Šarčević (1997: 72) and Schroth (1986: 55–6) maintain that the legal translator must not only understand the meaning of the words of the source text and what legal effects are intended, but also have the ability to use language effectively to achieve the same or sufficiently similar legal effects in the target text. For similar reasons, Dannemann et al. (2010: 81) dub this approach to translation a 'comparative drafting technique'. In discussing how EU translators and lawyer-linguists should go about acquiring such knowledge, Šarčević (2012: 96) looks specifically to the most prominent advocates of the functionalist tradition in comparative law, Konrad Zweigert and Hein Kötz. They make the case that only the *function* of legal institutions or rules can be compared usefully (Zweigert and Kötz 1998: 34–5, 43–4). The method of comparative legal research advocated by functional comparative law is thus one that compares how different legal systems solve particular problems which societies have in common (Zweigert and Kötz 1998: 39). Consequently, functional equivalents, as Šarčević calls them, are legal terms in different legal languages that may refer to different legal concepts or institutions but have the same or similar function in the respective legal systems (Šarčević 2012: 96–7).

From the foregoing we can infer that, if the EU institutions would opt for a fully familiarizing mode of multilingual legislative drafting, the legal knowledge required would play what I call a *positive* role. That is, it would require considerable knowledge to determine which legal terminology or style would generate the same legal effects or consequences in one or more Member States as those used in the draft text. This does not mean that finding such perfect legal equivalents is always possible, if ever. On the contrary, proponents of familiarization in legal translation generally deny the feasibility of 'perfect' translation (for example, Obenaus 1995: 248); Lindroos-Hovinheimo 2007: 369; Cao 2007: 34; Šarčević 1997: 47, 234). Some argue that, from a legal point of view, the meaning of legal terms of different national systems usually only partially overlaps since they denote legal concepts embedded in local legal cultures (for example, Šarčević 1997: 67–70, 230–34; De Groot 2006: 424). From the viewpoint of comparative legal analysis, Zweigert and Kötz (1998: 36) admit that no one would be capable of acquiring all the legal knowledge required for a perfect functional comparison, as this would require, in the words of Ernst Rabel, knowledge of 'the law of the whole world, past and present, and everything that affects the law'. Yet, notwithstanding the difficulty or impossibility of finding perfect legal equivalents, familiarization would require EU translators and lawyer-linguists to come at least as close as humanly possible. This reveals the limited potential of familiarizing EU translation in general. It seeks a perfect but practically unattainable degree of legal equivalence, leading proponents to admit that legal translation is necessarily a matter of approximation (Šarčević 1997: 70–71). The next section will make it clear that an exteriorizing approach to EU translation requires a different type and consequently a different degree of legal knowledge, thus leading me to conclude that the exteriorizing approach has a greater potential for success than familiarizing translation.

The Negative Role of 'Nominal Awareness' in Exteriorization

Unlike the often expressed view (for example, Garzone 2000: 5; Trosborg 1997: 153; Šarčević 1997: 12–25), the opposite of familiarization in translation does not necessarily amount to a servile or naïve commitment to reproducing the wording and syntax of the source text. Exteriorization is not merely a linguistic endeavour; legal knowledge does play a role. However, it is legal knowledge of a different kind. One could say that in a comprehensive exteriorizing approach to EU translation, legal knowledge would only play a *negative* role, that is, it pertains to terms that should not be used, even if a given term is the closest literal equivalent. For instance, whereas familiarization would require knowledge of a particular national legal term having the same legal effects or consequences as the terms in the original draft text, the aim of exteriorization would be to avoid the use of national legal terms. It shuns nouns and verbs with national legal 'baggage'. However, while EU translators or lawyer-linguists using the exteriorization approach would not need to search for the perfect functional equivalent in national legal terminology, they would still have to be aware of them in order to avoid them. The game of archery or target shooting serves as a metaphor. One could say that the familiarizing archer aims for the single bull's eye or inner ring of the target. After all, EU translators or lawyer-linguists strive to find the single most adequate legal equivalent in the national legal system of the respective Member State or States. They may question whether it is even possible to hit the bull's eye; but it remains their target nonetheless. In contrast, the exteriorizing archer hopes to *avoid* hitting the bull's eye. After all, exteriorization would require EU translators and lawyer-linguists to refrain from using terms that create an illusion of transparency.

Hence, exteriorization also requires knowledge of the Member State or States where the particular language version(s) will be applied. However, contrary to positive legal knowledge, negative legal knowledge does not necessarily require extensive knowledge of the national legal system or culture of the Member State(s). Instead, the knowledge required in such case could be described as 'nominal awareness', that is, mere awareness of the terms used in a particular legal system to designate specific national legal concepts. Along these lines, one cannot say that nominal awareness necessarily requires any specific legal, cultural and historical knowledge of the legal system of the respective Member State(s); one need not know the content of the legal concepts to which these terms are deemed to refer. Instead, in theory one would only need a comprehensive black list, a list of legal terms that are off limits. In this regard, even a legal dictionary containing definitions and/or explaining specific usages would already be superfluous. Instead, all that is needed is a list of national terms. This does not mean that exteriorization would result in a crude literal rendition that never requires adaptation. Recall that the objective of exteriorizing translation is to have the foreignness of the source text shine through in the target language. Exteriorization therefore rejects the use of any literal equivalent of a source term that happens to have national legal baggage, regardless of whether the translator regards the term as equivalent, legally or otherwise.

There is another reason why exteriorizing EU translation would entail more than mere literal translation: not everything goes. Avoiding the metaphorical bull's eye does not mean that the exteriorizing archer can just shoot his arrow in any direction. According to Schleiermacher (2004: 54), exteriorizing or foreignizing literary translation is of no value when it is random. A translation should 'sound foreign in a quite specific way'. In fact, the context of reception does play a role. The reason is that a particular legislative act of EU law is not foreign or exterior *of its own accord*; it is exterior relative to the national legal system of a particular Member State. The foreignness of EU law is therefore a domestic notion; a white sandy beach on a tropical island in the Pacific Ocean may be exotic to an average Dutchman, but not to the local resident. Ultimately, the translator would still translate *for* a particular target culture, as Venuti (2004: 331) argues. Using our archery metaphor, it can be said that aiming to avoid the bull's eye still involves the art of aiming. Whereas shooting the arrow in any random direction does not qualify as 'avoiding the bull's eye', aiming at one of the outer rings does. Consequently, extrapolating Venuti's point of view in literary translation (1995: 34), we can say that the exteriority of EU law still depends on the 'dominant target-culture values' of the local legal culture. The objective in exteriorizing EU translation would be to convey the exteriority of the meaning of EU law relative to a Member State's legal culture. However, the translator's sensitivity for the context of reception is primarily linguistic, not legal. That is to say, finding the appropriate neologisms requires high proficiency in the general language of the target Member State(s). In sum, an exclusively exteriorizing take on EU translation requires primarily linguistic skills, that is, a nominal awareness of the national legal language and an in-depth understanding of the general language or languages of the particular Member State. Obviously, this is easier said than done. It may occur that the most adequate words in a particular general language are already reserved by the national legal language (Dannemann et al. 2010: 70–71; De Groot 2012: 145). However, exteriorizing EU translators would not be searching for a single perfect word or phrase familiar to a Member State's legal culture. Instead, potentially multiple words may be comprehensible in the target language as exterior to the national legal language. Therefore, they would have multiple potential satisfactory solutions at their disposal, if necessary by using neologisms proper. Nonetheless, exteriorization should not be considered approximation. It would have been if it had set a real or hypothetical standard of perfection for translation, as is the case in familiarizing EU translation. However, since exteriorization precludes such measure, it is more likely to succeed in getting the job done by its own standards than familiarizing EU translation by its respective standards.

Practical Implications

As said above, it would be best for EU translation to take either a familiarizing or an exteriorizing approach. The reason is that pursuing a combination of both may lead to contradictory and thus unreliable results. The remainder of this chapter offers practical arguments against familiarizing and in favour of exteriorizing EU translation. If either approach were implemented, the knowledge and skills required by translators and lawyer-linguists would have several practical implications for the current institutional framework of EU translation.

First, as regards the current situation, EU translators in the EU legislative institutions may be highly qualified and experienced, but those having a legal background are in the minority. The same applies to the drafters of the original English text. Even lawyer-linguists, lawyers by trade, are primarily specialized in EU law and are not likely to be experts in the wide variety of policy fields regulated by EU legislation and have adequate knowledge of how the different national legal systems deal with these areas (see Guggeis and Robinson 2012: 52, 60, 72, 81). Therefore, familiarization would require extensive training in the national laws of the Member States not only for translators but also for lawyer-linguists.

Second, since legal translators and lawyer-linguists would be expected to focus their attention on specific legal systems to predict the legal effects of different language versions, the current configuration of language units would be less suitable for familiarization. Rather than assigning them to the 24 general languages, it would be better to divide them, at least the lawyer-linguists in all legislative institutions, amongst the 28 national legal systems of the Member States. Since each language version should be attuned to a specific national legal system, a special language version would have to be produced for each Member State. For example, lawyer-linguists would be responsible for finalizing two versions in the German language, one for Germany and the other for Austria. Moreover, for a multilingual Member State such as Belgium, they would prepare special Dutch and French versions, in addition to the Dutch and French versions prepared specifically for the Netherlands and France, respectively. Such institutional arrangements would be highly inefficient, if not preposterous, making a full-scale familiarizing approach to EU translation highly unattractive. Then again, if the EU would truly commit to a familiarizing approach and implement it consistently, such institutional changes would be indispensable for ensuring the best results in terms of readability and transparency. This unwelcome consequence demonstrates that familiarizing EU translation is undesirable.

Conversely, exteriorization in its fullest extent would lead to a more realistic and reasonable institutional configuration. First, since exteriorizing EU translation would be primarily linguistic translation, it would require little to no knowledge of the specific legal cultures of the Member States on the part of EU translators and lawyer-linguists. Therefore, the current level of translation skills and legal expertise would suffice. Second, since exteriorization would not require the language versions to be attuned to a specific national legal terminology and style, there would be no reason to produce as many language versions as there are national legal systems and languages. In fact, a fully exteriorizing approach would reduce a particular difficulty of familiarization, namely, finding adequate terminology for different Member States which apply the same language versions. For example, under the externalizing approach, a single French language version would simply need to avoid terminology and legislative styles that are too closely linked with any of the French legal languages of Luxembourg, France and Belgium. This might be a challenging task, but it beats drafting multiple French language versions or a single language version that uses legal terms familiar to all three legal cultures and are functionally equivalent as well. Therefore, based on considerations of practicality and efficiency, it would be better for EU translation to commit to an exteriorizing approach.

Concluding Remarks

This chapter compares the hypothetical implications in the event either a familiarizing or an exteriorizing approach were consistently applied to EU translation. The reality is, however, that EU translation currently uses both approaches concurrently. As a result, EU translators and lawyer-linguists simultaneously attempt to realize diverging objectives. Nonetheless, contemplating hypotheticals also tells us something about EU translation as it is carried out today. In particular, it highlights the different kinds of legal knowledge and comparative legal analyses required by current EU translation. Hence, when deciding how to strike a balance between sufficient textual correspondence and sufficient readability of the language versions of EU legislation, it may be concluded that more of the former poses less of a 'legal burden' than the latter. After all, the current knowledge and skills generally possessed by EU translators and lawyer-linguists, as well as the existing institutional arrangements, are better suited to achieving sufficient textual correspondence. At least this chapter offers an argument, albeit a practical one, suggesting that EU translation should lean towards greater textual consistency and the use of neologisms, and less towards fluent readability. Moreover, since exteriorization adheres to a constitutive notion of language, it does not seek perfect but unattainable solutions. Consequently, by its own standards, exteriorizing EU translation is more likely to succeed in expressing EU law consistently in 24 languages than familiarization.

References

Baaij, C.J.W. 2014. Legal translation and the 'contamination' of comparative legal research, in *Comparative Law: Engaging Translation*, edited by S. Glanert. Abingdon, Oxon and New York: Routledge, 104–22.

Cao, D. 2007. *Translating Law*. Clevedon: Multilingual Matters.

Chromá, M. 2004. *Legal Translation and the Dictionary*. Tübingen: Max Niemeyer Verlag.

Dannemann, G., Ferreri S. and Graziadei, M. 2010. Language and terminology, in *The Cambridge Companion to European Union Private Law*, edited by C. Twigg-Flesner. Cambridge: Cambridge University Press, 70–84.

De Groot, G.-R. 1996. Law, legal language and the legal system: reflections on the problems of translating legal texts, in *European Legal Cultures*, edited by V. Gessner, A. Hoeland and C. Varga. Aldershot: Dartmouth, 155–60.

De Groot, G.-R. 2006. Legal translation, in *Elgar Encyclopedia of Comparative Law*, edited by J.M. Smits. Cheltenham, UK and Northampton, MA: Edward Elgar, 423–33.

De Groot, G.-R. 2012. The influence of problems of legal translation on comparative law research, in *The Role of Legal Translation in Legal Harmonization*, edited by C.J.W. Baaij. Alphen aan den Rijn: Kluwer Law International, 139–59.

Garzone, G. 2000. Legal translation and functionalist approaches: a contradiction in terms? in *La traduction juridique, histoire, théorie(s) et pratique*, edited by J.-Cl. Gémar. Bern and Geneva: ASTTI and ETI, 395–414.

Guggeis, M. and Robinson, W. 2012. 'Co-revision': legal-linguistic revision in the European Union 'co-decision' process, in *The Role of Legal Translation in Legal Harmonization*, edited by C.J.W. Baaij. Alphen aan den Rijn: Kluwer Law International, 51–82.

Joint Practical Guide of the European Parliament, the Council and the Commission for persons involved in the drafting of European Union legislation. 2013. Available at: eur-lex-europa.eu/content/pdf/techleg/joint-practical-guide-2013-en.pdf.

Lindroos-Hovinheimo, S. 2007. On the indeterminacy of legal translation, in *Private Law and the Many Cultures of Europe*, edited by T. Wilhelmsoon, E. Paunio and A. Pohjolainen. Alphen aan den Rijn: Kluwer Law International, 367–84.

Lönroth, K.-J. 2008. Efficiency, transparency and openness: translation in the European Union. Speech at the XVIII World Congress of the International Federation of Translators in Shanghai, 12, 20. Available at: http://ec.europa.eu/dgs/translation/publications/presentations/speeches/20080801_shanghai_en.pdf.

Obenaus, G. 1995. The legal translator as information broker, in *Translation and the Law*, edited by M. Morris. Amsterdam and Philadelphia: John Benjamins, 247–61.

Onufrio, M.V. 2007. Harmonisation of European contract law and legal translation: a role for comparative lawyers. *InDret* 2/2004. Available at: http://www.indret.com/pdf/429_en.pdf.

Phillipson, R. 2003. *English-Only Europe? Challenging Language Policy*. New York: Routledge.

Schleiermacher, F.D.E. 2004. On the different methods of translating (Bernofsky, S., trans.), in *The Translation Studies Reader*, edited by L. Venuti. 2nd edition. London and New York: Routledge, 43–63.

Schroth, P.W. 1986. Legal translation. *American Journal of Comparative Law*, 34, 47–65.

Strandvik, I. 2012. Legal harmonization through legal translation: texts that say the same thing? in *The Role of Legal Translation in Legal Harmonization*, edited by C.J.W. Baaij. Alphen aan den Rijn: Kluwer Law International, 25–50.

Šarčević, S. 1997. *New Approach to Legal Translation*. The Hague: Kluwer Law International.

Šarčević, S. 2012. Coping with the challenges of legal translation in harmonization, in *The Role of Legal Translation in Legal Harmonization*, edited by C.J.W. Baaij. Alphen aan den Rijn: Kluwer Law International, 83–108.

Trosborg, A. 1997. Translating hybrid political texts, in *Text Typology and Translation*, edited by A. Trosborg. Amsterdam: John Benjamins, 145–58.

Varó, E.A. and Hughes, B. 2002. *Legal Translation Explained*. Manchester: St. Jerome Publishing.

Venuti, L. 1995. *The Translator's Invisibility: A History of Translation*. 2nd edition. Oxon: Routledge.

Venuti, L. 2004. Foundational statements, in *The Translation Studies Reader*, edited by L. Venuti. 2nd edition. London and New York: Routledge, 13–20.

Wagner, E., Bech, S. and Martínez, J.M. 2002. *Translating for the European Union Institutions*. Manchester: St. Jerome Publishing.

Zweigert, K. and Kötz, H. 1998. *An Introduction to Comparative Law* (Weir, T., trans.). 3rd edition. Oxford: Oxford University Press.

Chapter 8
Translating EU Legislation from a *Lingua Franca*: Advantages and Disadvantages

Annarita Felici

Introduction

Over the past decades English has become the most prominent language for global communication. Its prestige spans from international business to scientific development, social networks and entertainment. It is also the most learnt foreign language in the world, the official language of several countries and the working language or one of the main working languages of all international organizations. The EU is no exception. Despite its strong multilingual policy, English has gained the unofficial role of a *lingua franca* in the EU.

The widespread use of and the growing position of English as a *lingua franca* (henceforth: ELF) have given rise to a number of non-native varieties with some distinct differences from traditional British and American English. 'International English', 'world English', 'global English', 'sub-English' and 'globish' are some of the terms used to define a kind of general English which has evolved over the years into a vehicular language for worldwide communication.

Traditional studies on 'world English' refer to Kachru's classification (1985), which groups speakers and functions of English into three circles: an inner circle consisting of native-speaking countries (UK, United States, Ireland, Canada, Australia, New Zealand), an outer circle where English is an official language (Singapore, Hong Kong, India, etc.) and an expanding circle (China, Russia, Europe, etc.) where English is learnt as a second language. According to Kachru, the inner circle is norm providing because it contains proper varieties of English; the outer is in the process of defining its own varieties and is therefore norm developing. Finally, the expanding circle is norm dependent. The model has been widely criticized for its blurred classification into circles and for underestimating both the impact of international English in the world (Crystal 1997: 56) and the growing role of ELF in the expanding circle (Mollin 2006: 42). In addition, neither circle has a LSP dimension, thus missing typical and sensitive areas of *lingua franca* use.

The debate on ELF in the expanding circle dates back to the late 1990s, when some scholars (Jenkins 2007; Jenkins et al. 2001; Mauranen 2003; Seidlhofer 2001) started mentioning the possibility of a Euro-English variety with continental patterns. This was initially associated with the English used by non-native speakers within the EU (Jenkins et al. 2001: 13)[1] and somehow confused with Eurospeak. On the other hand, there is no consensus on whether it should be attributed the status of a variety. Other scholars (Grzega 2005: 52; McCluskey 2002: 43; Mollin 2006: 46–8) regard Euro-English features, with the exception of some EU administrative lexical units, as being more concerned with foreign language proficiency than with an established variety of English.

Nonetheless, the EU provides an ideal setting for the study of ELF. After the accession of the UK to the EEC and the enlargement of 2004, speakers of different backgrounds have increasingly used English in their daily communication. English is also the unofficial working language for drafting and for political negotiations and the pseudo-source language for most of the Union's translations. From a political point of view, a language traditionally shaped on the common law may represent a neutral and diplomatic tool, thus serving the legal needs of continental Europe. On the other hand, EU English remains a vehicular language drafted primarily by non-native speakers. This means that syntax, stylistic features and drafting conventions of one's own language may be easily imported into the *lingua franca*. The presence of native speakers is also not a guarantee of quality. The relatively closed environment of the EU and the patterns of communicative adjustment to the *lingua franca* often cause native speakers to lose touch with their mother tongue to the point that government jargon sounds absolutely natural.

Not surprisingly, translation work is particularly sensitive to the effects of this multilingual discourse community. If we add the impact of 'pivot languages'[2] on the operational side, the implications of using a *lingua franca* are doubled. Translators cannot rely on any controlled use of language and are faced with an unprecedented dynamic of languages in contact, where a target language becomes the source language for other languages (Burr 2013: 1490–91).

Departing from this standpoint, the present chapter examines the footprints of a *lingua franca* in EU legislative texts and their implications for translation. The next section proceeds with a brief overview of EU multilingualism at the crossroad of ELF and translation – two opposite trends if we regard the first as aiming at language reduction and the latter at its multiplication. A further section investigates EU legal English and the extent to which it qualifies as ELF. An analysis of some legislative text samples follows with the intent of highlighting pitfalls but also potential advantages of translating from such a *lingua franca*. The concluding remarks pinpoint the peculiarities of EU translation and how ELF requires us to revisit basic translation activities, thus bringing potentially new opportunities as well.

1 As stated by Jenkins et al., 'Because of the current role of "Euro-English" in the EU, it would be naive, certainly, to assume that legitimatisation, codification, and standardisation processes will not take place'.

2 The use of pivot languages refers to the translation into one of the most commonly used languages (often English, French and German) and then out of that languages into a lesser-used language. Italian, Polish and Spanish are also being used more frequently.

EU Multilingual Policy between ELF and Translation

Multilingualism is directly linked to the political nature of the Union and ensures equal rights and treatment for all 24 official languages. This is the basic principle enshrined in Council Regulation No.1/58, which provided in Article 1 that 'the official languages and the working languages of the institutions of the Community shall be Dutch, French, German and Italian'. This article has since been amended with a new language or languages at each enlargement; however, no definition of official and working language has ever been given. The pair suggests a synonymic use and a rather political move in placing the working languages '*de jure* alongside the official languages' (Burr 2013: 1473). A hint regarding the role of working languages is found only in Article 6, which states that the institutions of the Union 'may stipulate in their rules of procedure which of the languages are to be used in specific cases', thus implying that official and working languages are perhaps not always on the same level.

Along those lines, the equal authenticity of EU legislation compensates for the loss of sovereignty of the Member States and ensures democracy among them. In this sense, Article 55 of the consolidated version of the TEU, as amended, establishes that the Treaty has been 'drawn up in a single original' in all 24 languages, 'the text in each of these languages being equally authentic'. Looking at all these documents, it is difficult not to notice how 'original', 'official' and 'working' languages are considered substantially on the same level; something that is legally acceptable, but looks rather blurred from the point of view of linguistics and translation. On the other hand, most of these rules were drafted back in the late 1950s, when parallel drafting with six Member States and four official languages was still a feasible option.

The current practice is to negotiate and draft the base text in a commonly agreed language or *lingua franca*, which is increasingly English, and then translate it into all the other official languages. The process of negotiating and drafting the base text is rather complex and during the ordinary legislative procedure, more than one language may be used. The final translations are deemed to be consistent and to produce equivalent legal effects because, once authenticated, they acquire the force of law. As highlighted by Šarčević (1997: 117), the principle of equal authenticity is intended to confer indisputable authority on each of the authentic text, *de facto* eliminating the inferior status of translations. With 24 languages and 522 possible language combinations – 24 official languages that can be translated into 23 others – the use of a *lingua franca* and subsequent translations is an inevitable pragmatic solution.

In this regard, Article 6 of Council Regulation No.1/58 offers a valid diplomatic compromise to the actual implementation of EU multilingualism. Providing that the institutions may use a particular or a reduced number of languages in specific cases implicitly justifies ELF and the use of one or more working languages.

In practice, multilingualism is ensured and implemented via translation, bridging the gap between the functional needs of the Union and institutional democracy. In this way, the use of a *lingua franca*, which aims at reducing the linguistic regime, is informally neutralized by translation, thus achieving 'unity in diversity' and equal rights for all languages. Nonetheless, translation is not mentioned anywhere in the EU rules determining the use of languages. From a legal point of view, awarding official status to a translation would mean that some versions are more official than others. On the practical side, EU translation shows unprecedented features of languages in contact, be it ELF or the use of pivot languages. This is also due to the increased number of official languages, which makes it sometimes difficult to find translators from a given source language into another lesser-used language (e.g., from Greek into Croatian). Such practices raise inevitably the issue of text quality and highlight new unprecedented challenges for translation, requiring the use of intercultural communication to produce a collective target-language product from a fictitious source text.

EU Legal English: *Lingua Franca* or a New Variety?

Following the accession of Sweden and Finland and, more recently, the Eastern European countries, English has become the current *de facto* administrative *lingua franca*, shifting the balance from French to English. A publication of the Directorate-General for Translation[3] confirms that, in 2008, 72.5 per cent of texts in the Commission were originally drafted in English, 11.8 per cent in French, 2.7 per cent in German and 13 per cent in other languages. In contrast, 10 years earlier English and French shared 45.4 per cent and 40.4 per cent of the drafting respectively, thus showing that the use of English as the main drafting language has almost doubled. This trend is likely to increase because, as De Swaan (2004) put it, the more fragmented the linguistic landscape, the greater the need for a common means of communication. However, which English are we dealing with? Where does it appear in the circles mentioned above? And does it qualify as a new variety of legal English?

The dominant administrative language of Europe, English is the main working language of the institutions (with the exception of the CJEU) and the most prominent language for internal communication. In this regard, its role as a *lingua franca* and working language goes hand in hand because the need for a vehicular language implies an increase in its usage for practical purposes. Moreover, it has proved to be particularly attractive and instrumental from a political point of view. The EU context enhances the perception of English as a global and neutral language for several reasons, for example, the marginal role of Britain and the United States, non-native speakers outnumbering native speakers and last but not least, English being the language of a different legal tradition.

3 *Translating for a Multilingual Community* (2009). Available at: http://bookshop.europa.eu/en/translating-for-a-multilingual-community-pbHC3008600/ [accessed 24 September 2013].

These factors have inevitably contributed to an unmarked form of English devoid of cultural specificity; hence new terms such as *internal market*, *pigmeat*, *sheepmeat*, *planification*, etc. Others have acquired new meanings due to the influence of other languages, for example, *actual* meaning 'current', *in case of* used to replace the preposition 'for', *dispose of* with the new meaning of 'to have', *transpose* with the meaning of 'to implement'. These semantic changes can be attributed to the multilingual production of EU legislation and to the translation from one language into another during drafting and negotiations, as well as to the need for adapting English to the EU legal context. On the other hand, the first EU English texts were translations from French; hence both terminology and drafting style are inevitably shaped by the continental legal tradition and Romance language influence. Pointing to the broad and vague formulation of EU law, Robertson maintains that 'EU legal English looks more like civil law than common law style' (2012: 1233). However, he equally warns against assuming a close identity with the civil law tradition, thus regarding EU legal English as a new genre of its own. In short, the EU has developed its own drafting conventions and aims at differentiating its practice from that of other traditions.

From both a political and a linguistic point of view, the neutrality and morphological flexibility of English seem to lend themselves well to the goal of establishing a new European legal culture. Being the language of the common law, English theoretically has fewer chances than other languages to have an impact on the creation of new EU concepts. In this sense, it is perfectly in line with the *Joint Practical Guide* (2013: point 5.3.2.), which recommends avoiding terms closely linked to the national legal systems of the Member States.[4] The *Joint Practical Guide* also stresses that this new terminology must not be perceived as 'translation in a negative sense – but as a text which corresponds to a certain legislative style' (2013: point 5.4.). From a linguistic point of view, the limited inflection of English and its structural flexibility make it relatively easy to form new terms, sometimes blending different concepts into a single term, for example, *flexicurity*, the idea of a welfare state model that simultaneously ensures flexibility and security in the workplace. The indefinite semantics of English also ensures the neutrality of expressions, a trait which enhances the lack of cultural specificity advocated by the Union. The examples below highlight the inherent capability of English to express general terms and hypernyms. Abstract terms such as *mainstreaming*, *gender mainstreaming* and *cross-compliance* are much more effective and concise in English than in other European languages. In particular, the word *gender mainstreaming* requires a more detailed explanation in other languages, thus running the risk of introducing additional concepts or cultural specific nuances.

---

4 *Translating for a Multilingual Community* (2009). Available at: http://bookshop.europa.eu/en/translating-for-a-multilingual-community-pbHC3008600/ [accessed 24 September 2013].

Table 8.1 Extracts from IATE[5]

en	mainstreaming	gender mainstreaming	cross-compliance
fr	intégration; prise en compte systématique	intégration des questions d'égalité entre les hommes et les femmes; paritarisme; intégration des politiques d'égalité des chances	conditionnalité
de	generelle/durchgängige Berüchsichtung; Einbeziehung einer Fragestellung als Querschnittsthema	durchgängige Berücksichtigung der Gleichstellung von Frauen und Männern	Verpflichtungen, Auflagenbindung, Einhaltung anderweitiger Verpflichtungen
it	integrazione; mainstreaming	integrazione di genere; prospettiva uomo-donna; integrazione della dimensione delle pari opportunità per le donne e gli uomini	condizionalità
es	transversalidad; integración de las politicas	incorporación de la perspectiva de género; integración de la dimensión de género; integración de los objetivos de la igualdad de los sexos	condicionalidad

Along this line, one of the aims of the European scholars who drew up the Draft Common Frame of Reference (DCFR 2008)[6] is to create neutral terms in English for a European contract law. As Šarčević put it, 'a common effort has been made to avoid technical terms of English law, making it clear that the terms are not to be defined in accordance with English legal concepts. In essence, the goal is to create a new meta-language that is detached from English law and culture' (2010: 23).

The use of neutral forms of expression is also a diplomatic tool: the less specific words are, the higher the chances are that a compromise will be reached. In the EU legislative procedure the text is often perceived as a way to fix the result of political negotiations (Ioriatti Ferrari 2010: 275). Thus the use of a vehicular language with a relatively neutral semantics makes it possible to ensure a mix of national interests while remaining at the same time politically correct.

Finally, EU multilingual law is the product of translation and as such may also have something to gain from the use of broad neutral language. It is widely

5 The EU's multilingual term base at: iate.europa.eu.

6 See the text of the *Principles, Definitions and Model Rules of European Private Law. Draft Common Frame of Reference (DCFR)* at http://ec.europa.eu/justice/contract/files/european-private-law_en.pdf [accessed 15 September 2013].

agreed that general words can be more easily transferred and adapted to other languages. The increasing use of technological tools and the recent MT@EC, available both to translators and administrative staff, may equally benefit from the use of a 'deculturalized' language because it is easier for machines to process content deprived of cultural connotations.

All these factors highlight the strong functional character of EU English; however, going back to our initial questions, it proves rather difficult to classify EU English as a variety or to place it into one of the existing ELF categories. It has no place in Kachru's circles because his system does not take account of specialized usages of English. Even if his model were extended to include languages for special purposes, it is questionable whether it would accommodate EU legal English. In the European context, the notion of specialized language is quite blurred and legislative language often overlaps with specialized domains. For obvious reasons, EU English cannot be norm providing and after all multilingualism and language diversity are basic principles of the Union. Neither can it be norm dependent because the EU institutions strive to avoid terminology and forms linked to national legal systems.

The Europeanization of certain concepts, the increasing number of neologisms, the use of English terms with new meaning and the growing drafting initiatives clearly show the intent to develop a language reflecting the EU's needs and diversity. On the other hand, it would be going too far to regard EU legal English as norm developing because, with the exception of evident lexical influences, EU legal English has not yet evolved into a uniform drafting style. Nor does it look like Ogden's 'basic English' or other controlled forms of international English. EU drafting still appears to be influenced by the field of the particular policy, the nationality of the persons drafting the legislation, the degree of their knowledge of English and last but not least by the political interests of the Member States.

Translating EU Law from a *Lingua Franca*

The role of a *lingua franca* in EU multilingual translation has been addressed from various perspectives ranging from issues of language policy and cultural hegemony to aspects of translation quality. Less attention has been devoted to the translation of EU law from a *lingua franca* and the challenges it poses to professional translation.

As a result of the negotiations and interactions among speakers of different languages, the translation of EU legislative texts dismisses from the very beginning the traditional concepts of a source and target text. Their collective production in a common *lingua franca* and the large number of authors from different cultural and linguistic backgrounds may prevent professional translators from identifying the author's clear intention. Text intention is rather influenced by the intercultural communication process among the Member States and texts will inevitably reflect the dynamics of the intergovernmental cooperation resulting from a situation of languages and legal systems in contact. Even though European legislation is increasingly drafted in English, the pseudo-source text is the product of multilingual discussions and amendments, often shaped by the individual politics and legal background of the Member States. As noted by Dollerup, the source text becomes 'a fluid and changeable mass of text, composed of recycled translation, new linguistic material from both the core or tool languages as well as national languages incorporated in the core languages' (2004: 197). In this way, the source text(s) can be seen as an unstable textual net of relations shaped by the unique institutional environment of the EU. This 'special original' will serve as the source text of other translations, but once the final versions are authenticated, any fundamental distinction between source and target text is wiped out. From a legal point of view, EU authentic texts are neither 'original' source texts, dependent on a particular author, nor are they addressed to a specific target text reader or legal community. They represent EU law regardless of the source language and their uniqueness depends on the existence of similar independent texts in other languages.

As a matter of fact, the Court of Justice of the European Union (CJEU) talks about equivalent language 'versions' when it comes to multilingual interpretation of Union law. Therefore, it may sound irrelevant (and misleading) to talk about source and target language conventions. On the other hand, authentic texts gain such validity only after their enactment. As already mentioned elsewhere (Felici 2010: 104), prior to their publication in the Official Journal of the EU, these texts remain from a linguistic point of view the product of translation – indeed a translation process subject to the interplay of very special factors going beyond any translation norm.[7] EU multilingual legislation therefore poses new challenges to translation depending on the particular genesis and function of the legal text as well as on different institutional needs.

Pros and Cons: Some Linguistic Considerations

Linguistically speaking, the hybridity of EU text production and equal authenticity impose a neutral tone and a general language that is neither source nor target text oriented, but functions as a common denominator (Šarčević 1997: 255) in the shaping of multilingual legislation. In this regard, the use of a *lingua franca* and

7 In comparison, the translation of EU multilingual jurisprudence (judgments, opinions of the Advocates General, procedural documents, etc.) involves an even more complex process with French as the sole working language of the CJEU, often overlapping with pivot languages. On the use of pivot languages in the CJEU, formerly the ECJ, see McAuliffe (2012). It is noteworthy that opinions of the Advocates General are not binding and, as for judgments, the only authentic text is the judgment in the language of the case, which is always a translation if it is not French. On the linguistic regime of the CJEU and the authentic text of CJEU judgments, see Chapter 4 by Derlén in this volume.

certain features of EU legal English may be easily adapted to other EU languages and, to a certain extent, also simplify multilingual translation. It is a matter of fact that the lack of cultural specificity and technicality, as well as the broad formulation of certain provisions, may contribute in time to an easier transfer with quite equivalent meaning and effects. Generic concepts like 'recognition process', 'governance', 'right to health', 'right to accommodation' are not bound to any specific legal culture and are thus easily adjusted to any EU language.

The institutions have been trying to compensate for the lack of a common legal background with several drafting initiatives,[8] thus attempting to solve the problem from the bottom up primarily by tackling issues of language clarity. The need for simple, unambiguous language is particularly evident in the *Joint Practical Guide* which suggests reducing 'the legislative intention to simple terms' and using 'in so far as possible everyday language' to the point, 'where necessary, clarity of expression should take precedence over felicity of style' (2013: point 1.4.1.). The large number of calques and borrowings permeating all EU languages may also be regarded in this perspective. Words like *afforestation*, *milk quota*, *mobility*, *public security*, *structural funds* and *subsidiarity* may sound awkward to the lay citizen, but they have similar equivalents in most EU official languages, thus aiming at developing common ground politics and terminology. However, it is also important to distinguish between the clear intent to create a new 'acultural' EU language and linguistic ambiguities resulting from the literal reproduction of the *lingua franca* and translationese.

Syntactic features, word order and information structure, the use of modality and punctuation can be very sensitive to *lingua franca* contexts of usage. Considering the linguistic conformity of EU texts, they may have an equally important impact on legal communication and translation quality. Nonetheless, they have not received the same attention as the translation of legal concepts and EU terminology.

In the spirit of the Plain Language Movement, isolated initiatives in this direction have been promoted by translators at the Commission with the aim of simplifying drafting language and improving translation quality.[9] The *Joint Practical Guide* recommends a simple and concise drafting style;[10] however, EU legislative texts

---

8 *Joint Practical Guide, Declaration 39 of the Treaty of Amsterdam on the quality of the drafting of Community legislation, the Interinstitutional Agreement of 22 December 1998 on common guidelines for the quality of drafting of Community legislation, the Interinstitutional Agreement of 16 December 2003 on better lawmaking.* See also Strandvik's contribution in this volume (Chapter 9).

9 The Directorate-General for Translation (DGT) has been active with various initiatives to promote drafting clarity and consistency. See, in particular, *English Style Guide: A Handbook for Authors and Translators in the European Commission*, *Fight the Fog Campaign*, *How to Write Clearly*, *The Essential Guide to Drafting Commission Documents on EU Competition Law.*

10 Point 4 of the *Joint Practical Guide* (2013) recommends avoiding 'overly long articles and sentences, unnecessarily convoluted wording and excessive use of abbreviations'.

abound in embedded prepositional clauses, nominalizations, passive constructions and long convoluted sentences, all of which have a negative effect on multilingual transfer. The prohibition in Article 2(2) of Council Regulation 881/2002[11] is a good example of how adverb position, word order and the use of general terms in the English version may give rise to different interpretations of the same provision:

> 2. No funds shall be *made available, directly or indirectly, to, or for the benefit of*, a natural or legal person, group or entity designated by the Sanctions Committee and listed in Annex I.
>
> 2. Aucun fonds ne doit pas être *mis, directement ou indirectement, à la disposition ni utilisé au bénéfice* des personnes physiques ou morales, des groupes ou des entités désignés par le comité des sanctions et énumérés à l'annexe I.
>
> (2) Den vom Sanktionsausschuss benannten und in Anhang I aufgeführten natürlichen oder juristischen Personen, Gruppen oder Organisationen dürfen Gelder *weder direkt noch indirekt zur Verfügung gestellt werden oder zugute kommen.*
>
> 2. È vietato *mettere direttamente o indirettamente fondi a disposizione* di una persona fisica o giuridica, di un gruppo o di un'entità designati dal comitato per le sanzioni ed elencati nell'allegato I, *o stanziarli a loro vantaggio.*
>
> 2. Se prohíbe *poner a disposición* de las personas físicas y jurídicas, grupos o entidades señalados por el Comité de Sanciones y enumerados en el anexo I, *o utilizar en beneficio suyo, directa o indirectamente*, cualquier tipo de fondos.

As regards the scope of the prohibition, the question arises whether 'designated persons' linked to Al-Qaeda may benefit directly or indirectly from economic funds. According to the position of the adverbs *directly and indirectly* in the English version, the provision seems to prohibit both making funds available 'to' such persons (directly or indirectly) or 'for [their] benefit' by means of assistance in kind. In other words, spouses and family members linked to Al-Qaeda 'designated persons' are also prohibited to use the funds for the payment of bills, insurance and other family expenses. In other languages, *for the benefit of* is rendered differently, that is 'using for their benefit' in French and Spanish, and 'allocating funds for their benefit' in German and Italian, thus even covering ways of using such funds. The position of the adverbs *directly and indirectly* is more precise

11 This article refers to the opinion of Advocate General Mengozzi delivered on 14 January 2010 with reference to case C340/08 on the freezing of funds against persons and entities associated with Osama bin Laden. Available at: http://eur-lex.europa.eu/LexUriServ/LexUriServ.do?uri=CELEX:62008CC0340:EN:HTML [accessed 12 April 2013].

in French and Spanish, appearing to prohibit only 'making funds available to' designated persons but not their use 'for the benefit' of such persons. This means that spouses or family members would be different beneficiaries and therefore allowed to use the funds for their living expenses.

Other controversial usages concern the expression of modality, particularly *shall* and its multiple uses and interpretations by native and non-native speakers. In the enacting terms of binding acts, the *Joint Practical Guide* recommends using the present tense in French and the auxiliary *shall* in English (point 2.3.2.). This use appears often challenged as in Article 16(1) of Commission Regulation 2182/2002 below:

> 1. The maximum total value of Community assistance that can be granted under this Chapter *shall be equal* to:
>
> - 75 % of the eligible expenditure, for the measures referred to in Article 13(a) and (c);
>
> 1. La valeur totale du soutien communautaire octroyé en application du présent chapitre *peut atteindre*:
>
> - 75 % des dépenses éligibles, pour les actions visées à l›article 13, lettres a) et c);
>
> (1) Der Gesamtwert der in Anwendung dieses Kapitels gewährten Fördermittel der Gemeinschaft *beträgt höchstens*:
>
> - 75 % der förderfähigen Ausgaben für Maßnahmen gemäß Artikel 13 Buchstaben a) und c);
>
> 1. Il valore totale del sostegno concesso in applicazione del presente titolo *può giungere* al:
>
> - 75 % delle spese ammissibili, per le azioni di cui all'articolo 13, lettere a) e c);
>
> 1. El valor total de la ayuda comunitaria concedido en aplicación del presente capítulo *podrá alcanzar*:
>
> - el 75 % de los gastos subvencionables, en el caso de las acciones contempladas en las letras a) y c) del artículo 13.

While the English and German versions 'fix' the value of Community assistance at a maximum amount (*maximum/höchstens*), the French, Italian and Spanish only envisage the possibility of reaching this amount, thus potentially allowing an epistemic interpretation. The substantive content of the provision is clearly lost in French and Italian where the word *maximum* is not even mentioned. This also does not appear in Spanish, but the future *podrá* compensates for the weaker illocutionary force conveyed by *poder*. The clearest formulation is in German, where the use of the present indicative leaves no doubt about the declarative speech act and the amount of Community assistance. This example clearly shows how drafting guidelines and the inherent complexity of modality in different languages may lead drafters and translators to different interpretations.

Another constraint may be due to linguistic uniformity and to the mechanical transcoding of legal provisions. Ensuring linguistic uniformity is a necessity and facilitates the comparison of all language versions. In EU legislative texts, it is highly visible on a formal level, as well as in the attempt to recreate similar (if not identical) language structures in terms of word order and terminology. This is bound to have an impact on multilingual legal translation and interpretation.

An example of dubious linguistic conformity is the indefinite determiner *any* in Article 4(23) of Directive 2007/64/EC. The possibility of using *any* with both singular and plural nouns allows for a double reading in English which requires, for obvious syntactic reasons, an additional element in the other languages:

> 23. 'payment instrument' means *any personalised device(s) and/or set of procedures* agreed between the payment service user and the payment service provider and used by the payment service user in order to initiate a payment order;
>
> 23) «instrument de paiement»: *tout dispositif personnalisé et/ou ensemble de procédures* convenu entre l'utilisateur de services de paiement et le prestataire de services de paiement et auquel l'utilisateur de services de paiement a recours pour initier un ordre de paiement;
>
> 23. „Zahlungsinstrument" *jedes personalisierte Instrument und/oder jeden personalisierten Verfahrensablauf*, das bzw. der zwischen dem Zahlungsdienstnutzer und dem Zahlungsdienstleister vereinbart wurde und das bzw. der vom Zahlungsdienstnutzer eingesetzt werden kann, um einen Zahlungsauftrag zu erteilen;
>
> 23) «strumento di pagamento»: *qualsiasi dispositivo personalizzato e/o insieme di procedure* concordate tra l'utente di servizi di pagamento e il prestatore di servizi di pagamento e utilizzate dall'utente di servizi di pagamento per disporre un ordine di pagamento;
>
> 23) «instrumento de pago»: *cualquier mecanismo o mecanismos personalizados, y/o conjunto de procedimientos* acordados por el proveedor de servicios de pago y el usuario del servicio de pago y utilizado por el usuario del servicio de pago para iniciar una orden de pago;

The indefinite *any* may refer in English to both the personalised 'device' and the 'set of procedures', but not in French and Italian where the past participles (*personalisé/personalizzato*) clearly qualify the device and disambiguate the interpretation in its favour. If *any* is meant to refer to both the 'device' and the 'set of procedures', it would need to be specified as such as in German where 'any personalised' is repeated twice. A quite different solution is offered in Spanish by the optional plural of 'device(s)' unlike in French and Italian, but there is still no reference to the 'set of procedures'.

The complexity of the English indefinites may generate further ambiguities when embedded in convoluted syntactic structures, for example, in Article 6(1) of Directive 2005/29/EC concerning unfair business-to-consumer commercial practices in the internal market. The general trend of producing almost identical texts in content and form and the *lingua franca* context of production inevitably contribute to different encodings and decodings of the pseudo-source language. The most evident difference here is the interpretation of *in either case*, which is formulated as an adverb 'in any way/in any event' in German and Italian, and as an adjective 'both' in French and Spanish:

> 1. A commercial practice shall be regarded as misleading if it contains false information and is therefore untruthful or in any way, including overall presentation, deceives or is likely to deceive the average consumer, even if the information is factually correct, in relation to one or more of the following elements, *and in either case* causes or is likely to cause him to take a transactional decision that he would not have taken otherwise;

> 1. Une pratique commerciale est réputée trompeuse si elle contient des informations fausses, et qu'elle est donc mensongère ou que, d'une manière quelconque, y compris par sa présentation générale, elle induit ou est susceptible d'induire en erreur le consommateur moyen, même si les informations présentées sont factuellement correctes, en ce qui concerne un ou plusieurs des aspects ci-après et que, *dans un cas comme dans l'autre*, elle l'amène ou est susceptible de l'amener à prendre une décision commerciale qu›il n›aurait pas prise autrement;

> (1) Eine Geschäftspraxis gilt als irreführend, wenn sie falsche Angaben enthält und somit unwahr ist oder wenn sie in irgendeiner Weise, einschließlich sämtlicher Umstände ihrer Präsentation, selbst mit sachlich richtigen Angaben den Durchschnittsverbraucher in Bezug auf einen oder mehrere der nachstehend aufgeführten Punkte täuscht oder ihn zu täuschen geeignet ist *und ihn in jedem Fall* tatsächlich oder voraussichtlich zu einer geschäftlichen Entscheidung veranlasst, die er ansonsten nicht getroffen hätte;

> 1. È considerata ingannevole una pratica commerciale che contenga informazioni false e sia pertanto non veritiera o in qualsiasi modo, anche nella sua presentazione complessiva, inganni o possa ingannare il consumatore medio, anche se l›informazione è di fatto corretta, riguardo a uno o più dei seguenti elementi *e in ogni caso* lo induca o sia idonea a indurlo ad assumere una decisione di natura commerciale che non avrebbe altrimenti preso;

> 1. Se considerará engañosa toda práctica comercial que contenga información falsa y por tal motivo carezca de veracidad o información que, en la forma que sea, incluida su presentación general, induzca o pueda inducir a error al consumidor medio, aun cuando la información sea correcta en cuanto a los hechos, sobre uno o más de los siguientes elementos, *y que en cualquiera de estos dos casos* le haga o pueda hacerle tomar una decisión sobre una transacción que de otro modo no hubiera tomado;

The misinterpretation is probably due to the fact that *either* is sometimes distributive, essentially meaning 'both' or 'all', while at other times it is exclusionary, thus applying to only one element of a set. The long reference to both the 'false information' of the commercial practice and to its 'deceiving' factors is perhaps clearer in Spanish, where the additional demonstrative followed by the number 'dos' functions as an adjective ('in any of these two cases'), making the anaphoric reference explicit.

The final example below shows how different information structures and the use of punctuation may also give rise to slightly different meanings. Article 2(2) of Regulation 2777/2000 concerns Community financial support provided for tests carried out on animals with mad cow disease. Looking at the use of commas and at the German information structure, the question arises whether the Commission refund, a maximum of 15 euro per test-kit, applies to the tests 'carried out on animals slaughtered before the entry into force of the obligatory testing program' or whether this last condition refers in some versions to the maximum amount of '15 euro' for each of these tests:

> 2. The Community shall co-finance the tests referred to in paragraph 1. The financial participation by the Community shall be at the rate of 100 % *of the costs (VAT excluded) of the purchase of test-kits and reagents up to a maximum of EUR 15 per test in respect of tests carried out on animals slaughtered before the entry into force of the obligatory testing program as provided for in Article 1(3) of Decision 2000/764/EC, and in any case before 1 July 2001.*

> 2. La Communauté participe au financement des tests visés au paragraphe 1. La participation financière de la Communauté s'élève à 100 % des coûts (hors TVA) d›achat des kits de diagnostic et réactifs, *jusqu'à concurrence de 15 euros par test en ce qui concerne les tests effectués sur les animaux abattus avant*

l'entrée en vigueur du programme de dépistage obligatoire prévu par l'article 1er, paragraphe 3, de la décision 2000/764/CE, et dans tous les cas avant le 1er juillet 2001.

(2) Die Gemeinschaft kofinanziert die in Absatz 1 genannten Tests. Die Gemeinschaft erstattet *bis zu einem Höchstbetrag von 15 EUR je Test 100 % der Kosten (ohne MwSt.) für die Anschaffung von Testkits und Reagenzien für Tests an Tieren*, die vor dem Inkrafttreten des obligatorischen Testprogramm gemäß Artikel 1 Absatz 3 der Entscheidung 2000/764/EG und in jedem Fall vor dem 1. Juli 2001 geschlachtet werden.

2. La Comunità cofinanzia i test di cui al paragrafo 1. La partecipazione finanziaria della Comunità è pari al 100 % del costo (al netto dell›IVA) di acquisto del materiale occorrente, *compresi i reagenti, fino ad un massimo di 15 EUR per test*, relativamente ai test praticati su bovini abbattuti prima dell'entrata in vigore del programma di analisi obbligatorio previsto all'articolo 1, paragrafo 3, della decisione 2000/764/CE e comunque anteriormente al 1o luglio 2001.

2. La Comunidad cofinanciará las pruebas mencionadas en el apartado 1. La participación financiera de la Comunidad será del 100 % de los costes (excluido el IVA) que origine la compra de los lotes de pruebas y los reactivos, hasta un máximo de 15 euros por prueba *en relación con las pruebas realizadas en animales sacrificados antes de la entrada en vigor del programa obligatorio de realización de pruebas previsto* en el apartado 3 del artículo 1 de la Decisión 2000/764/CE, y en cualquier caso antes del 1 de julio de 2001.

The maximum amount of 15 euro seems to refer in French and Spanish exclusively to 'the test carried out on animals slaughtered before the entry into force of the obligatory testing program'. This is because the reference to the 15 euros is preceded by a comma, but is not followed by another comma as, for example, in Italian. The two delimiting commas result in an apposition in Italian so that the limitation to the obligatory testing program inevitably refers to the actual Community co-financing. Similarly, in German the maximal amount is placed at the beginning of the sentence and the 'obligatory testing program' is linked to the 'animals' (Tiere) slaughtered before the entry into force of this program. On the other hand, if we look at the English version, the lack of commas prevents the selection of one of the two readings, thus implying that Community co-financing seems to apply to both.

It may therefore be concluded that the use of ELF is not always synonymous with 'easy' and 'clear' communication. It is indeed functional and in a way inevitable; however, it can have a serious impact at discourse level both in terms of overall communication and when translating from ELF. The examples above show that syntax and discourse structures may hide serious traps in translation.

In this respect, linguistic conformity is of little help because world languages are structured differently and discourse is often subject to target language conventions.

Conclusion

In recent years, the difficulty of granting equal status to all EU languages in practice has led to the increased popularity of English as a current *de facto lingua franca*. English is used by the institutions for almost every communicative purpose: to negotiate and draft legislation, to communicate with the rest of the world including non-member countries, from an operational point of view as a source language and one of the pivot languages for translations, and last but not least, it is also the official or one of the official languages of three Member States of the Union (the UK, Ireland and Malta).

The present chapter has shown that, to a certain extent, ELF seems to be the sort of English that best serves the Union's needs in terms of providing acultural neutral expressions, ensuring efficiency, promoting uniformity of all language versions, translation memories and facilitating political negotiations. Helen Swallow, Head of the Editing Unit of the DGT, reports that editing in English cannot be extended to the same idiomatic language used in the UK as this would not fully satisfy the drafting needs of the Union (2013). The use of ELF and the translation from ELF need to be examined in the context of the production of EU legal texts, whose formulation favours generic forms untainted by the legal languages of the Member States. Neutrality is also ensured by the fact that English belongs to a different legal tradition, whereas EU law is essentially continental in nature. From the point of view of translation, a neutralized language is theoretically easier to transfer and may in principle promote better uniformity of all language versions. However, neutrality of expression does not mean Plain Language in terms of easy and clear drafting. EU legislative style is loaded with long encapsulated sentences that formally look the same but may lack uniform consistency as regards texture and discourse. The final section shows how the broad terms of ELF and the generalized use of certain forms can be ambiguous, thus resulting in different translations and consequently different interpretations of the provision in question. Whereas drafting in ELF meets the needs of the Union for a flexible language without cultural connotations, at this stage there are fewer advantages in terms of stylistic and syntactic features. Nevertheless, stylistic editing and studies on multilingual discourse structures can offer a broad area of research for developing legislative quality assessment and translation training. Translation technology would also benefit from such studies since information structure plays a key role in the output of machine translation.

Therefore, ELF can be regarded as both a problem and an opportunity for EU legal translation. The strong elements of 'deculturalization' and the uniform interpretation of all language versions challenge the traditional relationship of source and target texts, avoiding any reference to a specific source language community. The result is often a similar decontextualized translation, formally identical to its ELF 'original', but certainly not free from occasional linguistic deviations. In this sense, the specific context of EU text production highlights the need for a greater awareness of drafting and editing. Since source and target text quality are highly dependent on editing, this should no longer be considered a side activity of translation but rather a well-established service with a specific trained staff. In recent years, an Editing Unit has been set up within the Translation Service to deal with texts in English, whereas texts in other languages requiring verification are still dealt with by the respective translation units.

Last but not least, if ELF is expected to give rise to a new variety of legal English capable of expressing the reality of EU law alongside the national legal systems, multilingualism will place the same requirements on all other EU languages. In this respect, translation certainly has a role to play.

References

Burr, I. 2013. Article 55 in The Treaty on European Union (TEU). *A Commentary*, edited by H.J. Blanke and S. Mangiameli. Berlin/Heidelberg: Springer Verlag, 1461–525.

Crystal, D. 1997. *English as a Global Language*. Cambridge: Cambridge University Press.

De Swaan, A. 2004. *Endangered Languages, Sociolinguistics and Linguistic Sentimentalism*. Available at: http://deswaan.com/endangered-languages-socio linguistics-and-linguistic-sentimentalism/ [accessed 24 September 2013].

Dollerup, C. 2004. The vanishing original. *Hermes, Journal of Linguistics*, 32, 185–99.

Felici, A. 2010. Translating EU law: legal issues and multiple dynamics. *Perspectives: Studies in Translatology*, 18(2), 95–108.

Grzega, J. 2005. Reflections on concepts of English for Europe, British English, American English, Euro-English, Global English. *Journal for EuroLinguistiX* (JELiX), 2, 44–64.

Ioriatti Ferrari, E. 2010. Linguismo eurunionico e redazione della norma comunitaria scritta, in *Lingua e Diritto*, edited by J. Visconti. Milano: LED, 261–312.

Jenkins, J. 2007. *English as a Lingua Franca: Attitude and Identity*. Oxford: Oxford University Press.

Jenkins, J., Modiano, M. and Seidlhofer, B. 2001. Euro-English. *English Today*, 17(4), 11–19.

Joint Practical Guide of the European Parliament, the Council and the Commission for persons involved in the drafting of European Union legislation. 2013. Available at: http://eur-lex.europa.eu/content/pdf/techleg/joint-practical-guide-2013-en.pdf.

Kachru, B.B. 1985. Standards, codification and sociolinguistic realism: the English language in the outer circle, in *English in the World: Teaching and Learning the*

Language and Literatures, edited by R. Quirk and H. Widdowson. Cambridge: Cambridge University Press, 11–30.
Mauranen, A. 2003. The corpus of English as *lingua franca* in academic settings. *TESOL Quarterly*, 37(3), 513–27.
McAuliffe, K. 2012. Language and law in the European Union: the multilingual jurisprudence of the ECJ, in *The Oxford Handbook of Language and Law*, edited by P. Tiersma and L. Solan. Oxford: Oxford University Press, 200–216.
McCluskey, B. 2002. English as a *lingua franca* for Europe. *The European English Messenger*, 11(2), 40–45.
Mollin, S. 2006. English as a *lingua franca*: a new variety in the new expanding circle? *Nordic Journal of English Studies*, 5(2), 41–57.
Robertson, C. 2012. EU legal English: common law, civil law or a new genre? *European Review of Private Law*, 20(5–6), 1215–39.
Seidlhofer, B. 2001. Towards making 'Euro-English' a linguistic reality. *English Today*, 17(4), 14–16.
Swallow, H. 2013. *Quality in a multilingual setting: translation and editing at the European Parliament.* Paper presented at the First Legal Linguistics Workshop: Übersetzung und Textproduktion im Europarecht: Gibt es ein gemeinsames Ziel? Drafting and Translation in EU Law: Do They Work for a Common Goal? Cologne, 4–5 April 2013.
Šarčević, S. 1997. *New Approach to Legal Translation*. The Hague: Kluwer Law International.
Šarčević, S. 2010. Creating a pan-European legal language, in *Legal Discourse Across Languages and Cultures*, edited by M. Gotti and C. Williams. Bern: Peter Lang, 23–50.

Chapter 9
On Quality in EU Multilingual Lawmaking

Ingemar Strandvik[1]

Introduction

This chapter discusses the concept of quality and how it is applied within the multilingual lawmaking procedure in the European Union. In accordance with the ISO 9000 standard and the idea that quality is a matter of meeting needs and expectations, it is argued that it is natural for different actors and stakeholders to have different quality perceptions. A distinction is made between quality issues inherent in multilingual lawmaking and quality perceptions related to norms, beliefs and values. It is suggested that beliefs and values about legislative quality and legal translation determine how the work is organized, how drafting guidelines are applied and, consequently, what the resulting texts actually look like.

The author posits that, to be able to discuss the quality of EU multilingual lawmaking in a meaningful way, some conceptual issues need to be clarified, for example, what is meant by 'quality' and how legal translation should be practised in multilingual lawmaking. The findings from a case study on the translation of the Common European Sales Law (CESL) are cited as an illustration of best practice for ensuring high quality.

The chapter's conclusions suggest that, by focusing on the features that multilingual lawmaking has in common with other types of specialized translation or LSP translation, as it is frequently called, the principles of the EN 15038:2006 and the ISO 17100 translation standards could be applied to improve the procedures and workflow for multilingual lawmaking by integrating translators into the drafting process and making better use of their competences. Raising awareness and formal training in legislative drafting, terminology and translation could enable the different actors to distinguish more effectively between issues inherent in multilingual lawmaking, on the one hand, and norms, beliefs and values, on the other. While it is difficult to resolve the issues inherent in multilingual lawmaking, it is nevertheless useful to take a closer look at conflicting norms and working routines that can obstruct the desired communicative outcomes.

1 Quality Manager in the European Commission's Directorate-General for Translation. The opinions expressed are those of the author and should not be considered as representing the European Commission's official position.

What is Quality?

Based on the ISO 9000 standard for quality management systems, quality can be defined as 'the degree to which a set of inherent characteristics fulfils needs and expectations that are stated or generally implied'. When applying this definition in the context of EU multilingual lawmaking, we can draw at least four immediate conclusions. First, quality is not absolute. It is dependent on needs and expectations and as such is situation-specific and context-dependent. Second, the 'set of inherent characteristics' indicates that quality is the sum of a number of different quality characteristics which may need to be ranked in order of priority or may even be contradictory. Third, since different actors in the lawmaking process have different needs and expectations, they can perceive quality differently or prioritize the relevant quality characteristics differently. Finally, needs and expectations can be 'stated' or 'generally implied'. If they are 'stated', they are explicit, thus increasing the probability of reaching a common understanding, whereas needs and expectations which are 'generally implied' are regarded as 'custom or common practice for the organization, its customers and other interested parties' (ISO 9000: 3.1.2).

Does Quality Mean the Same to All?

If all the actors and stakeholders involved in EU multilingual lawmaking aim at *high quality*, does this mean the same to all of them? To answer this question it is necessary to review the different actors and stakeholders and examine their respective needs and expectations. The following list reflects the perspective as seen from the European Commission's Directorate-General for Translation (DGT).

The list starts with the *requesters*, the authoring Commission DGs sending texts for translation. The various Commission officials involved in drafting the source text are subject-matter experts who are seldom native speakers of the drafting language and rarely have any formal training in legislative drafting (Guggeis and Robinson 2012: 62). Their focus is necessarily on substance rather than form. They work in a largely monolingual context and have little or no competence to assess the quality of the 23 translated language versions.[2] At most, they can compare relevant features at surface level such as the layout, numbering, order of the footnotes, missing paragraphs, etc. Their main quality concern as regards the 23 translated language versions is therefore their very existence. Translation is a procedural requirement, an imposed part of the workflow that blocks the decision-

2 Before 2004, when there were 'only' 11 official languages, the authoring departments often managed to mobilize colleagues with language competence to check at least some of the language versions; however, with more than twice as many official languages, this is no longer practical. Today the DGT translators and revisers are mainly responsible for revising the translated language versions.

making process at certain stages if all language versions are not available.[3] The authoring DG therefore wants to avoid such procedural problems. Consequently, deadline compliance is a key quality criterion.

Editors, if they see the texts,[4] focus on the linguistic quality of the source texts with a view to making the language clear, correct and more concise, to give the readers a better understanding and perception of Commission documents. This may be done partly with the translators in mind, but it is mainly done because the source text will also become an official language version.

The *legal revisers* and *subject-matter lawyers* of the European Commission's Legal Service bear primary responsibility within the Commission for the overall drafting quality of draft legislation.[5] While the subject-matter lawyers focus on the substance, the material regulatory content (legal basis, conflicts with other provisions, proportionality, etc.), the legal revisers check the draft proposal before it is sent for translation, ensuring that the form complies with the legislative drafting rules and the text is written in clear, precise and concise language, using adequate and consistent terminology which is translatable into the other languages. After translation, they sometimes check each language version, but only in a small number of cases (cf. Guggeis and Robinson 2012: 61–3).

What matters most for the *in-house translators* is to ensure accurate and flawless transfer of the message. While they are also concerned with timely delivery (deadline compliance is around 99 per cent), that is usually not the main issue. In their role as institutional translators, they are loyal to the institution they work for and at the same time committed to acting as the voice of their language for the end-users (Koskinen 2008: 151, 154; cf. Abdallah 2012: 30–37).[6] In line with professional standards and ethics (cf. Drugan 2013: 43–4; EN 15038:2006:

3 The rules on language use are adopted unanimously by the Council (Article 342 TFEU). The most important are found in Regulation No 1 determining the languages to be used by the EEC (with subsequent amendments and derogations; OJ, 6.10.1958, at 385). For the internal Commission decision-making procedures, detailed rules are stipulated in the Commission's Rules of Procedure (OJ L 55, 5.3.2010, at 60), and particularly in Art. 6–4, 12–13 and 13/14–4 of the Rules giving effect to the Rules of Procedure. Commission practice is outlined in the communication 'Translation in the Commission: responding to the challenges in 2007 and beyond' (SEC(2006) 1489). In 2005, the Council decided that languages which are not official languages in the EU context could also be used by the institutions under certain conditions: see 'Council conclusion on the official use of additional languages within the Council and possibly other Institutions and bodies of the European Union' (OJ C 148, 18 June 2005, at 1).

4 Editing is not systematic. The DGT's editing unit gives priority to documents which come under the Commission's Work Programme and which are to be subsequently translated by the DGT, concern the Commission's core business, or are intended for publication.

5 See the website of the Legal Service of the European Commission: http://ec.europa.eu/dgs/legal_service/legal_reviser_en.htm#1.

6 Similar findings are found in internal studies, for example, the CESL case study referred to below and an internal ongoing project on excellence in translation.

5.4.1, ISO 17100: 3.1.3), they strive to make their texts as readable as possible (Koskinen 2008: 147). Although in-house translators focus mainly on their individual language version, they also pay considerable attention to the quality of the source text, insofar as it can affect the quality of the translated text. Spotted inconsistencies and errors are reported to the drafters so that new corrected versions can be sent for translation. The translators often examine other language versions as well, especially when in doubt.

The legislative institutions – the *European Parliament* (EP) and the *Council* – need correct, consistent and reliable texts on the basis of which the actual legislative decision-making process can take place. Trust in the accuracy of the content is key. The same applies to the *translators* of these institutions, who translate the amendments and redrafts resulting from this process.[7] For reasons of intertextuality, the same logic also applies to other *European institutions* such as the European Economic and Social Committee, the Committee of Regions and the European Central Bank, and to their *translators*.

Lawyer-linguists in the EP and the Council also check compliance with the EU's legislative drafting rules, however, at the end of the text production process. Moreover, and importantly, they focus on ensuring exact correspondence of all language versions (Guggeis and Robinson 2012: 62–3).

For their part, the *Member States*' national authorities and courts expect legislation that is factually correct and can be easily applied. In other words, the legislation should fit as seamlessly as possible into the national legal context and be sufficiently clear to be understood and applied by both the direct and indirect addressees.[8] At the same time, the Member States' representatives in the legislative process are sometimes more interested in achieving a certain substantive result to protect a national interest, rather than drafting a clear and precise text (Guggeis and Robinson 2012: 62).

Citizens and economic operators may not expect EU legislation to be an easy read; however, they do expect it to be linguistically and factually correct and not to be more difficult to grasp than national legislation.[9] A major issue for economic operators is to avoid excessive administrative burdens.[10]

7 In the Council, amendments are often negotiated on the basis of the English language version, and subsequently translated into the other languages. In the EP, MEPs table amendments in all official languages. For practical reasons, consistency between the languages is an issue in making such amendments and rewording fit the text in every language.

8 Member States have expressed their views on the quality of legislation in a series of conferences organized by the Legal Service of the European Commission. Reports of the conferences can be found at: http://ec.europa.eu/dgs/legal_service/seminars_en.htm.

9 See, for example, the Better Lawmaking initiative at: http://ec.europa.eu/dgs/legal_service/law_making_en.htm and Smart Regulation at: http://eur-lex.europa.eu/LexUriServ/LexUriServ.do?uri=COM:2010:0543:FIN:EN:PDF.

10 See http://ec.europa.eu/dgs/secretariat_general/admin_burden/index_en.htm.

The Directorate-General for Translation (DGT), as the Commission's translation service, has to operate with a wide quality concept that takes account of all these different quality aspirations, most of which are 'generally implied' (in the sense of ISO 9000). As a public administration, the DGT is by definition ultimately at the service of citizens. It should meet their needs but also ensure efficient use of the taxpayers' money. As part of the EU lawmaking machinery, it must meet the needs of the other institutions involved in the legislative procedure. As a translation service provider for the European Commission, its focus must also be on translation service quality, including aspects of customer satisfaction such as deadline compliance. As an administrative part of the European Commission, it must stay within the budget, while matching supply and demand. As part of the Commission, it must use its specific competence to help the Commission as a whole to achieve the overall political objectives, such as transparency and legitimacy. Last but not least, the legal obligations with regard to institutional multilingualism and multilingual lawmaking must be fulfilled.

Quality Issues Inherent in EU Multilingual Lawmaking

From the very beginning, Member States have accepted supranational lawmaking on condition that it is multilingual. The same is true for the gradual extension of European cooperation to new policy areas and the progressive integration process towards a political union. As emphasized in other chapters of this volume, the principle of multilingualism is enshrined in primary and secondary legislation and in case law (see Chapter 3 by Robertson and Chapter 4 by Derlén in this volume; cf. Baaij 2012: 2–8; Guggeis and Robinson 2012: 52–4).

Council Regulation 1/1958/EEC requires documents of general application to be 'drafted' in all official languages. Translation is not mentioned because the different language versions are not regarded as 'translations' but as authentic original language versions. From the legal point of view, all language versions of a legislative instrument have the same formal status and are equally authentic for the purpose of interpretation. Therefore scholars question the use of terms such as *original*, *translation*, *source text*, *target text* and sometimes even the term *language version* when referring to authentic legal instruments (Šarčević 1997: 64). Some contend that there are no source and target texts in the EU context, since once adopted all official language versions have the same legal status (see chapters 6 and 8 by Kjær and Felici, this volume). Furthermore, the meaning of any EU provision is created by all of the official language versions together and is thus interpreted collectively by the Court of Justice of the European Union (CJEU), without giving priority to a single language version, including the 'original'[11] (see chapters 4 and 6 by Derlén and Kjær, this volume).

11 See, for example, the judgment of 27 October 1977 in *Regina* v. *Boucherau*, Case 30/77 [1977] ECR 1999, where the Court stated that 'the different language versions of a Community text must be given a uniform interpretation and hence, in the case of divergence

An essential consequence of this is that all language versions *are* the law. They are not just information about legislation applicable elsewhere but are equally authentic and legally binding in all Member States. Consequently, the same basic quality criteria for legislation apply to all 24 texts, although 23 of them are 'drafted' by translators. For the purpose of the rule of law and legal certainty, these criteria include accessibility and predictability (cf. Schilling 2010: 49; Šarčević 1997: 71; *Joint Practical Guide* 1.2.). Accessibility presupposes that the text is available in one's language, whereas predictability goes further, implying that the text can be understood in one's language and is legally reliable in the sense that legitimate expectations can be derived from its application in legal processes. Upholding the fundamental right of non-discrimination on grounds of language, the criterion of predictability should apply to all equally authentic EU legislative texts, regardless of the language.

Furthermore, in multilingual lawmaking predictability presumes that all equally authentic language versions say the same thing. Or, more precisely, they should express the same legal intent, have the same meaning and produce the same legal effects. The presumptions of equal intent, meaning and effect of the equally authentic language versions are inherent in multilingual lawmaking and constitute essential elements of the most important quality criterion: the presumption that all the equally authentic texts of a single instrument will be interpreted and applied uniformly in all national jurisdictions where they are applicable (Šarčević 1997: 67–72).

Transparency and legitimacy: bridging the gap

To understand the Union's political objectives for institutional multilingualism and the quality of multilingual lawmaking, we need to go back some 20 years to the adoption of the Maastricht Treaty. This qualitative leap in European cooperation entailed the introduction of a political union with a single currency, co-decision, EU citizenship, etc. The increased supranationality and extension to new policy areas was not uncontested, resulting in complaints about 'democratic deficit', the need to 'bridge the gap between the EU and its citizens', the importance of 'drafting quality' and the 'quality of legislation'.

Up to that point, the quality of legislation had been more or less taken for granted. From then on, however, compliance with basic quality requirements for legislation became an issue. The institutions reacted to the criticism expressed in the Member States (Strandvik 2012a: 30–31) in a process of reflection that gave rise to a number of policy documents and drafting guidelines, as well as high-level declarations.[12] Ever since, such concerns have not been taken lightly.

between the language versions, the provision in question must be interpreted by reference to the purpose and general scheme of the rules of which it forms a part'.

12 See the chronological review of this reflection process on the website of the Legal Service of the European Commission at: http://ec.europa.eu/dgs/legal_service/legal_reviser_en.htm#2.

Openness and transparency strengthen people's trust in government, contribute to the legitimacy of the European project and encourage participation in political processes, thus strengthening democracy. Drafters in all EU institutions should always keep these concerns and considerations in mind as key quality criteria.

Drafting guidelines: theory and practice

One of the outcomes of the reflection on transparency and quality of legislation was the *Joint Practical Guide for Persons Involved in the Drafting of EU Legislation*, issued jointly by the legal services of the European Parliament, the Council and the European Commission in 2000.[13] Building on the recommendations in the *Interinstitutional Agreement on the Quality of Drafting of 1998*, it deals mainly with drafting, but also contains specific references to translation and terminology. Guidelines 1, 4 and 5 contain, among others, the following instructions:

- The texts should be clear, simple and precise (1.).
- Insofar as possible, everyday language should be used (1.4.).
- Overly long articles and sentences, unnecessarily convoluted wordings and excessive use of abbreviations should be avoided (4.).
- Overly complicated sentences, comprising several phrases, subordinate clauses or parentheses are to be avoided (5.2.2.).
- Texts must not be perceived as 'translations' in a negative sense. Texts peppered with loan words, literal translations or jargon are hard to understand, result in texts that are regarded as 'alien' and are the source of much of the criticism (5.4.).[14]

At first sight, these appear to be straightforward instructions for clear drafting. However, a closer look reveals that the application of all these drafting recommendations depends on the interpretation of vague words (*overly*, *excessive*, *unnecessarily*) and open-textured phrases (*as far as possible*, *to the extent possible*), all of which open the door for discretion.

Languages are structurally different, and both general and legal drafting conventions differ between languages. Moreover, as indicated above, different actors and stakeholders may have different needs and expectations. Therefore, even though all agree that sentences should not be too long, the syntax not too complex and the level of abstraction not too high, this does not mean that different stakeholders from different languages will agree on where to draw the line (cf. Prats Nielsen 2010).

13 Published in July 2013, the 2nd edition of the *Joint Practical Guide* is available at: eur-lex.europa.eu/content/pdf/techleg/joint-practical-guide-2013-en.pdf.

14 Criticism referring to the transparency reflection is discussed above. See also Strandvik (2012a: 30–31) and the reports from the Legal Service's series of seminars on quality of legislation at: http://ec.europa.eu/dgs/legal_service/seminars_en.htm.

As regards sentence length, let us have a look at a concrete example in recital 71 of the Commission's proposal for a Regulation on protective measures against pests of plants (COM(2013) 267), which reads as follows:

> In order to ensure uniform conditions for the implementation of this Regulation with respect to establishing a list of Union quarantine pests, establishing a list of the priority pests, setting out measures against specific Union quarantine pests, adopting measures for a limited time as regards the phytosanitary risks posed by pests provisionally qualifying as Union quarantine pests, recognising the protected zones recognised in accordance with the first subparagraph of Article 2(1)(h) of Directive 2000/29/EC and establishing a list of the respective protected zone quarantine pests, amending or revoking protected zones, amending the list of those protected zones, listing of Union quality pests and the plants for planting concerned, listing the plants, plant products and other objects whose introduction into and movement within the Union territory is to be prohibited, and the third countries concerned, listing the plants, plant products and other objects, and the requirements for their introduction into and movement within the Union territory, setting out equivalent requirements of third countries to the requirements for movement within the Union territory of plants, plant products or other objects, setting out specific conditions or measures concerning the introduction of particular plants, plant products and other objects into frontier zones of Member States, adoption of temporary measures as regards the introduction into and movement within the Union territory of plants for planting from third countries, listing of plants, plant products and other objects, whose introduction into, and movement within, particular protected zones is to be prohibited, listing requirements for the introduction into, and movement within, particular protected zones of plants, plant products and other objects, listing of the plants, plant products and other objects, and the respective third countries of origin or dispatch, for which a phytosanitary certificate is to be required for their introduction into the Union territory, listing of the plants, plant products and other objects, and the respective third countries of origin or dispatch, for which a phytosanitary certificate is to be required for their introduction into certain protected zones from those third countries, listing of the plants, plant products and other objects, for which a plant passport is to be required for their movement within the Union territory, listing of the plants, plant products and other objects, for which a plant passport is to be required for their introduction into certain protected zones, and setting out the format of the plant passport, *implementing powers should be conferred on the Commission*. [emphasis added]

Sentences like this with over 400 words are clearly an exception. Nevertheless, the recital is recent and the text passed a number of quality controls. Dozens of people read the passage and approved it, all fully aware of the role and function of recitals in EU legislation set forth in Guideline 10 of the *Joint Practical Guide*. Thus it can be assumed that the text reads exactly the way it is supposed to read.

In other words, the syntax was not considered too complex, for instance, because it corresponds to familiar drafting conventions at national or EU level or because other overriding quality considerations took precedence in producing this result.

In this case, the drafters considered it necessary to explicitly spell out all the situations in which implementing powers should be conferred on the Commission. Moreover, they felt it necessary to do this in one single recital. Questions of legislative drafting technique such as this are to be left to the discretion of the legislative drafting experts. Nevertheless, it is not clear why the recital is written in a single extreme left-branching sentence structure, with a large number of subordinate clauses preceding the main clause, a technique widely known to have a strong negative impact on readability. This is a purely linguistic drafting issue.

Interestingly, if we consult the different language versions, we see that most translators spotted this issue and simply moved the main clause, 'implementing powers should be conferred on the Commission', to the initial position in the recital. The resulting sentence still qualifies as an overly long sentence by any *linguistic* standards, but starts with the main clause and is therefore more readable. For greater clarity, some languages with cases (for example, German and Finnish) even added a colon after the main clause.

This example raises questions. The text is accessible to all addressees, but can it be read and understood in all languages? Do the various language versions comply with the quality requirements?

Whereas Cao (2007: 119) suggests that a 226-word sentence is not uncommon in common law countries, according to Swedish legislative drafting standards, sentences of 200 words violate the fundamental right of citizens to understand legislation and are thus unacceptable. Why should this factor not be taken into account? After all, the Swedish legal system is formally on equal footing with all other national legal systems of the Member States. What are the pragmatic consequences in terms of (lack of desired) reader response when such considerations are disregarded? Should legal traditions with reader-unfriendly drafting conventions be used as a model or should more receiver-oriented drafting conventions have priority in light of the above-mentioned political objective of 'bridging the gap' and the basic recommendation of the *Joint Practical Guide* that the source text should fit 'into a system which is not only complex, but also multicultural and multilingual'?

After 40 years of consistent plain language policy, the legal profession in Sweden has learned to express legal complexity in clear writing without jeopardizing legal precision, thus confirming Kimble's (1994–1995: 53) assertion that '[m]ost of the time, clarity and precision are complementary goals'. As Kimble remarked:

> Drafters usually do not have to choose between one or the other, the instances of actual conflict are much rarer than lawyers often suppose, and what's more, by aiming for both, the drafter will usually improve both.

The latest expression of this consistent plain language policy is the recent strategy and action plan for plain language in the judiciary (*Sveriges Domstolar* 2010; Strandvik 2012b: 145), which was adopted unanimously by all Swedish courts (*Remissammanställning*: Dnr 2009: 66) in the aftermath of the Government's Report on Citizens' Trust in the Judiciary (*Förtroendeutredningen* SOU 2008:106).[15]

As regards EU legislation, Guideline 5 of the *Joint Practical Guide* calls upon drafters to 'draft acts … framed in terms and sentence structures which respect the multilingual nature of Community legislation'. Drafters always need to be aware that 'the text must satisfy the requirements of Council Regulation No 1, which requires the use of all the official languages in legal acts'. Furthermore, 'this entails additional requirements beyond those which apply to the drafting of a national legislative text' (5.1.).[16] Although it is sometimes easier to draft complicated sentences rather than make the effort to express the ideas in concise and clear wording, the *Joint Practical Guide* makes it clear that this effort is essential in order to achieve a text which can be easily understood and *translated* (4.6.).

Where translators lack the authority to adapt the translations to comply with the basic quality requirements for legislation in the different target languages and cultures, the source text should be modified to facilitate translation. This is in keeping with the basic principle of language equality. However, who has the power to take such a decision and at what stage of the workflow? Furthermore, in light of the differences in national drafting conventions referred to above, which language has the privilege of using its own drafting conventions and how can that be reconciled with the principle of language equality?

Both drafting and translation are processes in which choices constantly have to be made. As seen above, in the context of EU multilingual lawmaking this involves knowing where to draw the line for the 'as-far-as-possibles'. In an attempt to answer these questions, it is useful to examine some norms, beliefs and values having an impact on the choices made.

Norms, Beliefs and Values

In Toury's opinion, 'translating is historically, socially and culturally determined, which is to say that it is norm-governed, just like any human behaviour' (1998: 13–14). From his point of view, norms involve 'the translation of general values or ideas shared by a community – as to what is right or wrong, adequate or inadequate – into performance instructions appropriate for and applicable to particular situations' (Toury 1995: 55). Quoting Davis, Toury says that in any social group, people create agreements on the acceptability or unacceptability of

15 See also interviews with the president and secretary of the Committee drafting the report, judges Heuman (2013) and Bohlin (2011).

16 For a more in-depth analysis of these 'additional requirements', see Strandvik 2014.

certain actions. Agreements are always negotiated and result in the establishment of conventions determining the behaviour of members of the group, many of which become behavioural routines. This process leads to the creation of predictable events, excluding certain choices in an attempt to create order and stability (Davis 1994: 97 quoted in Toury 1998: 14–15).

In her research, Koskinen draws two important conclusions on how beliefs and values have an impact on the norms applicable to EU translation. On the one hand, she concludes that different sets of conflicting norms seem to effectively hinder the desired outcome to improve readability. At the same time, she concedes that 'numerous tacit routines and pragmatic material solutions could rather accidentally contribute to an outcome no one desires', resulting in 'less than optimal translated communication' (2008: 148–9).

If we have a look at an example of such conflicting norms found in the Interinstitutional Swedish Style Guide for the translation of EU legal acts, we see that the general goal is 'to produce texts which stylistically deviate *as little as possible* from modern Swedish legislative texts' [emphasis added]. In this sense, the translator is encouraged to 'aim at an idiomatic Swedish without heavy or complex constructions that may figure in the source text' (*Att* översätta *EUrättsakter – anvisningar* 2007: 6). However, the section on gender-neutral drafting (2007: 101), in turn, states that 'the basic principle for translation is to follow the formulations of the source text'. Accordingly, 'if the author has chosen not to draft in a gender-neutral way, this should *normally* be reflected in the Swedish translation' [emphasis added]. Well aware of the governing norm in the target culture, the authors end by noting that 'both English and French source texts are more and more frequently drafted in a gender-neutral style'. In these recommendations, the words *normally* and *as little as possible* function in the same way as the 'as far as possibles' cited in the *Joint Practical Guide* above. Moreover, the general rule in the first recommendation is *de facto* contradicted by the concrete instruction concerning gender-neutral style. Similarly, despite the general recommendation to avoid 'heavy and complex constructions that may figure in the source text', the translator is bound by the so-called *sentence rule*, which imposes the same sentence breaks as in the source text, for the sake of enabling uniform referencing.

Similar (potentially) conflicting norms can be found in the *Joint Practical Guide*. For instance, as regards terminology, Guideline 6 advises drafters to express 'identical concepts … in the same terms, as far as possible without departing from their meaning in ordinary, legal or technical language' (6.). At the same time, drafters are warned in Guideline 5 to refrain from 'the use of expressions and phrases – in particular, but not exclusively, legal terms – too specific to the author's own language or legal system, [as this] will increase the risk of translation problems' (5.3.). With reference to the famous *CILFIT* ruling,[17] the latter warning

17 In *Srl CILFIT and Lanificio di Gavarda SpA* v. *Ministry of Health* (Case 283 ECR 1982, 3415, para. 19), the Court of Justice confirmed the autonomy of EU concepts: 'It must

is often applied not only to terms and expressions in the source text but also to those in the target texts. Moreover, the distinction between legal terms and standard LSP terms is far from obvious, since formally all terms in a legal act are legal terms (cf. Strandvik 2012a: 38). Note that the above Guidelines also use terms allowing discretion: *as far as possible, in particular but not exclusively, too specific*.

Translation and the Translator's Role and Status

Turning our attention to beliefs about translation, the question arises whether translation is a highly challenging, intellectually demanding task that, in addition to translation skills, requires language and subject-matter knowledge? Or is it merely a mechanical process of linguistic transcoding, a matter of substituting words and sentences in one language with corresponding words and sentences in the other? (cf. the discussion in Chapter 7 by Baaij, this volume). The position taken on this matter affects not only the translator's status but also the organization of the text production and in particular the appearance of the resulting texts.

In descriptions of the EU lawmaking process, as a rule, little or no attention is paid to translation (Koskinen 2008: 151; Strandvik 2012a: 31). This sometimes gives the impression that the only intellectual input in the text production process is provided by the authors of the draft proposal and by Council and EP lawyer-linguists who are responsible to ensure the concordance of all language versions. Translation is mostly taken for granted. The language versions just happen to be there, when the draft legislation is submitted to the Council and the EP (see Cao 2007: 151; Guggeis and Robinson 2012: 62). This anonymity is not specific to the EU but has been identified by scholars in other areas as well (Abdallah 2012: 41–2).

In the field of translation studies, it has been clear at least since the 1970s or 1980s that translation entails much more than linguistic transfer from one language to another (cf. Chesterman 1989; Baker 1992; Munday 2008; Pym 2010). The role of the LSP translator as a highly competent and present actor in the text production process is no longer contested, neither in the academic world nor in the profession. Indeed, this state of the art is reflected in the professional standards EN 15038:2006 and ISO 17100, which draw heavily on the functionalist school with its focus on communicative purpose, text genre conventions, subject-matter knowledge and specifications or translation briefs. Accordingly, the basic unit of translation is the text; meaning is translated, not words, and the yardstick for revising or evaluating a translation is the purpose of the communication.

also be borne in mind, even where the different language versions are entirely in accord with one another, that Community law uses terminology which is peculiar to it. Furthermore, it must be emphasized that legal concepts do not necessarily have the same meaning in Community law and in the law of the various Member States.' See the discussion on the autonomy of EU concepts in chapters 6 and 10 by Kjær and Engberg in this volume.

Is Legal Translation in Multilingual Lawmaking a Form of LSP Translation?

Those who maintain that legal translation is not a form of LSP translation often argue that legal translation is unique because of the lack of one-to-one equivalents in the languages of different legal systems and because legal languages use words from ordinary language, but with a specialized meaning. However, the absence of one-to-one equivalents is typical for the terminology in any social or human science, as opposed to the natural sciences. Furthermore, most languages for special purposes use words from ordinary language as terms with a specialized meaning. Another common belief is that only lawyers are able to translate legal texts. However, the importance of subject-field knowledge applies to all domains of LSP translation. The more subject expertise a translator possesses, the easier it is for him or her to understand the source text and the intention behind the wording, to read between the lines, navigating between words and meaning to achieve an appropriate level of literalness in the target text without getting trapped in the wording of the source text.[18]

Legal translation can be regarded as a form of LSP translation. However, one must not forget that there are many types of legal texts and that even legislative texts are translated for different purposes. For instance, like other types of LSP texts, translations of legislation in comparative law are usually made strictly for informative purposes. On the contrary, in multilingual lawmaking, it is the legal status of the texts that makes such translations unique. As emphasized above, all the language versions of EU legislation are legally binding texts. Hence, they do not merely inform us about the law, they *are* the law (cf. Šarčević 1997: 6–7).

Fidelity

As seen above in the *Joint Practical Guide*, the legal services of the European Parliament, the European Commission and the Council agree that, as a legal and political quality requirement for EU legislation, all language versions of a piece of legislation should deviate as little as possible from the target cultures' drafting conventions (5.4.). As regards the issue of fidelity, the above recommendation is in apparent contrast to the traditional view that in legal translation 'fidelity to the original text must be the first consideration' (Šarčević 2012: 85 citing the UN instructions for translation 1984: 3).

As for translators in EU multilingual lawmaking, of course they should be faithful. The question is to what and to whom? To the authors, who frequently do not draft in their mother tongue, work under extreme time pressure, are perhaps unaware of the institutional drafting guidelines or do not attempt to apply them

18 This perception has been confirmed in recent interviews in DGT News (11–2013), in the CESL survey (see below) and in interviews in an ongoing internal project on excellence in translation. Cf. also EN 15038 and ISO 17100 on translation and the translator's competence.

correctly? To the text drafted under such conditions? Or to the institution, with a view to ensuring that its guidelines are applied and its communicative purposes adhered to, thus achieving the communicative intent? Or perhaps to the end-users of the text by focusing on applying the drafting conventions of the target languages to produce texts that are understandable and predictable?

If quality means meeting the needs and expectations of all relevant stakeholders involved, the answer should be a mix of these considerations, a mix that may vary depending on the situation, the language, the drafting conventions and the text type concerned. Fidelity to the source text may well remain the first consideration, but it should not be the only consideration. In multilingual lawmaking, if adhering to a strict literal approach to translation prevents the translator from complying with the basic quality requirements that apply to legislation in the target language, further considerations are needed and concrete action should be taken (*Joint Practical Guide* 5.5.2.).

Interpretation

Another 'belief' in the field of legal translation is that translators should understand the source text but not overstep their authority by interpreting it in the legal sense (Šarčević 1997: 87). However, is it always possible to make a clear distinction between the act of understanding and interpretation by translators, on the one hand, and by legal professionals, on the other?

In the field of comparative law, De Groot and Van Laer contend that 'translators of legal terminology are obliged to practice comparative law' (De Groot and Van Laer 2008: 2). Husa (2012: 162) argues that legal translation is possible only if those who translate 'understand' the legal language and legal culture(s) of the source and target language(s). He further states that there are different levels of understanding involved and that deeper legal cultural knowledge is crucial for solving issues relating to terminology or deeper legal meanings (2012: 163). Referring to Gadamer, Husa holds that understanding and interpretation are indissolubly bound together: 'What the text says and what the text means cannot always be separated which indicates that the roles of a translator and a lawyer cannot always be separated either' (2012: 173). To produce a text that leads to the same results in practice, the translator must be able to 'understand not only what the words mean and what a sentence means, but also what legal effect it is supposed to have, and how to achieve that legal effect in the other language' (Schroth 1986: 55–6, cited in Šarčević 1997: 72). Husa (2012: 179) puts it in the following way:

> A jurist does not try to reach a textual end-product which would be analysed from the point of view of the function of the language as such but "what the text says legally", not how it says it.

Guggeis and Robinson, in turn, contend that it would be rare for lawyer-linguists to question the choice of technical terms (2012: 71) since they lack technical expertise and do not have the research resources available to translators. They further state that the 'checking' of legal terminology by lawyer-linguists does not entail extensive legal research or comparative law studies, rather checking to ensure that the terminology is appropriate and consistent throughout the text concerned and with that in other parts of EU law (2012: 72). Leaving aside the issues of the status and visibility of the translators, and where to draw the line between understanding and interpreting and between legal terminology and 'normal' LSP terminology, it seems clear that it is the translators who do the bulk of the terminological work and multilingual legal drafting in 23 of the 24 official languages.

After these reflections on the theoretical framework, we turn to a case study showing how a high profile translation assignment was organized by the Commission with a view to ensuring high quality.

Case Study: Translation of the Common European Sales Law (CESL)

The lack of a uniform contract law at EU level is widely considered to constitute a concrete or potential obstacle for the Single Market (cf. Baaij 2012: 2–7). This is nothing new for legal scholars who have carried out numerous research projects financed by the EU for decades with a view to harmonizing national laws in the area of private law, especially contract law. What was new is that the Commission itself decided to take action after finalization of the academic Draft Common Frame of Reference (DCFR),[19] the predecessor of the political CESL. In 2010, in a Green Paper on policy options for progress towards a European Contract Law for consumers and businesses (COM(2010) 348), the Commission listed different options regarding the legal nature and application of the future instrument, ranging from hard harmonization of national laws to a 'toolbox' for the legislator to use when negotiating future proposals or an 'optional instrument' which would co-exist with existing national contract laws. After consultation on the Green Paper, which triggered hundreds of reactions, the Commission finally decided to create an optional instrument in the form of a regulation setting forth a uniform set of contract law rules, which would be available to businesses and consumers in all EU languages and would strive for autonomous interpretation Union-wide. The proposal for the Regulation on a Common European Sales Law was adopted by the Commission on 11 October 2011.[20]

Aware of some interesting aspects of the assignment and the fact that the quality of the translations will play a key role in the success of the optional instrument, I

19 *Principles, Definitions and Model Rules of European Private Law, Draft Common Frame of Reference* (DCFR) (2009). For details, see Chapter 5 by Pozzo in this volume.

20 COM(2011) 635 final, Proposal for a Regulation of the European Parliament and of the Council on a Common European Sales Law.

decided to carry out a case study to examine how a high profile translation project is handled by the Commission when the needs and expectations of all actors in the multilingual lawmaking procedure are geared towards achieving the highest quality possible.

How the CESL Project was Carried Out

Awareness of the complexity of the project and its high political priority led to thorough preparation in both the drafting and translation stages. The Commission created an expert group on European contract law consisting of 17 members from 15 Member States with a mandate to draft the optional instrument by extracting the basic contract rules from the Draft Common Frame of Reference (DCFR). This text was further edited by a drafting committee (composed of three experts, two of whom were native speakers of English, and one Commission official from the Directorate-General for Justice, the authoring Directorate-General (DG)). Thereafter it was sent to the Legal Service, where two legal revisers checked and revised the language of the text prior to translation. The comments and discussions generated during the drafting process resulted in modifications of the English draft proposal. The final draft proposal was expected to coincide to a large extent with the text in the corresponding chapters of the DCFR, which at the time existed in English only.

At the same time, the Commission launched a parallel translation project to have select chapters of the DCFR translated into the five 'big' languages (French, German, Italian, Polish and Spanish) via a tender won by a German university. The coordinator of this parallel project was also a member of the expert group on European contract law. One of the tasks of this project was to produce a multilingual glossary that could be used by the DGT translators of the CESL. Moreover, the translators of the DCFR were to proceed in the same order, chapter-wise, as the DGT translators with the aim of creating as many synergies as possible.

Equally thorough preparations were undertaken to ensure high quality of the translations of the CESL. Contacts were established at an early stage between the authoring DG and the DGT, which appointed a project manager (lead translator) to discuss with DG Justice how to ensure successful handling of the file. For its part, DG Justice provided briefing sessions for the translators and revisers to clarify the project's background, purpose, challenges and procedure. For the first three chapters, the translators were given extensive reference material consisting of:

1. annotations by the legal experts with explanations, examples and contextual information;

2. a comparative table with the wording of the new CESL proposal side by side with the corresponding wording of the DCFR and other existing reference instruments;[21] and
3. the new CESL provisions in different colours, showing the origin of different parts of the text, that is, whether the wording was new or whether it had been lifted from the DCFR, the Consumer Rights Directive or other reference instruments.

Apart from the translation briefs provided by the authors, all translators involved in the project participated in the knowledge-sharing networking that takes place for all important projects via an electronic routing slip called 'Note/Elise'. This workflow-related database enables all translators and revisers working on a particular document to exchange questions and relevant information, such as clarifications by the author or errors and inconsistencies spotted. When information is posted, a notification is sent to all other translators working on the file. Such knowledge-sharing is useful, among other things, as a means of ensuring a common understanding of the text, thus promoting multilingual consistency. Subsequently, relevant information was transferred via this tool to colleagues in the EP and the Council for reference.

The Survey

Against this background, I carried out a modest survey to determine whether the translators involved in this legally complex project were aware of its importance, whether the high profile of the project had resulted in special treatment and whether there were any lessons to be learned. The survey was intended to motivate the translators to reflect on their working methods and identify some of the challenges of multilingual lawmaking, with a view to raising awareness of the important role of translation in EU multilingual lawmaking.

The translators and revisers involved in the project were asked whether translating or revising this file had been 'business as usual' and whether any specific problems had come to light while dealing with the file. Translators from 11 languages replied with input in writing. I later interviewed eight of them to discuss their replies and the competence profile required for this type of translation. The respondents also provided examples of terminological issues encountered. The findings were discussed in a follow-up seminar.

21 Principles of European Contract Law (PECL), the UNIDROIT Principles of International Commercial Contracts (PCC), the UN Convention on Contracts for the International Sale of Goods (CISG) and the Consumer Rights Directive 2011/83/EU.

Translator profiles

Of the 11 respondents, all but two were lawyers; the two non-lawyers had 17 and 27 years of experience translating EU legislation. If we extrapolate this to the non-respondents, it could be assumed that, in most language departments, lawyers or very experienced translators were assigned to this complex legal translation. On the other hand, it could also indicate that it was the lawyers and most experienced translators who replied, since they were more aware of the specifics of the assignment.

One of the lawyers had the privilege of working closely with her country's representative in the above-mentioned expert group on European contract law. Another was a former legal reviser from the Commission's Legal Service. Others worked closely with their respective colleagues in the Legal Service, who subsequently revised the texts. In several language departments, two lawyers shared the assignment, for instance, a Belgian and a Dutch lawyer produced the Dutch version, thus ensuring that the translation would be adequate for the end-users in both countries.

As to the question whether you need to be a lawyer to translate such a complex legal text, some replied 'yes', others 'no'. One lawyer commented that the fact that he is a lawyer does not mean that he is a specialist in contract law. Thanks to advance planning and early briefings by the authoring DG, one of the non-lawyer respondents had enrolled in a course in contract law at the Open University, committing her own time months ahead to prepare for the assignment. All respondents agreed that a translator always needs knowledge of the subject matter, the more the better. This applies to all LSP translation, not just legal translation.

Business as usual?

As regards the question whether the CESL translation assignment was business as usual, the reply was 'yes' *and* 'no', or rather 'no' *and* 'yes'. If we distinguish between procedure and substance, the answers could be summarized in the following way.

As to the *procedure*, all agreed that the project preparations were clearly not business as usual. The thorough editing of the original, the training sessions and the abundant reference material were clearly examples of best practice. However, in one aspect the procedure ended up being business as usual, namely the need to translate under mounting time pressure, with new versions arriving as the deadline approached. The planned schedule for simultaneous delivery of chapters of the source text and translations of the corresponding chapters of the DCFR was delayed, as a result of which some of the initially planned synergies did not materialize. The results of the overall synergies from this parallel project were also questioned by some language departments after the event.

As regards the *substance*, most respondents initially replied that this was clearly not business as usual. Compared with 'normal' legislative proposals, this project had a much greater 'legal' component, contract law being part of the core of any legal system. Therefore, considerable effort was required to make the translation sit comfortably within the national context. At the same time, however, it was argued that the principles of contract law were familiar, and that this matching exercise was what they actually did on a daily basis: attempt to strike a balance between EU law and national law, recognizing the fact that EU law is a legal order in its own right with an independent set of rules which are to be interpreted and applied by national courts but on their own terms and not in the light of national legislation.

Terminology

The survey confirmed that the respondents worked in accordance with well-established international standards for terminological work by carrying out conceptual analysis prior to translation instead of translating legal terms mechanically by methods of literal translation (cf. Strandvik 2012a: 36–7). The translators seem to have done their best to build on existing national terms, using reference material and consulting legal experts to determine when and to what extent this was appropriate. However, this did not necessarily apply to the same terms and, even when it did, different translators came up with different solutions, for instance, as regards the term *good faith and fair dealing*.

Conclusions from the Survey

Despite the modesty of the survey, some conclusions can be drawn. First of all, it raises the recurring question of the *ideal competence profile* of the legal translator. Should he/she be a lawyer or a linguist? What kind of lawyer and/or what kind of linguist? Is a lawyer specialized in criminal law more competent to translate contract law than a non-lawyer with solid experience in legal translation? Is a linguist a person who has studied linguistics, a person who has studied his/her mother tongue, a person who has studied foreign languages or a person with translator training? The resulting competence is definitely not the same. Another question is whether the ideal legal translator exists or whether it is perhaps more effective to focus on teamwork. The latter would entail ensuring that each translator has sufficient knowledge of the subject matter and experience to identify problems and that all required competences to solve them are covered by someone in the team or somewhere in the process. This would be in line with Husa's argument: '[T]oday we should think what kind of interactive teams we should build [rather] than to cling on to an outdated "one person fixation", which leads to futile dichotomy' (2012: 180).

As regards the work of lawyer-linguists, Guggeis and Robinson (2012: 70) remark that it is only by working closely together in a constructive spirit that they have been able to meet tight deadlines and fulfil their responsibility of ensuring that the final texts are of the highest standard. This survey suggests that the same applies to translators.

Second, is there an *ideal working method*? Should the working methods be the same for all languages? Even if the strategy is the same as regards terminology, is it possible to apply it throughout the entire text in an identical way in all languages?

The respondents' replies point in a different direction, suggesting that, even if the strategy is the same, the choices made by translators of multilingual legislation depend on the text in question and the way it relates to each language, culture and national legal system. Translators of different languages encounter different problems depending on the relationship between EU law and their national legal system. Moreover, it is even questionable whether translators of the same language can work the same way. Depending on the competences of individual translators, they will need to consult different experts for different reasons to ensure that various problems are addressed properly.

For the same reasons, however useful the reference material, it was not useful in the same way for all languages and all translators, due to individual preferences and competence profiles and to differences between the legal systems. Whatever tools, reference material or competence profile you have, the intellectual matching exercise required to reach a satisfactory end result must still be carried out.

The responses suggest that solutions to translation problems in EU multilingual lawmaking depend on the concrete issues encountered in the text, thus implying that a continuum of methods is used, ranging from 'word-for-word translation' to 'sophisticated comparative law analysis', but always with a strong commitment to make the text *work* in the national context. This requires a clear understanding of the pragmatic, extra-linguistic aspects of law, enabling the translator to look beyond the surface structure of the source text and grasp how the text will operate in the legal sense (cf. Baaij's hypothetical translation strategies in Chapter 7, this volume).

This brings us back to the quality criteria of predictability. Endorsing the idea that law is communication, the *Joint Practical Guide* recommends: 'Since regulations have direct application and are binding in their entirety, their provisions should be drafted in such a way that the addressees have no doubts as to the rights and obligations resulting from them' (2.2.1.) and 'Each category [of addressees] is entitled to expect that legislation will use language that they can understand' (3.1.).

How does all this fit in with the idea of creating a new neutral legal language? (on this topic, see Dannemann (2014) and Šarčević (2014); also Pozzo in Chapter 5, this volume). The complexity of the balance to be struck was clearly explained in the briefings given by the authoring services. On the one hand, interference from national legal orders and their terminology was to be avoided. At the same time, however, it was stressed that the text must be comprehensible to the addressees. Since the CESL is to be an optional instrument, it was clear that the potential users (businesses and consumers) must be able to understand the text; otherwise, they would not trust it and never opt for it, thus dooming it to failure. This motivated the translators to take account of the linguistic, cultural and legal expectations of the addressees of their respective language versions.

Third, the survey shows *solid compliance with the professional standards* EN 15038:2006 and ISO 17100 on the part of the DGT. The task was assigned to translators with a strong specialization in legal translation and the project management adopted a fully integrated teamwork approach, including knowledge-sharing with both the authors and internal and external legal experts, as well as among the translators themselves, through translation briefs, reference material, training sessions and consultations. This integrated working method is clearly best practice and complies with what Šarčević cites as conditions for the successful translation of legislation (1997: 109; 2012: 102–3).

Lastly, in light of the *working arrangements and time allocation* and considering the purpose of the CESL and the complexity of the subject matter, the question arises whether it takes less effort by translators to produce a high quality language version than is required by drafters to produce a high quality source text. The expert group worked on the source text for years, whereas in terms of resource allocation, the translation phase was more or less business as usual, although admittedly with more reference material. Therefore, it would not be surprising if the resulting language versions could be further improved, despite the commitment, competence and professionalism of the translators involved.

If this is the case, then the translation of the CESL provides interesting material for further research. If there are different views on the quality of different language versions, this may be due to objective imperfections, to the different (or perhaps inappropriate) profiles of the translators, to insufficient translation briefs or knowledge-sharing between the different actors, to different conceptual approaches to the translation strategy, or simply to time pressure. Or it could even be due to opposition to the legislative initiative as such.

Overall Conclusions

There is no doubt that the current mechanism of EU multilingual lawmaking works. The question is whether it works as well as it should and as well as it could. Different actors are likely to have different views on this, partly because they have different needs and expectations, partly because they come from different legal and drafting traditions with different norms and conventions. In light of the key role of translation in EU multilingual lawmaking, it is appropriate to ask whether translation and multilingualism receive sufficient attention in the workflow or whether they are taken too much for granted.

Legal Translation as LSP Translation: Applying the Standards

We have seen that legal translation in multilingual lawmaking entails constant decision-making. How to interpret all the 'as-far-as-possibles'? How to strike the right balance between fidelity to the source text, the authors, the institution and to the end-users of the texts? Applying the principles of the professional standards EN 15038:2006 and ISO 17100 may provide the magic recipe. By emphasizing the aspects that EU multilingual lawmaking shares with other types of LSP translation instead of the differences, it becomes apparent that these professional standards can and should be applied to all EU translation, including translation in multilingual lawmaking. This applies in particular to subject-field specialization, systematic revision, structured use of translation briefs and knowledge-sharing among the different actors. Such *modus operandi* would enable the actors to work more effectively together. In that respect, the CESL project can to some extent serve as a model of best practice.

The purpose-driven approach is not only a matter of professional translation but is also crucial from the legal point of view, in particular for the proper functioning of multilingual lawmaking. Of course, the wording of the source text matters. However, as we have seen, what matters even more in multilingual lawmaking is that all language versions express the intended meaning and achieve the intended legal effect. It hardly suffices to rely exclusively on the formal correspondence of the linguistic expression to ensure that all the language versions will produce the same legal effects, thus promoting uniform interpretation and application of the single instrument in practice.

Raising Awareness: Untangling Norms, Beliefs and Routines

Institutional multilingualism and multilingual lawmaking are always complex activities whose complexity increases in proportion to the number of languages. There are no simple solutions. What is needed is awareness of this complexity, plus a toolbox of different solutions to be applied appropriately to the issue at stake. As the CESL case study shows, this does not necessarily mean that the solutions will be the same for all languages. Our perception of translation plays a role in this respect as it is likely to influence the status of the different actors and the working arrangements, that is, whether and to what extent we opt for flexible networking-oriented professional settings with translators integrated into the workflow on par with the other actors, or whether we prefer industrial one-size-fits-all solutions with translators in isolated compartments.

If Koskinen's analysis is correct that working routines and conflicting norms obstruct achievement of the political goals of the EU institutions, then it would be advisable to attempt to make a distinction between challenges that are inherent in multilingual lawmaking, on the one hand, and norms, beliefs and mere working routines, on the other. Raising awareness and providing formal training in legislative drafting, terminology and translation could promote better understanding of these issues. We may not be able to eliminate the challenges inherent in legal translation; however, by raising awareness about them, we can try to approach them differently, untangle and review our norms, beliefs and values, and update our working routines.

References

Abdallah, K. 2012. *Translators in Production Networks*. Joensuu: Publications of the University of Eastern Finland.

Att översätta EUrättsakter – anvisningar (Interinstitutional Swedish Style Guide for the Translation of EU Legal Acts). 2007. Available at: http://ec.europa.eu/translation/swedish/guidelines/documents/swedish_style_guide_dgt_sv.pdf.

Baaij, C.J.W. 2012. The significance of legal translation for legal harmonization, in *The Role of Legal Translation in Legal Harmonization*, edited by C.J.W. Baaij. Alphen aan den Rijn: Kluwer Law International, 1–24.

Baker, M. 1992. *In Other Words*. London: Routledge.

Bohlin, F. 2011. Interview in *Språklagen i praktiken* (The Language Act in Practice). Stockholm: Språkrådet (Swedish Language Council), 45–8.

Cao, D. 2007. *Translating Law*. Clevedon: Multilingual Matters.

Chesterman, A. (ed.) 1989. *Readings in Translation Theory*. Helsinki: Oy Finn Lectura Ab.

Dannemann, G. 2014. System neutrality in legal translation, in *Translating the DCFR and Drafting the CESL: A Pragmatic Perspective*, edited by B. Pasa and L. Morra. Munich: Sellier European Law Publishers, 117–22.

Davis, J. 1994. Social creativity, in *When History Accelerates: Essays on Rapid Social Change, Complexity and Creativity*. London and Atlantic Highland, NJ: The Athlone Press, 95–110.

De Groot, G.-R. and Van Laer, C.J.P. 2008. The quality of legal dictionaries: an assessment. Maastricht University. Available at: http://ssrn.com/abstract=1287603.

Draft Common Frame of Reference (DCFR) *Principles, Definitions and Model Rules of European Private Law*, full edition. 2009. Munich: Sellier European Law Publishers.

Drugan, J. 2013. *Quality in Professional Translation – Assessment and Improvement*. London: Bloomsbury.

EN 15038:2006. European Standard on Translation Services – Service Requirements. Available at: http://www.cen.eu/cen/Members/Pages/default.aspx.

Förtroendeutredningen. Ökat förtroende för domstolarna. 2008. Stockholm. SOU 2008:106.

Guggeis, M. and Robinson, W. 2012. 'Co-revision': legal-linguistic revision in the European Union 'co-decision' process, in *The Role of Legal Translation in Legal Harmonization*, edited by C.J.W. Baaij. Alphen aan den Rijn: Kluwer Law International, 51–81.

Heuman, S. 2013. *Sättet att skriva domar måste hänga med sin tid*, interview in Advokaten 1/2013. Available at: http://www.advokatsamfundet.se/Advokaten/Tidningsnummer/2013/Nr-1-2013-Argang-79/Sattet-att-skriva-domar-maste-hanga-med-sin-tid/.

Husa, J. 2012. Understanding legal languages: linguistic concerns of the comparative lawyer, in *The Role of Legal Translation in Legal Harmonization*, edited by C.J.W. Baaij. Alphen aan den Rijn: Kluwer Law International, 161–81.

Interinstitutional Agreement of 22 December 1998 on common guidelines for the quality of drafting of Community legislation. OJ C 73, 17 March 1999, 1.

ISO 9000:2000 Quality management systems – Fundamentals and vocabulary. Available at: www.iso.org.

ISO 17100 Translation services – Requirements for translation services (Draft).

Joint Practical Guide of the European Parliament, the Council and the Commission for persons involved in the drafting of European Union legislation. 2013. Available at: eur-lex.europa.eu/content/pdf//techleg/joint-practical-guide-2013-en.pdf.

Kimble, J. 1994–1995. Answering the critics of plain language, in *The Scribes Journal of Legal Writing*, Lansing, 51–85. Available at: http://plainlanguagenetwork.org/kimble/Answering2.pdf.

Koskinen, K. 2008. *Translating Institutions: An Ethnographic Study of EU Translation*. Manchester: St. Jerome Publishing.

Munday, J. 2008. *Introducing Translation Studies*. London: Routledge.

Prats Nielsen, A. 2010. EU-kommissionen översätter grönböcker: En studie i begriplighet – möjligheter och begränsningar, Examensarbete Språkkonsultprogrammet, Stockholms universitet.

Pym, A. 2010. *Exploring Translation Theories*. London: Routledge.

Remissammanställning: Förtroendeutredningens betänkande (SOU 2008:106) Ökat förtroende för domstolarna – strategier och förslag, Ds 2009: 66.

Schilling, T. 2010. Beyond multilingualism: on different approaches to the handling of diverging language versions of a Community law. *European Law Journal*, 16(1), 47–66.

Strandvik, I. 2012a. Legal harmonization through legal translation: texts that say the same thing? in *The Role of Legal Translation in Legal Harmonization*, edited by C.J.W. Baaij. Alphen aan den Rijn: Kluwer Law International, 25–49.

Strandvik, I. 2012b. La modernización del lenguaje jurídico en Suecia: ¿enseñanzas aplicables a otras tradiciones? in *Hacia la modernización del discurso jurídico*, edited by E. Montolío. Barcelona: Publications de la Universitat de Barcelona, 131–49.

Strandvik, I. 2014. Is there scope for a more professional approach to EU multilingual lawmaking? *Theory and Practice of Legislation, Legislative Drafting and Linguistics*, 2(2), 211–27.

Sveriges Domstolar (Swedish Courts). 2010. *Strategi för utformning av domar och beslut* (Strategy for the Drafting of Court Rulings and Decisions) and *Handlingsplan för genomförande av strategin* (Action Plan for the Implementation of the Strategy). Dnr 783-2010.

Šarčević, S. 1997. *New Approach to Legal Translation*. The Hague: Kluwer Law International.

Šarčević, S. 2012. Coping with the challenges of legal translation in harmonization, in *The Role of Legal Translation in Legal Harmonization*, edited by C.J.W. Baaij. Alphen aan den Rijn: Kluwer Law International, 83–107.

Šarčević, S. 2014. Legal translation and legal certainty/uncertainty: from the DCFR to the CESL proposal, in *Translating the DCFR and Drafting the CESL:*

A Pragmatic Perspective, edited by B. Pasa and L. Morra. Munich: Sellier European Law Publishers, 45–68.

Toury, G. 1995. *Descriptive Translation Studies and Beyond*. Amsterdam and Philadelphia: John Benjamins.

Toury, G. 1998. A handful of paragraphs on 'translation' and 'norms', in *Translation and Norms*, edited by C. Schäffner. Clevedon: Multilingual Matters, 10–32.

PART III:
Terms, Concepts and Court Interpreting

Chapter 10
Autonomous EU Concepts: Fact or Fiction?

Jan Engberg

Legal Concepts as Knowledge

In this chapter I study an aspect of legal concepts in EU multilingual law from the point of view of Knowledge Communication. Adopting a Knowledge Communication perspective means basically two things:

1. That the study builds on the assumption that legal concepts are instances of specialised knowledge communicated through natural language.
2. That descriptions of the characteristics of a legal concept must be in accordance with what we know about general characteristics of concepts communicated this way.

Regardless of whether they exist in mono- or multilingual legal orders, legal concepts are inherently language-based, as law cannot exist and develop in ways other than through language. Only via language are lawyers and other users of the law, such as the citizens of a society, able to exchange knowledge about the legal concepts underlying the rules of a legal system. Therefore, no law without language (cf. comments by Graziadei in Chapter 2). Consequently, it is generally relevant to investigate to what extent the way in which lawyers conceptualize law and aspects of law is in accordance with or at odds with the characteristics of language-based concepts. As a concrete example, language-based concepts are inherently dynamic. This characteristic challenges traditional ideas in the legal community of statutory interpretation, which generally presuppose more conceptual stability. In previous work I have looked at the impact of this clash on the way we view statutory interpretation and legal translation, on the one hand (for example, Engberg 2009, 2010, 2011), and the functioning of a supranational legal order like EU law, on the other (Engberg 2012). In this chapter, I apply this general perspective of legal communication to the specific situation of concepts in EU multilingual legal communication and to what is claimed to be a central characteristic of the EU legal order: conceptual autonomy. The aim of the study is to investigate the question whether the conceptual autonomy of EU concepts formulated in different languages for purposes of interlingual and intercultural communication of the law is fact or fiction from the point of view of Knowledge

Communication, and, second, to identify the relevant prerequisites for such a claim to prevail.

In the following, I start by presenting the idea of autonomous EU concepts in more detail. This presentation is followed by a discussion of two lenses that can be used to study legal concepts as instances of (language-based) knowledge. These lenses – culture and interpersonal communication – correspond to different factors influencing relevant knowledge. Each of them has a different take on knowledge and its development, with an ensuing different view of the idea of autonomous legal concepts, which I will elaborate. Based on these factors, I venture a conclusion pointing out the relevant conditions and assumptions for language-based concepts of knowledge as a prerequisite for a concept to be autonomous.

EU Concepts as Autonomous

This section deals first with the characteristics of conceptual autonomy in the EU. The second part takes a closer look at the consequences of the multilingual character of EU legal communication.

What Does it Mean that EU Concepts are Autonomous?

The claim that concepts of EU law are autonomous is regarded as a fundamental principle essential for its development as a supranational legal order and as a prerequisite for its uniform application:

> The autonomy of the EU legal order is of fundamental significance for the nature of the EU, for it is the only guarantee that Union law will not be watered down by interaction with national law, and that it will apply uniformly throughout the Union. This is why the concepts of Union law are interpreted in the light of the aims of the EU legal order and of the Union in general.[1]

Accordingly, in order to function as a supranational legal order, its concepts must also be interpreted at a supranational level. Such a specific interpretation is essential to ensure that the impact of EU concepts on the daily legal life of EU citizens is not tainted by national differences. If the EU wants to guarantee specific freedoms for its citizens, its concepts must be 'untouchable' by interpretations of the national courts of the Member States (see Chapter 4 by Derlén in this volume).

This idea of the autonomy of EU law, which led to the idea of the autonomy of its concepts, is based on the case law of the Court of Justice of the European Union (CJEU), as it is called today (van Rossem 2013: 15; see also Chapter 6 by Kjær, this volume). In the landmark decision *Costa* v. *Engel* (1964), the Court established the autonomy of EU (then Community) law by maintaining the following:

1 Cited at: http://eur-lex.europa.eu/en/editorial/abc_c05_r1.htm.

> It follows from all these observations that the law stemming from the treaty, an *independent source of law*,[2] could not, because of its special and original nature, be overridden by domestic legal provisions, however framed, without being deprived of its character as Community law and without the legal basis of the Community itself being called into question. (emphasis added)[3]

In the development of the case law since 1964, the idea of autonomy has acquired the role of a 'premise upon which such fundamental principles of EU law [as primacy, fundamental rights protection or judicial review] are built' (van Rossem 2013: 18). Consumer protection can be mentioned as another area where the European Union intends to guarantee special rights to its citizens (Health & Consumer Protection 2005). Autonomy or independence has been continuously emphasized in CJEU case law, prominently in the *CILFIT* case: 'It must also be borne in mind, even where the different language versions are entirely in accord with one another, that Community law uses terminology which is peculiar to it.'[4] This statement conveys the idea that EU terminology is specific at EU level. The Court continues: 'Furthermore, it must be emphasized that legal concepts do not necessarily have the same meaning in Community law and in the law of the various Member States.'[5] This emphasizes the independence not only of the terms themselves, but also of their meanings: only interpretations specific to an EU context have a direct bearing on the meaning of EU concepts.

The idea of autonomy was originally seen as relevant in connection with internal relations between EU law and the national legal systems of the Member States, that is, for the purpose of establishing the EU legal order as independent of and with direct effect on the national legal systems. In the further development, conceptual autonomy was also established as relevant in the external relations between EU law and parts of international law (van Rossem 2013: 16). However, this chapter deals only with internal relations, as this is where the aspects of EU translation and multilingualism play a major role.

We can thus conclude that the idea of EU law as a supranational legal order with autonomous concepts has a very central, even fundamental, character in the argumentation of the CJEU and of the EU as such. The question is how we can coordinate this with the characteristics of Knowledge Communication as a necessary basis for the existence and development of legal concepts.

2 The (original) French version of the judgment uses the expression *une source autonome* – hence the talk of 'autonomous' concepts. The idea is also framed as 'conceptual independence'.

3 Case 6/64 [1964] ECR 585, at 594.

4 Case 283/81 [1982] ECR 3415, para. 19.

5 Case 283/81 [1982] ECR 3415, para. 19.

What do Differences between Formulations in Different Language Versions Mean for EU Conceptual Autonomy?

The question dealt with in this subsection is connected to the fact that EU legislative texts are drafted in all EU official languages and that these language versions are equally authentic (EEC Regulation 1/1958, Art. 1, 4). This means that in the process of interpretation one has to take all language versions into account instead of relying on a single language version (see Derlén in Chapter 4 of this volume).

As an example, let us take a look at the definition of consumer in Article 2(2) of Directive 97/7/EC on the protection of consumers in respect of distance contracts, which is potentially of general importance for the daily legal life of citizens (emphasis added below):

> en: "consumer" means any natural person who, in contracts covered by this Directive, is acting for purposes which are *outside his trade, business or profession*;
>
> de: Im Sinne dieser Richtlinie bezeichnet der Ausdruck … "Verbraucher" jede natürliche Person, die beim Abschluß von Verträgen im Sinne dieser Richtlinie zu Zwecken handelt, *die nicht ihrer gewerblichen oder beruflichen Tätigkeit zugerechnet werden können*;
>
> da: I dette direktiv forstås ved … forbruger: enhver fysisk person, der i forbindelse med de af dette direktiv omfattede aftaler *ikke handler som led i sit erhverv*;
>
> fr: Aux fins de la présente directive, on entend par … "consommateur": toute personne physique qui, dans les contrats relevant de la présente directive, agit à des fins *qui n'entrent pas dans le cadre de son activité professionnelle.*

The technique behind the definition in this directive is to define 'consumer' negatively, that is, to distinguish between situations where natural persons are acting as 'consumers', on the one hand, and situations where they are acting in the context of what in the French version is called '*activité professionnelle*', on the other. In this directive a consumer is a person who enters into contractual relations relating to distance contracts, but does not meet certain criteria and may therefore be distinguished from persons acting within the confines of their '*activité professionnelle*' and therefore be granted special rights. In the following, I will refer to these two categories as 'consumers' and 'non-consumers'.[6] The reason

6 I am aware that it is not in accordance with legal tradition to use the expression *non-consumers*. The formulation has been chosen because it mirrors the topic of this chapter, which focuses on the concept of *consumer/Verbraucher/forbruger*. Using one of the three terms in the English definition in Directive 97/7/EC would hide the problem to

for choosing a negative technique for defining 'consumer' is that special laws on consumers emerged at EU and national level considerably later than the national rules for persons acting in their '*activité professionnelle*'. Thus, when it became relevant to make the distinction, the 'non-consumer' concept already existed and the negative definition technique was the obvious solution for defining 'consumer'. For example, the German Commercial Code (HGB), which contains positive definitions of *Kaufmann*, that is, of traders and business persons, was adopted in 1900, the same year as the German Civil Code (BGB). At that time, the BGB did not contain any definition of *Verbraucher*.[7] Such a definition was incorporated into the BGB during the reform of the German law of obligations in 2002, at which time major changes were made in the rules governing consumer contracts as a reaction to, among other sources, Directive 97/7/EC cited above. Following the formulation in the German version of this and other consumer directives, the definition of consumer in the BGB is also negative in the sense described above.

The interesting aspect of the definition in Directive 97/7/EC above (in italics) is the fact that the different language versions use one (Danish, French), two (German) or three (English) elements to characterize situations in which a person is not acting in the capacity of a consumer. The relevant question in our case is how to accommodate the use of different elements in the definitions with the idea of conceptual autonomy: how is it possible to perceive a concept as autonomous if the definitions in the various language versions contain different essential elements? Will the interpretation not depend on the different formulations of the definition and different categorizations in each language and thus lead to different interpretations in the respective language versions? I venture an answer to the question in the concluding section of this chapter.

The differences in the formulation of the definitions reflect differences already existing in the national legal systems, as is illustrated by the following examples from the relevant Danish and German statutory definitions in earlier legislation:[8]

> da: § 3 (2). Som en forbrugeraftale betegnes en aftale, som en erhvervsdrivende indgår i sit erhverv, når den erhvervsdrivendes ydelse hovedsagelig er bestemt

---

be described: the category in opposition to the English term *consumer* is described in this directive by three words denoting the three different elements constituting the definition of 'non-consumer'. In the absence of a single English term which would adequately convey the broad concept, EU drafters and translators opted to use more specific terms which cover the various situations. This problem is treated in detail by Šarčević (2014: 54) who also describes the historical development of the terms used to designate the concept covered by the French term *professionnel* across definitions of consumers in directives until today.

7 Before the reform of the BGB, earlier consumer directives had been transposed by specialized laws. Accordingly, the definition of *Verbraucher* in the BGB is not the first introduction of the concept in German law. Since the historical development of the German concept is not of central interest for our discussion, no further details are provided here.

8 No translation is provided because the content of the provision is not relevant for the argumentation of this study.

til *ikke-erhvervsmæssig anvendelse* for den anden part (forbrugeren) og den erhvervsdrivende vidste eller burde vide dette. (emphasis added)[9]

The Danish definition defines consumer contracts concluded at the home of the consumer (*Dørsalgsloven*) and is not related to any EU directive. In fact, a directive covering the subject matter was not enacted until 1985.[10] The above definition uses the same negative technique as in Directive 97/7/EC and it also uses one element only (*ikke-erhvervsmæssig anvendelse*) to characterize a 'non-consumer'.

de: § 2. Unternehmer ist, wer eine *gewerbliche oder berufliche Tätigkeit* selbständig ausübt. (emphasis added)[11]

The German definition of 'non-consumer' is from an early version of the German Value Added Tax Act. For our purpose it is interesting to note that the two alternative elements we saw in the definition of the later directive are already present here.

As we can see, the elements of 'non-consumer' used to define consumer in Directive 97/7/EC originate from the traditional national conceptualizations: in the Danish tradition, 'non-consumers' are defined by means of a single characteristic shared by the relevant situations and expressed by different combinations of words, in which the word *erhverv* is central. In the German tradition, on the other hand, 'non-consumers' are defined by using two alternative elements expressed by the two words *gewerblich* and *beruflich*. These are the same words used in the formulation of the definition in the German version of Directive 97/7/EC. This demonstrates that the differences between the language versions of the definitions in the directive are due to differences in the conceptualization of 'non-consumers' in the respective national legal system.

The task of this study is therefore to explain how (or whether), from the perspective of Knowledge Communication, the EU can be said to have an autonomous consumer concept despite the fact that 'consumer' seems to be defined differently in different language versions and that these differences are rooted in the traditional conceptualization of situations in which a person is not acting in the capacity of a consumer in the national legal systems of the Member States. To this end, I will present two of the central factors influencing the meaning of a concept understood as knowledge. First, however, I will introduce the idea of meaning based on knowledge underlying the Knowledge Communication approach.

9 *Lov om visse forbrugeraftaler* No. 139 from 1978.

10 Council Directive 85/577/EEC of 20 December 1985 to protect the consumer in respect of contracts negotiated away from business premises.

11 *Umsatzsteuergesetz 1951*, Bundesgesetzblatt 1951–45, 791–6.

Knowledge Communication and Meaning

The Knowledge Communication approach to legal communication is based on the concept of meaning as conceptual structures, a concept from cognitive linguistics. '[T]he conceptual approach of cognitive linguistics is concerned with the patterns in which and processes by which conceptual content is organized in language' (Talmy 2011: 223). An aspect of special interest for the purpose of this study is the fact that cognitive linguistics 'addresses the interrelationships of conceptual structures, such as those in metaphoric mapping, those within a semantic frame, those between text and context, and those in the grouping of conceptual categories into large structuring systems' (Talmy 2011: 623). This means that the study of semantics within the field of cognitive linguistics concerns the way knowledge (seen as interrelated concepts) is structured cognitively, that is, how knowledge is represented in the minds of the linguistic actors involved in relevant linguistic activity. In other words, 'The meaning of a word like *house* simply is the concept we have of houses' (Riemer 2010: 239).

Adopting this approach has consequences for the study of legal concepts which by necessity are language-based. First, in order to discover what a concept looks like we need to investigate what knowledge elements (that is, conceptualizations) constitute the conceptual representation activated by relevant individual language users when understanding or using the words conventionally connected to the concept. Concretely, in the case presented above one would investigate what knowledge elements (= elements of the concept) different individuals activate when using or being confronted with the word *consumer/forbruger/Verbraucher*. The interesting thing is that this turns the question of meaning into an empirical question, rather than a question of individual interpretation.

Second, it also gives us the possibility to operationalize the idea that a legal concept is autonomous. What does it mean for a concept to be autonomous from the perspective of meaning as conceptual structures? I claim that a concept can be regarded as autonomous from this perspective if it actually activates its own knowledge element when used or perceived in relevant texts. The knowledge element may be related to similar national concepts, but it has to contain the trait that it is independent and thus potentially different from the national concepts. Thus this approach turns it into an empirically testable question, that is, whether a concrete concept is actually perceived as autonomous or not.

We have now seen two consequences of what happens when the general statement of the inherent interrelation of law and language (in Knowledge Communication terms) is taken seriously for the way meanings are viewed and may be established. As an ensuing consequence of choosing a cognitive linguistics approach, it becomes difficult not to raise the question how the knowledge of individuals develops. This is due to the fact that meaning is seen as based on knowledge and conceptual structures which are represented and therefore empirically accessible in individuals, as stated above. This, in turn, raises the question what factors influence the conceptual representations of individuals.

Especially in an emerging legal order such as EU law, the situation is that new concepts begin to exist.

A number of factors may be influential in the process of emerging concepts. The focus in this chapter is on two factors: the factor of *culture*, linked to a particular national language, and the factor of *interpersonal communication*. As will be shown, these factors may also be conceived as descriptive lenses. Interestingly, observing the complex question studied here through either lens renders a different picture of the possibility of the autonomy of EU concepts.

Factors of Influence: Descriptive Lenses

The general constructivist insights that have existed since Kant apply to both of the two descriptive lenses, namely, that the world may (very well) exist independently of human perception of it; however, we only have access to the world by way of our perception (*Anschauung* instead of access to *das-Ding-an-sich* according to Kant). Thus we can only talk about and shape the world according to our perception of it. As the main means for articulating our perception (and thus our knowledge) of the world, our language plays a major role in the perception process. This language cannot have a mere representational character, representing the world as it actually is (*Ding-an-sich*), for this would presuppose access to this actual world, which we do not have. Instead, it is an active shaper of our perception of the world (*Anschauung*) (Legrand 2008: 188).

Language is characterized as a collective tool for communication, that is, a tool for communication which lives by the fact that it is shared by people within the same linguistic community. Having a very important collective character, (national) languages are often seen as carriers of (national) cultures: a language is regarded as the expression and carrier of the special cultural characteristics of the nation. At the same time, however, language can empirically be found only in communicative settings, that is, in settings involving individual people. Moreover, a language exists only as long as it is carried and used by individuals.

Language may thus be said to have both a collective and an individual dimension simultaneously, a characteristic which also applies to language as a tool for perception. The two descriptive lenses presented here are characterized by emphasizing one or the other side of this duality when studying the emergence or development of meaning: either the collective dimension, which focuses on the power of language to shape culture through the perceptions of individuals, or the individual side, which focuses on the creative power of interpersonal communicative activities of individual language users on collective perceptions.

First Lens: Culture

A propagator of the position of the collective side of language as a shaping factor is Professor Pierre Legrand, who has also inspired a number of other researchers, especially in the field of comparative law. To keep this chapter relatively brief, in this subsection I focus on the ideas of Legrand and related researchers, knowing that the position is radical in its approach to the importance of the collective dimension of language. However, for this reason it demonstrates very clearly the consequences of choosing this type of descriptive lens for viewing the conceptual autonomy of EU legal concepts.

In this approach, language as a collective object plays a decisive role in the understanding of language-based concepts: 'What one experiences in world is actually *constituted* by language' (Legrand 2008: 189; emphasis in original).[12] The language a person speaks (as his/her mother tongue) is seen as something pre-existing and therefore as a dominant factor determining individual interpretation. Hence, individual interpretations are performed on the basis of shaping forces that the individual cannot escape:

> The meanings that the interpreter brings to the act of interpretation were internalized by him as he was thrown into a tradition (linguistic, legal and otherwise) that constituted him as the individual that he is (and as a member of the tradition). The basic point is that the individual's sphere of understanding is, in important ways, inherited and that it arises irrespective of any subjective preferences. (Legrand 2008: 220)

In the field of law, this means that a concept specific to a particular national legal system and expressed in the culture-carrying language of this nation may never be made fully available to receivers from other cultures via translation (Beck 2011: 71, 80). The fact that different legal systems are incommensurable is due, among other things, to linguistic incommensurability (Legrand 2008: 210).

Seen through this lens, the idea underlying this study that legal concepts expressed in different languages can be autonomous in relation to potentially similar concepts in the national legal systems of the Member States, is undefendable (Glanert 2006: 262–7). The main reason for this view is that languages will resist supranational concepts because these concepts are foreign to the underlying culture-bound meanings carried by the national language. Thus, an EU concept expressed in the national language will necessarily be interpreted according to the national legal culture and therefore cannot be autonomous. This factor, among other things, is due to the fact that lawyers are educated inside national legal systems. Consequently, they are introduced to specific conceptualizations of the world (*Anschauungen*) which are traditionally more or less different across national legal systems.

The consequences for the autonomy of EU legal concepts are negative in my reading. Applied to the concrete example presented above, it can probably be said that *consumer*, *forbruger* and *Verbraucher* could hardly be interpreted as one and the same concept due to the different cultural background of the terms in the

12 Cf. Graziadei in Chapter 2, Kjær in Chapter 6 and Baaij in Chapter 7 of this volume.

three different national languages. Likewise, it would be practically impossible to postulate autonomy for the concept because the distinctive cultural perceptions underlying the respective national languages cannot be ruled out. Therefore, autonomy cannot be established.

However, the prerequisite of the negative result when viewing our problem through this lens is that we accept the idea that the collective dimension of language dominates. As we will see in the next subsection, this does not necessarily have to be the case.

Second Lens: Interpersonal Communication

Viewed through the previous lens, culture is regarded as a collective phenomenon influencing interpretation and forcing specific viewpoints, thus limiting the interpretive forces of the interpreter. Moreover, national culture is viewed as a monolithic entity resistant to any influence by the individuals making up the national community, as the latter is inseparably linked to the national culture. Accordingly, the emphasis is on the impact of culture on the individual.

Other researchers studying cultural aspects have chosen an alternative balance between the collective and the individual. For example, the anthropologist Fredrik Barth is interested in the cultural worlds of different groups and how they perceive the world. Like the researchers in the previous subsection he supports the constructivist idea that what we know shapes our perceptions (Barth 2002: 1). However, instead of regarding the concept of 'culture' as the basic and overarching factor, he investigates what 'culture' is based on, that is, its origins and how it develops. For this venture, he makes a distinction between culture and knowledge: 'Knowledge is distributed in a population, while culture makes us think in terms of diffuse sharing' (Barth 2002: 1). Significant for the argumentation in this study is his distinction between *knowledge* as something which is distributed among individuals and clearly held by individuals, on the one hand, and *culture* as something that is shared and is thus mainly collective: 'The knowledge component of our being is conceptually separable from our relationships and group memberships, the social dimensions of our lives' (Barth 2002: 2). In a second step, he looks at how we may conceptualize this knowledge that individuals possess, making them see the world in a specific way that is similar among the members of a particular culture. One important aspect is that such individual knowledge can only emerge through personal experience by the knower. However, this process is not limited to real experiences in which the individual interacts with the world. An important source of knowledge is provided by the individual's own inferences drawn on the basis of direct experiences, as well as on the basis of inferences drawn and presented by others about the world (Barth 2002: 2). In other words, individual knowledge emerges from one's personal experiences and insights, as well as from learning from the experiences and insights of others. And the last factor is in no way a minor source:

> As a consequence, much of our knowledge we have accumulated by learning from others including, indeed, the criteria for judging validity that we have learned to use. Though it is experience-based, most knowledge thus *does not become private in any individual sense*. This makes a great deal of every person's knowledge conventional, constructed within the traditions of knowledge of which each of us partakes. (Barth 2002: 2; my emphasis)

The most interesting consequence of these thoughts for the problem studied here is that it underlines the important role played by the individuals of a cultural community in upholding and developing their culture and shows us the mechanism behind culture. As a collective phenomenon culture gets into the knowledge stock of the individual via direct experiences, on the basis of which the individual draws inferences, but also, and very importantly, on the basis of communicative processes through which we get access to the (cultural) insights of others. Knowledge is generated in socially embedded communicative situations.

This shows us that interpersonal communication may have an important impact on the development of an individual's knowledge. We should not forget that such knowledge constitutes the basis of meaning of legal concepts in the Knowledge Communication view relied upon here (see above). An interesting consequence of this view lies in the fact that the balance between individual and collective is not necessarily as favourable to the collective as it is deemed to be by the propagators of the position presented in the subsection on the culture lens. An individual's knowledge which is not in accord with the culturally shared knowledge may actually influence the latter through further communicative processes. The culture may eventually change if the members of the group linked to the culture acquire new insights and start talking differently.

Coming back to our concrete example, we reach a different conclusion about conceptual autonomy on the basis of these ideas, compared with those in the subsection on culture: the individual may actually influence culture and the collective through interpersonal communicative actions. Therefore, if a legal practitioner learns through communicative interaction with university teachers or lawmakers that the terms *consumer*, *forbruger* and *Verbraucher* in an EU context are linked (1) to the same legal concept which is (2) autonomous and thus distinct from similar concepts in the national legal systems, and accepts the insight of others, then the legal practitioner will communicate on the basis of this acquired knowledge. Consequently, the legal practitioner will have the potential to influence the knowledge of everyone else communicating in the field. That will then also at least potentially alter the shared cultural insight about the meaning of the terms *consumer*, *forbruger* and *Verbraucher*, which will gradually become linked to different chunks of knowledge depending on the setting (national versus EU) in which they are applied. Thus, we have shown how the state of affairs required in order for EU conceptual autonomy to exist under the conditions of Knowledge Communication set out above may come about in a system of language-based legal concepts.

Conclusion: Combining the Lenses

In my opinion, it is necessary to combine the two lenses in order to arrive at a serious answer to the question whether the autonomy of EU legal concepts is fact or fiction. The two lenses emphasize two different aspects. The *cultural-based lens* focuses on problems originating from the fact that the EU does not have its own national identity, tradition and therefore culture. The EU has decided not to have one language, but to function as a unit based on the interaction between many languages with equal official status. For this reason, it will have to influence and shape meanings in the different national languages. A clash with existing cultural understandings is therefore pre-programmed and has to be taken into account, theoretically as well. This is a kind of cultural struggle, a struggle to influence and harmonize the national legal cultures and the way they categorize the world. In a setting such as that of the EU, national legal cultures are likely to perform the kind of resistance that Glanert (2006) attributes to language.

The lens oriented towards *interpersonal communication*, on the other hand, focuses on opportunities for development which arise because the knowledge of individuals is in reality influenced by sources other than the national culture and language. Individuals may receive relevant input from other sources as well, including the EU lawmaker. If enough people share a specific aspect as part of their knowledge, this may also influence the way they use their national language – and thus the shared cultural knowledge linked to this language.

In combination, the two lenses show relevant difficulties and possibilities in respect of the problem studied here: interpersonal communication may be regarded as a possible motor for engendering knowledge at the level of individual knowers, which may help overcome the resistance typical of national cultures. Accordingly, by combining both lenses we can document the viability of establishing autonomous, language-based legal concepts and the strong barriers that have to be overcome. Since the concept studied here (*consumer*, *forbruger*, *Verbraucher*) is negatively defined in relation to 'non-consumers', the problem of establishing a common and autonomous concept may not be too difficult. In my opinion, it would be more difficult to achieve the same for the concept of 'non-consumer'. Here the task is to create an autonomous EU concept on the basis of formulations that presuppose three differently shaped concepts: the Danish concept consisting of one element (*erhvervsmæssig*), the German concept consisting of two alternative elements (*gewerblich oder beruflich*) and the English concept consisting of three alternative elements (*trade*, *business* or *profession*). In future empirical studies, it would be interesting to examine the relevant conceptual structures to see how they are conceptualized by legal practitioners in the EU.

Finally, it is difficult to regard conceptual autonomy in EU law as a characteristic that its concepts carry from the time they are introduced in a particular piece of supranational legislation. This is due to the fact that interpersonal communication works as a motor over time rather than in an instance. As a result, it creates conceptual autonomy as an emerging characteristic: we learn that known concepts from national law can also acquire a supranational, autonomous meaning over a period of time. In my view, legal theory will have to cope with this state of affairs in its conceptualization of conceptual autonomy in a supranational law like that of the EU.

References

Barth, F. 2002. An anthropology of knowledge. *Current Anthropology*, 43(1), 1–18.

Beck, S. 2011. Strafrecht im interkulturellen Dialog. Zur Methode der kulturbezogenen Strafrechtsvergleichung, in *Strafrechtsvergleichung als Problem und Lösung*, edited by S. Beck, C. Burchard and B. Fateh-Moghadam. Baden-Baden: Nomos, 65–86.

Engberg, J. 2009. Methodological aspects of the dynamic character of legal terms. *Fachsprache*, 31(3–4), 126–38.

Engberg, J. 2010. Knowledge construction and legal discourse: the interdependence of perspective and visibility of characteristics. *Journal of Pragmatics*, 42(1), 48–63.

Engberg, J. 2011. Rechtsübersetzung als Wissensvermittlung – Konsequenzen aus der Art rechtlichen Wissens, in *En las vertientes de la traducción/ interpretación del/al alemán*, edited by S. Roiss, C. Fortea Gil, M.A. Recio Ariza, B. Santana López, P. Zimmermann Gonzalez and I. Holl. Berlin: Frank & Thimme, 393–406.

Engberg, J. 2012. Word meaning and the problem of a globalized legal order, in *Oxford Handbook of Language and Law*, edited by L.M. Solan and P.M. Tiersma. Oxford: Oxford University Press, 175–86.

Glanert, S. 2006. Zur Sprache gebracht: Rechtsvereinheitlichung in Europa. *European Review of Private Law*, 14(2), 157–74.

Health & Consumer Protection, Directorate-General. 2005. *Consumer Protection in the European Union: Ten Basic Principles*. Brussels: European Communities.

Legrand, P. 2008. Word/world (of primordial issues for comparative legal studies), in *Paradoxes of European Legal Integration*, edited by H. Petersen, A.L. Kjær, H. Krunke and M.R. Madsen. Aldershot: Ashgate, 185–233.

Riemer, N. 2010. *Introducing Semantics*. Cambridge and New York: Cambridge University Press.

Rossem, J.W. van 2013. The autonomy of EU law: more is less? in *Between Autonomy and Dependence*, edited by R.A. Wessel and S. Blockmans. den Haag: T.M.C. Asser Press, 13–46.

Šarčević, S. 2014. Legal translation and legal certainty/uncertainty: from the DCFR to the CESL proposal, in *Translating the DCFR and Drafting the CESL: A Pragmatic Perspective*, edited by B. Pasa and L. Morra. München: Sellier European Law, 45–68.

Talmy, L. 2011. Cognitive semantics: an overview, in *Semantics*, edited by C. Maienborn, K. von Heusinger and P. Portner. Berlin: de Gruyter, 622–42.

Chapter 11

Basic Principles of Term Formation in the Multilingual and Multicultural Context of EU Law

Susan Šarčević

Introduction

This chapter deals with the formation of terms to designate EU legal concepts and institutions for the purpose of EU multilingual lawmaking in general, and by candidate countries during the pre-accession period, in particular. For the most part, EU term formation falls into the category of translated-oriented terminology management, which is text driven, as opposed to systematic terminology management, which is subject-field driven (Wright and Wright 1997: 148). The texts to be translated include EU instruments of primary and secondary law comprising the bulk of the Union *acquis*. The sensitive task of creating terms to translate EU legislation is particularly acute in the candidate countries where one of the tacit conditions for accession is the translation of the entire *acquis*, a Herculean undertaking requiring the creation of the entire vocabulary of EU law in the national language over a relatively short period of time (see Wagner et al. 2002: 107–11; Šarčević 2001: 34–49; 2004: 129–37). This often results in *an ad* hoc approach to terminology formation in which concepts are named on a term-by-term basis without an overall strategy.

In the absence of written rules prescribing strategies for the formation of EU terms, translators and terminologists are caught in a constant tension between creativity and conformity. On the one hand, they are encouraged to take on the role of 'cultural pioneers' by being creative with their language, exploiting its best possibilities to express new concepts, thus giving a 'cultural dimension to the translation of the *acquis*' (Gozzi 2001: 32). On the other hand, the pressure to conform to the other languages by harmonizing terms across languages, at least visually, curtails their linguistic creativity and ability to satisfy target user expectations (cf. Koskinen 2000: 53). Arguing for a more systematic approach to EU term formation, this chapter attempts to identify some basic principles and propose criteria for effective term creation, taking account of the unique relationship between EU and national law.

Since the effectiveness of the equivalents in translation-oriented term formation depends to a large extent on the source terms, the stage is set by pointing out some basic criteria for choosing the source terms in the original drafting language of the base text of EU legislation. Examples with 'flaws' are cited to show the impact of the choice of source terms on the effectiveness of the equivalents and the overall communication process in general. The main section on the formation of EU secondary terms (equivalents) attempts to shed light on the underlying thought process leading to successful term creation. Attention is focused above all on the basic dilemma whether effective communication is best served by aligning a term on the other language versions or by creating a term that aims to satisfy target user expectations, thus favouring creativity over conformity. Focus is then shifted to the term–concept relationship, stressing that all term formation is an onomasiological exercise. For best results a multilingual approach to EU term formation is recommended. In support of this approach, examples are cited from as many languages as is practical, including both the 'old' and 'new' languages. The final section focuses on the 'new' languages and the importance of achieving terminological consistency as a precondition for the proper functioning of EU law. The creativity/conformity dichotomy is revisited in the concluding remarks, emphasizing the different cultural perspectives in pre- and post-accession term formation.

In Retrospect

Having chosen a multilingual regime based on language equality, the founding fathers of the European Communities entrusted legal experts, translators and terminologists with the difficult task of creating a new vocabulary with signs in the four national languages of the six founding States to name the new institutions and express legal concepts of the new supranational legal order. The language of Community (today EU) law has often been described as a 'jargon' of peculiar and artificial terms (Pym 2000: 7; Koskinen 2000: 53); however, this is intentional so that the terminology can be easily distinguished from terms of national law. The legal language of each of the Member States consists of two sub-languages, one with signs designating concepts and institutions of national law, and the other with signs representing concepts and institutions of EU law. Accordingly, EU terms constitute a parallel set of signs, which, however, needs to be supplemented by and coordinated with the signs and concepts of each national language in order to guarantee the proper functioning of EU law and its successful integration into the national legal systems. It is precisely this interplay of EU law with national law that makes the choice of EU terms such a difficult one (Šarčević 2012: 89; 2006: 135; Kjær 2007: 79).

According to terminology scholars, 'terms are located within the tension between the need for efficient communication and the requirements of representing the concepts of a domain' (Kageura 2002: 15). In my opinion, the criteria for choosing terms or signs to represent EU legal concepts are dictated by the need for effective communication in the multilingual and multicultural context of EU law.

Legal terminology is particularly sensitive because it leads to legal effects. The terms in equally authentic EU legislation are attributed official status and as such become the building blocks of EU law, which has direct effect on Union citizens. In light of the specific communication process of EU law, which is made by the EU institutions but applied in the Member States, the ultimate goal is to create a transparent and coherent vocabulary of EU terms in each national language, which will co-exist with the terms of the respective national law and ensure effective communication by promoting the uniform interpretation and application of EU law by the national administrators, lawyers and especially judges in the 28 Member States. EU multilingual law can be effective only if all Union citizens are guaranteed equality before the law, regardless of the language version of the legislation in question.

Greatly simplified, the task is to choose a sign in the national language that will send a clear signal to the target receivers indicating the default reference system according to which the term is to be interpreted, that is, the reference system from which the term derives its meaning, in our case, EU law. Misinterpretations occur when the chosen sign is not transparent or easily recognizable as an EU sign or has multiple references[1] and when the underlying concept is not clearly defined, has several definitions or is not defined at all, as is frequently the case in EU law. Compared to the conceptual systems of the national legal orders, which have been shaped by a lengthy history and cultural tradition, the young conceptual system of EU law is in a constant state of flux and development. After only 60 years of existence, EC/EU law is developing at a fast pace and has considerably expanded the number of its policy fields and intensified the degree of harmonization of national laws, gradually building its own conceptual system in the process, albeit fragmented. Due to the numerous conceptual gaps, EU law is still very much dependent on the terms and concepts of the national legal systems of the Member States, and as Kjær suggests, probably always will be (2007: 76). Therefore, choosing an adequate sign for a given EU concept requires not only linguistic sensitivity at the level of the term but also in-depth knowledge of the conceptual systems of both EU and national law. Above all it is essential to examine not only how a potential term fits into the conceptual structure of a particular EU text, related texts and EU law as a whole, but also how the term fits into the context of national law. This applies to the choice of equivalents, as well as to the choice of the source terms in the base text, the latter of which is often crucial for the overall success of a piece of legislation.

Criteria for Choosing the Source Terms

In EU multilingual lawmaking, the base text is drafted in one language by legal experts and technical drafters and then translated into the other official languages

1 On multiple references as an obstacle to the interpretation of EU terminology, see Šarčević and Čikara (2009: 201–8); also Kjær (2007: 80).

primarily by translators of the Commission's Directorate-General for Translation (DGT) (see Chapter 9 by Strandvik in this volume). French served as the main drafting language of Community legislation up through the 1980s and was still on par with English in the late 1990s.[2] Thereafter, it rapidly lost ground to English, especially after the historic accession of the 10 new Member States in May 2004, which included Cyprus, the Czech Republic, Estonia, Hungary, Latvia, Lithuania, Malta, Poland, Slovakia and Slovenia. This was followed by the accession of Bulgaria and Romania in 2007 and, more recently, the accession of Croatia in 2013. It is important to keep in mind that English did not become an official language until the accession of the United Kingdom and Ireland on 1 January 1973.

It has been said that the actual number of truly innovative EC/EU concepts is relatively small (Schübel-Pfister 2004: 116), for instance, the *Union acquis* (formerly *acquis communautaire*), *democratic deficit*, *comitology*, *public undertaking*, *flexicurity*. For the most part, concepts have been borrowed from one or more of the national legal systems or from international law. When borrowing concepts, the original meaning is either retained or modified or, like a transplant, gradually acquires a specific European meaning through secondary legislation or especially rulings of the Court of Justice of the European Union (CJEU). As for the terminology, the foreign term is sometimes retained and borrowed into the other languages or renamed, preferably with a neutral term which is easily translated into the other languages and will not evoke misleading or negative connotations in the target readers of the national legal systems (Šarčević 2012: 105; see Dannemann 2012: 109–13).

Since French was the original drafting language, it is not surprising that French law has played a major role as a source of EC/EU concepts. In the initial phase of development, the Community legislator often made a double *faux pas* by retaining the national term of a borrowed concept and by failing to define the concept for the purpose of the particular instrument and Community law in general. For example, the term *détournement de pouvoir* (abuse of power) first appeared in the Treaty establishing the European Coal and Steel Community of 1952.[3] Although the term was not defined, it had apparently been borrowed from French administrative law (Schübel-Pfister 2004: 165). The other language versions followed suit by using their corresponding national terms or functional equivalents:[4] *Ermessensmissbrauch* (de), *sviamento di potere* (it) and *misbruik*

2 In 1987, 70 per cent of legislative proposals were still drafted in French; this fell to 40 per cent at the end of the 1990s, while 47 per cent were drafted in English. In 2010 the dominance of English climbed to 77 per cent and has continued to increase since then; see *Translation and Multilingualism* (2012: 7).

3 Unlike the Rome Treaties of 1958, the Treaty establishing the European Coal and Steel Community, which entered into force on 23 July 1952, was authentic in French only.

4 Elsewhere I define *functional equivalent* as 'a term designating a concept or institution of the target legal system having the same or similar function as a particular concept of the source legal system' (Šarčević 1997: 236).

van bevoegdhedi (nl), which, however, differ in content and scope. In the first relevant dispute concerning the meaning of the term, Case 3/54 *ASSIDER* v. *High Authority*,[5] the Court of Justice applied the criteria used by the French *Conseil d'Etat* to characterize an occurrence as a *détournement de pouvoir*, although Advocate General Legrange had made a comprehensive comparative study of the relevant criteria applied in all six Member States. Shortly thereafter the Court began to modify its stand, shifting the criteria towards the broader German concept of *Ermessensmissbrauch*.[6] However, it was not until much later that the Court finally succeeded in defining European criteria to be used when determining whether a situation qualifies as an abuse of power in EC/EU administrative law (see Strinz 1999: 193).

Even when a European definition has been achieved, the use of national terms to designate EU concepts creates a multiple reference which sends conflicting signals to the receivers and is thus a potential source of misinterpretation. On the one hand, it can occur that the receivers do not recognize the sign as an EU term, in which case they will automatically interpret it in accordance with their own national law, leading to different results in practice. This is a major problem, especially after the accession of new Member States whose judges and administrators must be re-educated to learn to recognize EU terms and to interpret and apply them in accordance with their European meanings. In other cases where national judges and administrators do recognize the sign as an EU term but also as a national term, as in other instances of polysemy, they must determine by the context whether reference is being made to EU or national law. This creates what Goffin, formerly of the Terminology Section of the DGT, called a competitive situation (1999: 2136), which endangers the uniform application of EU law in the Member States. For the sake of achieving uniform application, all references to EU law must be interpreted as such, taking account of the provision in the context of EU law as a whole. This point was made in the *CILFIT* case (1982), where the Court stressed that 'Community law uses terminology which is peculiar to itself'. Accordingly, even if the same terms are used, 'its legal concepts do not necessarily have the same meaning as they have in the law of the various Member States; moreover, every provision of Community law must be placed in its context and interpreted in the light of the provisions of Community law as a whole'.[7]

As a general rule, it can thus be said that the use of national terms to designate EU concepts should be avoided whenever possible, as it creates multiple references, running the risk that receivers will interpret the term in accordance with their national law. In this sense, Guideline 5 of the *Joint Practical Guide* cautions drafters (translators and terminologists) to use 'concepts or terminology

5 Case 3/54, *ASSIDER* v. *High Authority* [1954] ECR 123.

6 Judgment of 16 July 1956 in Case 8/44 *Fédération Charbonnière de Belgique v. High Authority* [1954–56] ECR 245.

7 Case 283/81 *Srl CILFIT and Lanificio di Gavardo SpA* v. *Ministry of Health* [1982] ECR 3415, para. 19.

specific to any one national legal system ... with care'. Going a step further, it explicitly states that '[legal] terms which are too closely linked to national legal systems should be avoided' (point 5.3.2.). In particular, technical terms of national law should not be used in the base text, or in any of the language versions for that matter. For example, since the concept of *faute* 'has no direct equivalent in other legal systems', it proposes using neutral terms such as *illégalité* or *manquement*, depending on the context (point 5.3.2.).

In his classic analysis of *vocabulaire juridique*, Cornu maintains that technical terms constitute only a small percentage of the vocabulary of a legal language, whereas the majority of terms are words from general language whose meaning has been expanded or limited. As a result, the latter are at least partially comprehensible to lay persons (1990: 68). In the interest of enhancing transparency and thus comprehensibility, the EU legislator frequently uses words from general language, many of which already have legal meanings in the national laws but belong to the common core of terms shared by most national legal systems. Although such terms are assigned a new EU meaning, for example, the instruments of secondary law: *regulation*, *directive*, *decision*, *recommendation*, *opinion*, they have the advantage of being relatively transparent and are also easily translated. Moreover, they do not require a high learning curve and can be easily remembered, thus ensuring that they will be recognized as EU terms from the context and interpreted in accordance with their European meaning. However, as emphasized in the *Joint Practical Guide*, such terms must not be assigned a meaning 'contrary to their ordinary meaning' (point 14.1.).

Whenever possible, neologisms (newly coined words) are created to designate the new reality of EU law. Often artificial and strange sounding, EU neologisms are effective because they are easily recognizable as EU terms and can thus be readily distinguished from national terms. As Gozzi points out, 'If a term appears to be useful for resolving conflicting views in negotiations or drafting an act, it is adopted, no matter how unusual or unorthodox it may sound' (2001: 32). Neologisms should be concise, precise and as transparent as possible. As stated in Rirdance and Vasiljevs (2006: 19), 'It is important to get as close as possible to the main and specific features of the concept being [named]. All newly coined terms have to be correct, consistent and comply with the rules of the national language'.

Despite the desire to achieve transparency, this is not always possible. In fact, Gozzi admits that EU neologisms are 'often completely incomprehensible to native speakers' (2001: 32). A good example is the neologism *avocat général*, the European institution modelled on the *Commissaire du Gouvernement* in the French *Conseil d'Etat*. Currently there are nine Advocates General who submit opinions to the Court of Justice in the form of a non-binding proposal based on a fully independent survey of the question of law in the case at hand. As is recommended, the original foreign term has been replaced by a neutral term; however, it fails to convey the essential characteristics of the underlying institution. As a result, like the French neologism itself, the equivalents are non-transparent (not semantically motivated) although they successfully reproduce the source term: *Advocate*

General (en), *generaladvokat* (da), *Generalanwalt* (de), *abogado general* (es), *julkisasiamies* (fi), *avvocato generale* (it), *advocaat-generaal* (nl), *Advogado-Geral* (pt), *generaladvokat* (sv), *генерален адвокат* (bg), *generální advokát* (cs), *kohtujurist* (et), *főtanácsnok* (hu), *generalni pravobranilec* (sl), *nezavisni odvjetnik* (hr).[8]

From my experience teaching EU terminology to Croatian judges, I can confirm that, although the Croatian hybrid term *nezavisni odvjetnik* [back translation = independent advocate] is considered a good equivalent, it evoked no mental associations that could enable the judges to grasp even the function of this institution, which is unknown in Croatian law. On the contrary, it was inconceivable to them that an 'advocate' would be engaged to write an independent and non-binding opinion before the judge delivered the binding judgment! This shows the importance of creating relatively transparent source terms. On the other hand, according to Gozzi, even if a neologism designating an EU legal concept or institution lacks transparency, this does not mean that it cannot be effective (2001: 32), that is, once the learning process has been mastered. This applies not only to the source terms but also to the equivalents, which brings us to the main section on the formation of EU secondary terms, as Bratanić and Lončar call them in Chapter 12.

Formation of EU Secondary Terms

In the multilingual and multicultural context of EU law, translators and terminologists have the challenging task of finding or creating adequate equivalents in their national language to convey the 'source' term and, to the extent possible, the underlying EU concept. Although EU secondary term formation is one of translation, the term–concept relationship remains of primary importance. In essence, the goal is to create parallel terms in all languages that will be interpreted in accordance with the EU conceptual system, thus promoting the uniform interpretation and application of EU law in all Member States. In addition to identifying some basic principles and criteria to be taken into account by translators and terminologists with a view to achieving this goal, this section attempts to shed light on the underlying thought process that is an integral part of successful EU term formation.

Striking a Balance between Creativity and Conformity

According to best practices in term formation, the basic linguistic criteria for creating EU secondary terms are set forth in the standard of linguistic correctness in ISO 704: 2009: 'A term shall conform with the morphological, morpho-syntactic

8 The terms are from IATE, the EU's multilingual term base available at: iate.europa.eu. The Croatian term (hr) has been added.

and phonological norms of the language in question.' However, in practice there are conflicting pressures on EU translators and terminologists to conform to the other languages. Therefore, the basic question that arises when forming EU secondary terms is whether effective communication is best served by aligning a term on the other language versions or by creating a term that aims to satisfy target user expectations, thus favouring creativity over conformity. Each strategy has its pros and cons. Returning to the example of *avocat général* cited above, we note that 10 of the 15 languages have opted for conformity with the other languages by using calques (literal translations) to translate the source term, thus achieving formal uniformity across languages linking them to the common concept. On the other hand, the Slovene (sl) and Croatian (hr) terms are hybrids, whereas the Finno-Ugric languages – Finnish (fi), Estonian (et) and Hungarian (hu) – use a single descriptive word with native roots. The 10 'harmonized' terms fall into the category of EU internationalisms, which, according to Pym, are mostly based on Latin but also Greek stems, prefixes and suffixes (2000: 4; on EU internationalisms, see Šarčević 2004: 129–37; 2006: 137). As in the above example, conscious efforts are always made to match up the French and English terms as closely as possibly, with allowances for their specific morpho-syntactic features.

The general need to create EU terms that are easily recognizable and uniform across languages led to the widespread use of EU internationalisms. Despite the advantage of harmonizing EU terms, Goffin has confirmed that it is up to each language unit to decide on a case-to-case basis whether to use an EU internationalism or to create a term with domestic roots (1999: 2135). In keeping with the ISO standard, each language unit is encouraged to select a term that best suits its morpho-syntactic characteristics so as not to destabilize the national language. It is well known that the ability to assimilate 'foreign' elements differs from language to language, sometimes within the same family. As regards the Germanic languages, English freely admits and assimilates lexical elements from other languages, whereas German, Dutch, Danish and Swedish are less flexible and thus more resistant to 'foreign' elements (Šarčević 2004: 131). The various levels of resistance are visible in the following equivalents from IATE for the term *cohésion sociale*. In this case the internationalisms are loanwords formed by borrowing lexical units of Latin origin and naturalizing them in the receiving language. As usual, the 'purest' internationalisms are found in the Romance languages: *cohesión social* (es), *coesione sociale* (it), *coesão social* (pt) and *coeziune socială* (ro). In the Germanic languages, the picture is mixed. While the internationalism is fully adopted in English – *social cohesion* – the Dutch and German offer two variants: *sociale cohesive*, *sociale samenhang* (nl) and *sozialer Zusammenhalt*, *soziale Kohäsion* (de). According to German language policy, terms with German roots are preferred, but precision and transparency have priority. Danish also offers two variants but uses only domestic roots to express *cohesion*: *social samhørighed*, *social sammenhængskraft* (da). The same applies to the Swedish equivalent: *social sammanhållning* (sv). Although the Slavic languages are generally able to assimilate foreign elements, the equivalents in Slovene, Czech and Polish vary considerably: *socialna kohezija* (sl), *sociální soudržnost* (cs), *spójność społeczna* (pl). As expected, the non-Indo-European languages are the most resistant to foreign elements: *sosiaalinen yhteenkuuluvuus* (fi), *notesotsiaalne* ühtekuuluvus (et), *társadalmi kohézió* (hu).[9]

Although conformity across languages is not mandatory, in numerous cases, there are strong arguments to demonstrate solidarity by adopting the internationalism, for instance, when choosing designations for the main institutions and legal instruments. This advice has been clearly heeded as regards the terms chosen to name the *Commission européenne/European Commission*. The entries in IATE show that 23 of the 24 language units have chosen the internationalism, the only exception being Hungary, which opted for the hybrid term *Európai Bizottság*.[10] This is in keeping with its general strategy to avoid the use of lexemes of foreign origin whenever possible, adopting internationalisms only if there is no adequate equivalent in Hungarian. However, unlike the Finns who keep foreign-derived neologisms to a minimum with a view to appeasing user expectations,[11] the Hungarians' main concern is to protect their small language from an onslaught of foreign borrowings, especially English. In this sense, Somssich and Varga (2001:75) concede that they favoured words with Hungarian roots even if the foreign terms had already been accepted in colloquial Hungarian. In such cases, however, they admitted that it is hard to achieve user acceptance of the Hungarian translation, even if it is relatively good.

In Croatia the situation is considerably more complex as it takes on not only linguistic and cultural but also political overtones. In essence, Croatia's independence in 1991 sparked a linguistic evolution aimed at returning the language to its historical roots and cultural heritage by purging the numerous borrowings and calques that had been assimilated over the years (see Šarčević and Čikara 2009: 198). Needless to say, this puristic trend has had a major impact on the formation of EU terms in Croatian. As regards the policy on the use of internationalisms, the translation manual compiled by the Translation Coordination Unit (TCU) of the then Ministry of European Integration states that terms with Croatian roots have priority over internationalisms; however, exceptions are permitted (*Priručnik za prevođenje* 2002: 156). Whereas this general rule seems rather harmless on its face, its strict application in practice resulted in a general 'ban' even on the use of terms of Latin and Greek origin, thus making the process of EU term formation

9 Note that the Hungarian equivalent assimilates *cohesion* (*kohézió*), but not *social* (*társadalmi*). According to Gambier, Finnish also uses the neologism *kohesio* but prefers *yhteenkuuluvuus* for a less specialized readership (1998: 301). Maltese, also a non-Indo-European language, is not represented here.

10 Although Croatian policy strongly favours the use of words of Croatian origin, an exception was made in this case. As a result, the European Commission is *Europska komisija*; however, commissioner is *povjerenik*.

11 According to Gambier (1998: 298), EU internationalisms are often unnatural sounding and difficult to pronounce in Finnish.

considerably more difficult. As a result, finding an adequate Croatian equivalent for otherwise easily translatable terms became a real challenge. For example, when searching for an optimal equivalent for the term *Directorate-General*, linguists rejected the internationalism *generalna direkcija*, as well as the hybrid term *opća direkcija*. Instead, the TCU chose the term *opća uprava*; however, that term was rejected by lawyers because it exists in Croatian administrative law, but with a different meaning. It appears that German lawyers had also rejected the term *Allgemeine Verwaltung* for the same reason. In the end, the compromise term *glavna uprava* was selected together with the Croatian lawyer-linguists in Brussels. Although the adjective *glavna* (= main) is not the most precise solution, no harm is done in this case, as it is a name and not a legal concept. Otherwise, a loss of precision can negatively affect the content or scope (or both), leading to different results in practice.

As in Germany (see examples in Šarčević 2006: 137), an internationalism and a term with Croatian roots have sometimes been used as synonyms, at least until the latter was given priority as a result of user acceptance or usage in Croatian harmonized legislation. For instance, the terms *konkurencija* and *tržišno natjecanje* were both used for 'competition' even after the first Croatian Competition Act (*Zakon o zaštiti tržišnog natjecanja*) was adopted in 1995. Later the term *konkurencija* lost favour. As a result, the term *tržišno natjecanje* appears in the authentic Croatian version of the Treaty on Functioning of the European Union (TFEU)[12] and is used in all compounds. However, a problem arises when attempting to form other derivatives, which is a distinct disadvantage of using puristic terms. According to the international standard in ISO 704:2009, for the sake of coherence, terms should be used which are capable of generating derivatives – verbal forms, various types of compounds and syntagmatic units, an adjective and adverb. However, it is impossible to create a verb, an adjective and adverb from a noun like *tržišno natjecanje*, thus requiring a reversion to words with Latin roots: for example, *to compete = konkuriati*, *competitive = konkurentan*, *competitiveness = konkurentnost*. In this example, the shift to derivatives with Latin roots does not create a problem of comprehension; however, this is not always the case.

In this context it is necessary to emphasize that relying on linguistic criteria alone when building a legal vocabulary can endanger the communication process, leading not only to different but also to unwanted or harmful results in practice. As Goffin reminds us, EU term formation is subject to the requirements for special-field domains (1999: 2135). Therefore, as in all special-field domains, specialist knowledge must also prevail in EU term formation. Accordingly, legal criteria have priority when determining the adequacy of a term in a particular legal context. As an example of what can happen when linguistic considerations prevail, I cite a serious mistake made by the Croatian Government Office for Linguistic Revision, which is responsible for the final linguistic revision of legislative

12 *Ugovor o funkcioniranju Europske unije*; available at: http://eur-lex.europa.eu/legal-content/HR/TXT/?uri=CELEX:12012E/TXT.

texts prior to their enactment by the Croatian Parliament. Insisting on the use of puristic terms, it made the mistake of replacing an established legal term with a term of Croatian origin but with a different meaning. This occurred in the final linguistic revision of the Croatian Obligations Act in 2005 when it changed the term *bankarska garancija* (bank guarantee) to *bankarsko jamstvo* (bank warranty) without consulting legal experts. This mistake brought about a serious substantive change which had to be officially corrected by an amending act (see Šarčević and Bajčić 2011: 29).

Thus it follows that legal criteria must always have priority over linguistic preferences when choosing terms to designate EU legal concepts. Accordingly, it can generally be said that legal criteria should also prevail when deciding whether to favour creativity over conformity with the other languages in each individual case. After all, legal reliability is a *conditicio sine qua non* in the formation of an EU legal vocabulary. However, ensuring legal reliability in EU term formation depends on the specific circumstances in each national legal system. Therefore, legal reliability can be ensured only by an onomasiological approach, which includes conceptual analysis at both EU and national level.

EU Term Formation as an Onomasiological Exercise

Although the principles of terminology theory confirm that term formation is an onomasiological exercise starting at the level of the concept (see Bratanić and Lončar, Chapter 12, this volume; Cabré 1999: 38), this is sometimes neglected in practice. The example above shows the potential danger when terminologists, translators or revisers make terminology decisions using a semasiological approach that starts and often stops at the level of the term, in other words, without taking account of conceptual considerations. In particular, EU translators and terminologists are warned against 'blindly' accepting internationalisms without investigating whether the term already exists in their national legal system but with a different meaning. As mentioned earlier, as a rule, terminologists and translators should avoid using terms of national law to designate EU concepts. However, this is not always possible.[13] Moreover, the flipside is true: if an adequate national term already exists, that term is to be used. Creating a new term for an existing term results in multiple references, posing a threat to uniform interpretation. Literal equivalents, the most commonly used type of equivalent in EU term formation (Šarčević 2004: 130), are often abused in this respect. On the one hand, literal equivalents, such as *marché intérieur/internal market* and *single currency/monnaie unique*, are particularly effective as they are transparent and can be easily identified as EU terms across languages. However, when terminologists and translators rely on literal equivalents without making the necessary conceptual background checks, they run the risk of creating a 'competing' term for a concept that already exists

13 On whether to form new terms or use national terms, see Šarčević (2012: 98–102); also Šarčević and Čikara (2009: 201–8).

in their national legal system. For this reason, the literal approach that dominates EU translation and legal translation in general has been criticized, among others, by the comparatist Peter de Cruz, who emphasizes that the 'translation of a legal text is much more than simply providing mere synonyms or literal equivalents for terms'. In his opinion, 'translators need to be very conversant not just with the operation of "registers" … legal registers and legal terms *per se*, but with the overall legal system into which the concepts fit' (1999: 163).

As for EU term formation, translators and terminologists have the double burden of creating a vocabulary that is coherent within EU law as a whole and also compatible with their national terms and concepts. However, since they are usually not specialists in EU law and have no training in their national law, they often lack the knowledge and skills to make informed decisions. For example, when translating the expression *unfair terms* in Directive 93/13/EEC on unfair terms in consumer contracts, the Italian translator simply aligned the Italian equivalent on the French term, using the expression *clausole abusive*, although the French adjective *abusif* has the same meaning as *vessatorio*, which is more faithful to the original intent of the directive and is compatible with Italian law. As a result, the list of terms cited in IATE as equivalents for *unfair terms* includes, among others, *clause abusive* (fr), *cláusula abusiva* (es), *cláusula abusiva* (pt) and *clausola abusiva* (it). The Italian term *clausola iniqua* is also cited.[14] While this casts doubt on the reliability of the terms cited in IATE, a much more harmful situation would have occurred if the misleading term had been transposed into Italian law. According to Pasa and Benacchio (2005: 84), it is fortunate that the translator's mistake was detected during transposition; otherwise, there would have been serious repercussions if it had become a part of the terminology and organization of the Italian Civil Code. As they report, 'The term *abusive* has "slipped past" the Italian legislator a few times'.

From the above it follows that making informed terminology decisions requires considerable competence on the part of terminologists and translators. In particular, they should possess adequate knowledge of both EU law and their national law, as well as comparative law skills, enabling them to determine whether a potential equivalent exists in their national legal system and, if so, to conduct a comparative analysis of the characteristics of the European and national concepts to determine the adequacy of the potential national equivalent. While the use of comparative law methods is widely accepted in legal translation (see Chapter 5 by Pozzo in this volume), the adequacy of a functional equivalent must be tested in each case depending on the communicative purpose (Šarčević 1997: 241–7; 2012: 97; cf. De Groot 2012: 142–6). Nonetheless, in my opinion, the use of the functional approach of comparative law is highly useful when carrying out terminological research as it focuses on concepts and not terms, as in the literal approach (see

14 The terms, with the exception of English, are in singular in this entry. The plural form, which appears in the Italian translation of Directive 93/13/EEC, is cited in another entry: *clausole abusive*.

Šarčević 2012: 96–8). For best results, conceptual analysis should be carried out by an interdisciplinary team of linguists and legal experts to guarantee the reliability of equivalents.[15]

As seen earlier, the use of functional equivalents is not recommended for the designation of EU concepts as it creates multiple references, often leading to different results in practice in the Member States. Exceptions to this general rule are permitted when it is clear from the context that reference is being made to the EU concept or institution. Sometimes the word *European* is added, leaving no doubt as to the intended reference. Take the example of *European Ombudsman*, which in its modern meaning as a Parliamentary Ombudsman was originally a Swedish institution. The term itself dates back to an indigenous Swedish, Danish and Norwegian word of old Norse. The English term is a naturalized borrowing used colloquially in the UK for the national institution, which is formally called the *Parliamentary Commissioner for Administration*. The French term *Médiateur européen* is derived from the French national institution *médiateur de la République*. Similarly, a number of other languages use their national functional equivalent, for example, Swedish (*Europeiska ombudsmannen*), Danish (*Den Europæiske Ombudsmand*), Dutch (*Europese Ombudsman*), Finnish (*Euroopan oikeusasiamies*), Spanish (*Defensor del Pueblo Europeo*), German (*Europäischer Bürgerbeauftragter*), Czech (*evropský veřejný ochránce práv*) and Slovene (*Evropski varuh človekovih pravic*) (see http://www.ombudsman.europa.eu). In this case the use of functional equivalents is useful because the function of the European and national institutions is identical.

Although the purist trend in Croatia rejects borrowings, the Croatian lawyer-linguists in Brussels favoured the hybrid borrowing *Europski ombudsman* over the Croatian functional equivalent *Europski pučki pravobranitelj*, which was commonly used in the media and was generally preferred. As a result, the term *Europski ombudsman* appears in the authentic Croatian version of the TFEU (Art. 228). As such, it is one of the few borrowings in the entire Croatian vocabulary of EU terms. While the choice of the borrowing is surprising, it reflects the fact that the Croatian terminology has been created on the basis of the English. If a multilingual study of the other equivalents and their sources had been carried out, I believe that the functional equivalent would have been given priority in this case.

A Multilingual Approach to EU Term Formation

As in the majority of the new Member States from Central and Eastern Europe, the translation of the *acquis* in Croatia was mostly an English-only project, with other source-language texts being consulted only in cases of ambiguity or doubt

15 On the use of conceptual analysis in EU term formation and translation, see Šarčević (2012: 93–8); in legal translation, see Sandrini (2009: 152–63); also Schübel-Pfister (2004: 113); Šarčević (1997: 237–41); for the purpose of term formation in local, national and international scenarios, see Rirdance and Vasiljevs (2006: 24–8).

(Šarčević 2001: 36). The same strategy applied to the formation of EU terms, which in my opinion is unfortunate as the Croatian language and Croatian law are much closer to German. When teaching legal translation to Croatian lawyers and linguists, in my first lesson I always stressed the fact that Croatian law is a civil law system belonging to the Germanic tradition. Moreover, the first Croatian civil law terms were created by translating the Austrian ABGB, which entered into force in the Croatian language (*Opći građanski zakonik*) in 1853 (see Šarčević 1997: 35). Similarly, the first Croatian criminal law terms were essentially translations of the Austrian StGB dating back to 1803; the Croatian text (*Kazneni zakon o zločinstvih, prestupcih i prekršajih*) entered into force in 1852. It is noteworthy that Latin was the official language of the law on Croatian territory until 1847, which, according to Mattila, was one of the last nations in Europe to make the switch to its vernacular language (2013: 167). Recent history also confirms the affinity to the German language and German and Austrian law. During the transition to a market economy entire German laws were 'translated' into Croatian. This, however, depends on the area of law. As elsewhere, English terms dominate in areas such as banking, finance, capital markets and others (Barbić 2013: 53).

From the very beginning I recommended a multilingual approach to EU term formation and translation of the *acquis*, encouraging Croatian translators and terminologists to consult and compare other language versions in addition to the English, especially the French, German and one or two Slavic languages, preferably Slovene because of the similarities of the legal systems. In my opinion, such approach respects the multilingual and multicultural dimensions of EU legislation and leads to visible improvements not only in the linguistic quality of the target language and terminology but also its reliability (see Šarčević 2001: 44–7). As we recall, one of the main goals is to create EU terms that are coherent with one's national legal system. However, the overuse of calques and loanwords of English source terms sometimes has the opposite effect, even to the point of threatening to destabilize the national legal language. As for the Croatian terminology and translations, it became evident that a number of erroneous loanwords in directives could have been detected if the terminologists, translators or revisers had consulted other language versions, especially German. Without such comparative work, some faulty terminology has been enacted into law in the Croatian transposing acts. For example, the term *transaction* appears as *transakcija* instead of *pravni posao* (*Rechtsgeschäft*) in several provisions of the Capital Markets Act and the Consumer Credit Act. As a result, some bank transactions are nowadays commonly referred to as *transakcija*. Although EU English is not the English of the common law (see Chapter 8 by Felici), it uses some general terms of legal English which resemble civil law terms but have different meanings. According to Barbić (2013: 61), the influence of such English calques and loanwords is particularly harmful because some of them are being accepted in their English meanings, thus posing a threat to the conceptual coherence of Croatian law. As an example, he cites the adjective *materijalan*, which is increasingly being used in legal expressions in Croatian legislation in the sense of the English term *material* (= essential), which departs considerably from the traditional meanings of *materijalan* in various contexts of Croatian law, which correspond to the usage of *materiell* in German law.

One of the most obvious disadvantages of an English-only approach to term formation and translation of the *acquis* is the fact that in many cases, the English term is a translation of the French. As mentioned above, French remained the 'original' drafting language of most legislation for a long time after English became an EU official language. Although subsequently authenticated translations are equally authentic as well, everyone knows that making a translation of a translation is risky business, thus casting doubt on the interpretative value of subsequent translations (see Šarčević 2002: 256–9; 1997: 207). Elsewhere I pointed out that, after Sweden and Finland acceded to the Union, in a preliminary ruling in 1998 in the case *Bayerische Hypotheken– und Wechselbank AG*,[16] the Court of Justice ruled in favour of the German text, which allowed a broader interpretation than the English text. A comparison of the other language versions revealed that all coincided with the German text, with the exception of the Swedish and Finnish texts, which follow the English text. My main concern was not the ruling of the Court of Justice but rather the implications for the interpretative value of the Swedish and Finnish translations of the *acquis*, which were based mainly on the English texts (Šarčević 2002: 260–61). Today the situation is even more acute in light of the dominance of English in the new Member States. As for Croatian judges, at least in the initial phase, most of them will base their decisions on the relevant provision in the Croatian text, unless it is ambiguous or unclear. When they do consult another language version, it will probably be the English text. If the English text has a defect and served as the source text, as in the case cited above, then any discrepancy with the other language versions will go undetected. To make the situation even more absurd, today it could happen that the number of translations with undetected defects will constitute the majority. A solution to this problem would be to use an 'historical' method of interpretation allowing judges to compare only the authentic texts in force at the time of the occurrence of the event leading to the dispute at hand.[17]

It would be wrong to imply that all the new Member States applied a strict English-only strategy when forming EU terminology and translating the *acquis*. Taking a look at the equivalents in IATE for the *Court of Justice*/*Cour de justice*, we see that a number of new Member States followed the German term *Gerichtshof*, while others made an independent choice: *Съд* (bg), *Soudní dvůr* (cs), *Euroopa Kohus* (et), *Bíróság* (hu), *Trybunał Sprawiedliwości* (pl), *Curtea de Justiţie* (ro), *Súdny dvor* (sk), *Sodišče* (sl). No consensus was reached on the name

16 Case C/45/96, *Bayerische Hypotheken– und Wechselbank AG* v. *Edgard Dietzinger* [1998] ECR I/01199.

17 Derlén (in Chapter 4 of this volume) cites this historic approach as an 'innovative' method used by national courts in the past and even by Advocate General Jacobs in the *Henriksen* case.

of the Court in Croatian. In fact, it was usually 'mistranslated' as *Sud pravde*, a literal translation of the English.[18] While *Sud Europske unije* is the accepted designation for the institution, that is, *Court of Justice of the European Union*, it was argued that *Sud* (= Court, also the Bulgarian solution) is inappropriate as a designation for the *Court of Justice*, which is now one of the three constitutive parts of the CJEU, as it would not be recognizable as the Luxembourg Court in a non-EU context. Lacking a better solution, the lawyer-linguists in Brussels opted for *Sud*, which appears in the authentic Croatian version of the TFEU; however, *Europski sud* is currently cited in IATE. While other language versions were consulted when proposing potential equivalents for the institutions and some key concepts, these were clearly exceptions in Croatia. On the contrary, Czech translators and terminologists made a point of consulting several languages on a regular basis when forming EU terminology and translating the *acquis* in the pre-accession period.

Drafted in 1999, the first edition of the Czech manual 'Rules for Translating EC Law' (*Pravidla pro překládáni práva ES*), which contains over 100 pages of mandatory terms and phrases, was based on English only. However, the second edition was expanded to include French and German source texts and terminology (Obrová and Pelka 2001: 107). Encouraging its freelance translators to adopt a multilingual approach, the Czech Coordination and Revision Centre (CRC) (*Koordinačni a revizni centrum*) sent the source text to the translators in English, French and German. The translators returned the translation to the department coordinator together with a list of terms for approval, which was later uploaded into the common database, accessible by all translators and revisers. Following a strict regime, all revisers were required to assess the quality and accuracy of the Czech translation by comparing it with all three source languages. To ensure high quality, the revisers were required to have one of the source languages at A level, the second at B level and the third at C level. The revised translation was then sent to the departmental coordinator for the final terminological clearance or for further editing and terminological change proposals. Since different Czech equivalents were often proposed for the same concept, depending on the source language used, it was up to departmental experts and lawyer-linguists to choose the most adequate Czech equivalent (Obrová and Pelka 2001: 105).

According to Obrová and Pelka (2001: 99–107), the initial phase of translation and term formation in the Czech Republic was characterized by an *ad hoc* approach; however, after the CRC was established in 1998, it immediately began to introduce systematic methods of term management, thus ensuring high quality and reliable terminology, which is not only coherent but also consistent. In their opinion, the

18 The literal translation can also be considered a mistranslation for historical reasons. According to the Croatian legal historian and lexicographer Mažuranić, one of the historical meanings of *pravda* was *sud*. Therefore, using the word *pravda* in the name of the court is redundant. See the entry in Mažuranić (1975: 1078).

most important factor in the final phase is to have consistent terminology, which can be achieved only by standardization.

Achieving Terminological Consistency through Standardization

While creativity is encouraged in EU term formation, too many cultural pioneers is not a good thing. Terminological consistency is a golden rule in EU term formation and legal translation in general, especially in such an immense and serious undertaking as the translation of the *acquis*. For this reason, Guideline 6 of the *Joint Practical Guide* emphasizes that the same terms are to be used to express the same concepts (point 6.2.). This applies not only to the 'provisions of a single act, including the annexes, but also to the provisions of related acts, in particular implementing acts and all other acts in the same area. In general, terminology must be consistent with the legislation in force' (point 6.2.2.). Accordingly, synonyms have no place in EU legal vocabulary or in any legal vocabulary for that matter. In particular, the use of synonyms in legislative texts is misleading as it implies that reference is being made to a different concept (Šarčević and Bajčić 2011: 21–2; Šarčević 2004: 136). Therefore, once a term has been approved as an official equivalent for a given concept, translators are obliged to use it even if they do not regard it as the best solution.

According to best practices of term management, the mandatory usage of terminology can be achieved only through standardization, which has the effect of linking a term to a given concept (Cabré 1999: 199–201). However, this does not mean that concepts cannot and will not change. Particularly in EU law, legal concepts are constantly in flux and subject to change. On the other hand, once a term has been assigned to a specific concept, changing the term would destabilize the whole system. For a standardized terminology it is also desirable that a term be attributed to a single concept. In this sense, Guideline 6 of the *Joint Practical Guide* discourages polysemy: 'Identical terms must not be used to express different concepts' (point 6.2.). This, however, is difficult to achieve in the field of law. Therefore, it frequently occurs that the same EU term is used to denote different concepts in different areas of law, which users should be able to recognize by the context.

For the purpose of standardization in the pre-accession period, EU terms in the national language should be approved (and/or proposed) by an interdisciplinary body of subject experts, terminologists and other linguists, preferably one that has been authorized by the national government (Šarčević and Bajčić 2011: 25; Rirdance and Vasiljevs 2006: 19; in general Cabré 1999: 200). Dissemination via a central terminology database is essential in order to ensure accessibility to all users. In retrospect it can be said that most of the new Member States of the 2004 enlargement followed these practices. As a rule, the national Translation Coordination Unit (TCU) responsible for organizing translation of the *acquis* also established and maintained the national EU terminology database. In some cases, the national TCU approved the terminology as well, for example, the Czech CRC mentioned above and the Hungarian TCU established at the Ministry of Justice in 1997. The staff of the Hungarian TCU, which consisted of four to nine terminologists and lawyer-linguists, was responsible for the final linguistic and legal-linguistic revision of the translations and for resolving problematic terms, the latter in cooperation with the expert working group appointed in 2000 by the participating ministries, national authorities, universities and the Hungarian Academy of Sciences (Somssich and Varga 2001: 71). The Hungarian TCU is still active today, and the Terminology Council of the Hungarian Language was established in 2005 to standardize national terminology (in Rirdance and Vasiljevs 2006: 45).

Terminology work is on a high level in Lativa where the Latvian Translation and Terminology Centre (TTC) invested much time and resources at the initial stage of its activity to lay the groundwork for developing and standardizing EU legal terminology and setting standards for translating the *acquis* into Latvian. Work on developing a uniform terminology database began in 1998, one year after the TTC was established. A terminologist assigned to each draft translation collaborated closely with translators, revisers and sector experts outside the TTC. To ensure consistent and reliable terminology, only terminology was used which had either been approved by the Terminology Commission of the Latvian Academy of Sciences (TC of LAS), was used in Latvian legislation or had been established in general practice (Lejasiasaka 2001: 121). The TC of LAS, which currently consists of 26 subject-field sub-commissions, has been responsible for proposing, approving and standardizing Latvian terminology since 1919! According to Rirdance and Vasiljevs, 'The TC of LAS [was] the main arbiter to decide about borrowing or not borrowing English terms from EU documentation and creating new Latvian terms if the corresponding terms could not be found in present vocabulary' (2006: 81). In light of the long tradition of high terminology standards in Latvia, it is not surprising that Tilde of Riga was the driving force behind the EUR TermBank Project, which resulted in the central Euro TermBank database that links the languages of new Member States to other terminology banks and resources of countries and organizations in the public domain inside and outside the EU.[19]

Summing up, it can be said that standardization is a precondition for achieving compulsory terminology usage, thus resulting in terminological consistency, a requirement for ensuring effective communication in EU law. Candidate countries can learn from the experiences of others, but in the end each country must choose its own strategy for term formation and strive to apply best practices of term

19 While the start-up countries included Estonia, Hungary, Latvia, Lithuania and Poland, the number of languages participating in the database has grown to 34, including Russian and Chinese. One of the main goals is to strengthen the linguistic infrastructure in new EU Member States through the harmonization, collection and dissemination of public terminology resources; see Rirdance and Vasiljevs (2006: 11).

management under the circumstances dictated by its specific pre-accession situation in respect of resources and available specialists, both linguists and lawyers. In any case, the vital role played by terminologists and translators should not be underestimated. Once authenticated, the 'translations' become equally authentic legally binding texts and the terms therein have a direct impact on the application of EU law in the particular country. To modify or replace 'erroneous terminology' in EU legislation, a corrigendum must be adopted by the institution(s) that issued the act. If the 'misleading or incorrect terminology' was used in subsequent acts as well, 'it can only be changed when the acts concerned are codified or recast' (Somssich et al. 2010: 75).

Concluding Remarks: The Cultural Dimension of the Creativity/Conformity Dichotomy

In the limited space available, it has been possible to identify only some of the basic principles and criteria for successful EU term formation for the translation of EU legislation in general and in particular for the translation of the *acquis* by candidate countries. Instead of concluding by assembling a catalogue of the basic principles and criteria discussed throughout the chapter, I find it more useful to briefly revisit the basic dilemma facing all translators and terminologists when forming EU secondary terms, that is, whether effective communication is best served by aligning a term on the other language versions (conformity) or by creating a term that aims to satisfy target user expectations (creativity). This basic issue deserves further comment as it sheds light on the cultural dimension in EU term formation and the question of loyalty, which seems to differ in the pre- and post-accession periods.

As regards the pre-accession perspective, from my experience in Croatia and that of others involved in the translation of the *acquis* in earlier candidate countries, it can be said that the members of the national TCUs were committed to cultivating a cultural dimension of term formation that went beyond merely respecting the requirements of language correctness. Torn between time pressures and their drive for perfectionism (Obrová and Pelka 2001: 113), their main goal in EU term formation was to coin new terms which would be reliable and satisfy target user expectations at home (Somssich and Varga 2001: 75). Hence, they favoured creativity in their own language over conformity with the other languages as a means of guaranteeing effective communication. After all, pre-accession term formation is concerned primarily with 'vertical' linguistic issues, that is, within a single language, as opposed to 'horizontal' issues across languages or 'all the languages taken together in parallel', as Robertson puts it (Chapter 3, this volume). Therefore, it is quite natural that their first priority or loyalty was to their national language and culture. As 'outsiders', there was little to no pressure to consider horizontal issues such as achieving conformity across languages. This seems to change rather drastically after translators and terminologists are recruited by the DGT and become 'insiders'.

A Finnish translation scholar who joined the DGT after graduating from translation school and later returned to academia, Koskinen acknowledges that, once inside the institution, 'translators are not free to use just any strategy' but must conform to 'a code of practice' that dictates a literal translation strategy. Despite the EU values of cultural and linguistic diversity, translators are under pressure to forget about the cultural turn in translation studies and to avoid target-receiver culture-specific features, adopting instead a 'preference for surface-level similarity, which is assumed to guarantee that readers of the various translations all get the same message'. Accordingly, equivalence is often taken to mean 'linguistic correspondence, or literal rerendering', thus reducing the notion of equivalence to a 'mere visual equivalence' without quality requirements: 'what is important is that all versions *look* the same' (Koskinen 2000: 54–6; see also Koskinen's ethnographic study of EU translation, 2008). From Koskinen's remarks, it follows that all linguistic diversity, even at the level of the term, is regarded as a potential threat to uniform interpretation and is thus discouraged. Since the EU requirement of strict interlingual correspondence conflicts with the cultural approach in translation studies, EU translators and terminologists need to forget about enlightened theory and use traditional methods which their teachers had made them unlearn (cf. Pym 2000: 12). In their role as 'insiders' they are expected to be loyal to the institution and its policy of '*a*cultural communication', as Koskinen calls it (2000: 54). While vertical linguistic issues remain important, it appears that horizontal considerations prevail, thus tilting the balance in favour of conformity across languages in the interest of achieving uniform interpretation Union-wide.

As regards terminology, Koskinen remarks: 'The specific EU culture has produced a new variant of each language, molding its structures and introducing a variety of new words', which 'have not met with unanimous support back home' (Koskinen 2000: 53; on the development of an EU culture, see Koskinen 2008: 80). In her opinion, the 'small' EU languages are particularly vulnerable, especially Finnish, which at that time was the only official non-Indo-European language. While citizens' complaints about the 'strange and unnatural sounding' Finnish words did not go unnoticed, the reply was standard: 'No matter how strange the result of such linguistic experiments may appear at first glance, experience shows that very often words coined in (and by) the European Institutions are soon accepted by the most (Euro)sceptics' (Gozzi 2001: 32). In other words, users at home have no choice but to accept the new EU idiom and rhetoric from Brussels. This raises several questions: does this rather harsh stance imply that all post-accession decisions on terminology are made in Brussels and do EU translators and terminologists need to adjust their loyalty priority?

It appears that the EU institutions have softened their policy and are now open to establishing a formal coordination system for the channelling of linguistic remarks from individual Member States. In this regard, Somssich et al. (2010: 46–9) report a 'boom' in coordinated decision-making on terms to be used in EU legislative texts as a result of initiatives taken mostly by new Member States. For example, some of the TCUs established during the pre-accession period have remained active, albeit with a reduced staff, and cooperate with the EU institutions on terminology issues and/or actively participate in the consolidation of their national EU terminology. This is the case, for instance, in Latvia, Hungary and Romania. In Poland, the Polish Language Council assists the Polish unit of the DGT. In Slovenia, a project was launched in 2009 to establish a national mechanism for the authentication of Slovene terminology, which forwards terminology to the Slovene Government Office for European Affairs, the central coordination body for linguistic cooperation with the EU institutions. In Finland, a network for the translation of EU legislation was established in 2009 to facilitate cooperation between Finnish translators of the EU institutions and national officials. Thanks to the network, contacts are quickly established between Finnish translators and subject experts on terminology issues before a text is formally adopted. In Ireland, the Irish Terminology Committee supports Irish translators at the EU institutions by making recommendations for new terms and reviewing terms proposed for inclusion in the IATE database (see Somssich et al. 2010: 48–9).

While the new coordination system has not brought about any visible change in the position of the EU institutions on the question of conformity across languages, at least it provides a link between EU translators and terminologists and their colleagues and subject experts at home, thus ensuring that they remain up-to-date on language usage and have feedback on issues such as user acceptance. Most importantly, it rekindles their loyalty to their national language and culture, preventing them from becoming totally submersed in the EU culture of sameness. This has the positive result of reminding them of their duty to promote effective communication in EU law by striking a proper balance between creativity and conformity.

References

Barbić, J. 2013. Jezik u propisima, in *Jezik u pravu*, edited by J. Barbić. Zagreb: Hrvatska akademija znanosti i umjetnosti, 49–77.

Cabré, M.T. 1999. *Terminology: Theory, Methods and Applications*. Amsterdam: John Benjamins.

Cornu, G. 1990. *Linguistique juridique*. Paris: Montchrestien.

Dannemann, G. 2012. In search of system neutrality: methodological issues in the drafting of European contract law rules, in *Practice and Theory in Comparative Law*, edited by M. Adams and J. Bonhoff. Cambridge: Cambridge University Press, 96–119.

De Cruz, P. 1999. *Comparative Law in a Changing World*. London: Cavendish Publishing.

De Groot, G.-R. 2012. The influence of problems of legal translation on comparative law research, in *The Role of Legal Translation in Legal Harmonization*, edited by C.J.W. Baaij. Alphen aan den Rijn: Kluwer Law International, 139–59.

Gambier, Y. 1998. Mouvances eurolinguistiques. Cas de la Finlande, in *Europe et traduction*, edited by M. Ballard. Arras: Artois Presses Université, 295–304.

Goffin, R. 1999. Terminographie bei der Europäischen Kommission, in *Fachsprachen / Languages for Special Purposes,* edited by L. Hoffmann, H. Kalverkämpfer and H. Wiegand. Band 2. Berlin: Walter de Gruyter, 2124–38.

Gozzi, P. 2001. Experiences in countries preparing for membership, in *Legal Translation: Preparation for Accession to the European Union*, edited by S. Šarčević. Rijeka: Faculty of Law, University of Rijeka, 23–34.

Joint Practical Guide of the European Parliament, the Council and the Commission for persons involved in the drafting of European Union legislation. 2013. Available at: eur-lex.europa.eu/content/pdf/techleg/joint-practical-guide-2013-en.pdf.

Kageura, K. 2002. *The Dynamics of Terminology: A Descriptive Theory of Term Formation and Terminological Growth*. Amsterdam: John Benjamins.

Kjær, A.L. 2007. Legal translation in the European Union: a research field in need of a new approach, in *Language and the Law: International Outlooks*, edited by K. Kredens and S. Goźdź-Roszkowski. Frankfurt am Main: Peter Lang, 69–95.

Koskinen, K. 2000. Institutional illusions: translating in the EU Commission. *The Translator*, 6(1), 49–65.

Koskinen, K. 2008. *Translating Institutions: An Ethnographic Study of EU Translation*. Manchester: St. Jerome.

Lejasiasaka, I. 2001. Development and use of uniform Latvian terminology at the Translation and Terminology Centre. *Terminologie et Traduction*, 2, 118–29.

Mattila, H. 2013. *Comparative Legal Linguistics*. Farnham: Ashgate.

Mažuranić, V. 1975. *Prinosi za hrvatski pravno-povjestni rječnik*. Drugi dio. Zagreb: Informator. Originally published 1908–1922. Zagreb: Jugoslavenska akademija znanosti i umjetnosti.

Obrová, P. and Pelka, J. 2001. Translation of EC law into Czech. *Terminologie et Traduction*, 2, 94–117.

Pasa, B. and Benacchio, G.A. 2005. *The Harmonization of Civil and Commercial Law in Europe*. Budapest: Central European University Press.

Priručnik za prevođenje pravnih akata Europske unije. 2002. Ministarstvo za europske integracije. Zagreb. Available at: www.mvep.hr/files/file/prirucnici/MEI_PRIRUCNIK.pdf.

Pym, A. 2000. The European Union and its future languages: questions for language policies and translation theories. *Across Languages and Cultures*, 1(1), 1–17.

Rirdance, S. and Vasiljevs, A. (eds) 2006. *Towards Consolidation of European Terminology Resources: Experience and Recommendations from Euro TermBank Project*. Riga: Tilde.

Sandrini, P. 2009. Der transkulturelle Vergleich von Rechtsbegriffen, in *Legal Language in Action: Translation, Terminology, Drafting and Procedural Issues*, edited by S. Šarčević. Zagreb: Globus, 151–65.
Schübel-Pfister, I. 2004. *Sprache und Gemeinschaftsrecht*. Berlin: Duncker & Humblot.
Somssich, R. and Varga, K. 2001. Consistency and terminology in the translation of Community legislation in Hungary. *Terminologie et Traduction*, 2, 58–81.
Somssich, R., Várnal, J. and Bérczi, A. 2010. *Lawmaking in the EU Multilingual Environment*. Brussels: European Commission. Directorate-General for Translation.
Strinz, R. 1999. *Europarecht*. Heidelberg: C.F. Müller Verlag.
Šarčević, S. 1997. *New Approach to Legal Translation*. The Hague: Kluwer Law International.
Šarčević, S. 2001. Preserving multilingualism in an enlarged European Union. *Terminologie et Traduction*, 2, 34–50.
Šarčević, S. 2002. Problems of interpretation in an enlarged European Union, in *L'interprétation des textes juridiques rédigés dans plus d'une langue*, edited by R. Sacco. Torino: L'Harmattan Italia, 239–72.
Šarčević, S. 2004. Creating EU legal terms: internationalisms vs. localisms, in *Terminology at the Time of Globalization*, edited by M. Humar. Ljubljana: ZRC SAZU, 128–38.
Šarčević, S. 2006. Die Übersetzung von mehrsprachigen EU-Rechtsvorschriften, in *Insights into Specialized Translation*, edited by M. Gotti and S. Šarčević. Bern: Peter Lang, 120–52.
Šarčević, S. 2012. Coping with the challenges of legal translation in harmonization, in *The Role of Legal Translation in Legal Harmonization*, edited by C.J.W. Baaij. Alphen aan den Rijn: Kluwer Law International, 83–107.
Šarčević, S. and Bajčić, M. 2011. Stvaranje hrvatskoga nazivlja za europske pojmove: Kako srediti terminološku džunglu? in *Hrvatski jezik na putu u EU*, edited by M. Bratanić. Zagreb: Institut za hrvatski jezik i jezikoslovoje / Hrvatska sveučilišna naklada, 21–32.
Šarčević, S. and Čikara, E. 2009. European vs. national terminology in Croatian legislation, in *Legal Language in Action: Translation, Terminology, Drafting and Procedural Issues*, edited by S. Šarčević. Zagreb: Globus, 193–214.
Translation and Multilingualism. 2012. Publication of the DG for Translation. Available at: ec.europa.eu/dgs/translation/publications/brochures/index_en.htm.
Wagner, E., Bech, S. and Martínez, J.M. 2002. *Translating for the European Union Institutions*. Manchester: St. Jerome.
Wright, S.E. and Wright, L. 1997. Terminology management for technical translation, in *Handbook of Terminology Management*, edited by S.E. Wright and G. Budin. vol. 1. Amsterdam: John Benjamins, 147–59.

Chapter 12
The Myth of EU Terminology Harmonization on National and EU Level

Maja Bratanić and Maja Lončar

Term Harmonization

According to the traditional Wüsterian approach which still generally prevails in terminology management, term harmonization is an essential requirement of any terminological activity, monolingual as well as multilingual. If terminology is not harmonized, it cannot ensure reliable, unambiguous and standardized professional communication. Another prime prerequisite of multilingual communication in the European Union is that terminology must be easily accessible. This is achieved primarily by IATE, the EU inter-institutional terminology database, and *EuroVoc*, the EU's multilingual thesaurus, as well as by a number of internal translation and documentation tools. In the context of EU multilingual legislation the need for harmonization at both the level of the term and the concept becomes a condition of legal certainty.[1]

Multilingual terminology harmonization therefore implies the establishment of equivalences across languages, and the regulation of synonymy and term variation within a single language. The procedures of term harmonization have been elaborated by several ISO standards, primarily by ISO 860:2007(E) entitled 'Terminology work – harmonization of concepts and terms', which provides methods and a workflow model for standardizing and harmonizing concepts, concept systems, definitions and terms.

As stated in the above ISO Standard, harmonization starts at the concept level and continues at the term level. Concept harmonization is generally defined as:

1 In this sense, the *Joint Practical Guide* (2013) makes a distinction between formal and substantive consistency. Point 6.2. on formal consistency reads: 'The terminology used in a given act shall be consistent both internally and with acts already in force, especially in the same field. Identical concepts shall be expressed in the same terms, as far as possible without departing from their meaning in ordinary, legal or technical language.' Substantive consistency is covered in points 6.3. and 6.4. The former reads: 'Consistency of terminology must also be checked with regard to the content of the act itself. There must be no contradictions inherent in the act'.

> an activity leading to the establishment of a correspondence between two or more closely related or overlapping concepts having professional, technical, scientific, social, economic, linguistic, cultural or other differences, in order to eliminate or reduce minor differences between them.

Differences and similarities between concepts and concept systems must be examined in order to determine the feasibility of harmonization. Ideally, the goal should be the harmonization of entire concept systems.

In reality, however, due to a number of linguistic and extra-linguistic factors, even when all efforts are made to coordinate terminologies as they develop, as is usually the case during the translation of the EU *acquis*, inconsistent terminologies continue to be created and used. Discrepancies between concepts within a single language and across languages are very often not apparent at the term level and are therefore difficult to diagnose before possible instances of miscommunication or outright damage in legal effects occurs.

The principle of the equal authenticity of all 24 official language versions further intensifies the impression of the infallibility of the translation procedure guaranteed by armies of highly trained translators and rigorous lawyer-linguist guards. The advantage of multilingual legislation has been confirmed by the highly justified conviction of many legal experts that 'multilingualism does not make the exercise of legal interpretation more difficult' since 'the same legal rule expressed in other languages might be a great help in understanding its intention, and therefore, in establishing its meaning' (Ćapeta 2009: 106). The problem with this assumption, however, lies in the fact that most translators, no matter how skilful and experienced, lack the background legal finesse required to detect the potential lexical and conceptual incongruity.

In contrast to other areas of special-language communication, terminology harmonization in the context of EU legal translation often turns out to be a myth, despite ample control mechanisms. This chapter attempts to identify the main linguistic and extra-linguistic causes of this phenomenon based on the example of the translation of the *acquis* by candidate countries, in this case Croatia, and to provide an overview, albeit not systematic, of various causes, both systemic and pragmatic, contributing to such mismatching.

EU Term Formation

Sager (1990: 80) differentiates between primary and secondary term formation. Primary term formation is a monolingual activity involving the lexicalization of a new concept. In secondary term formation new terms are created for existing concepts. It therefore starts from an existing term and can be either monolingual or multilingual. In the first case it is usually the result of a monolingual revision of terminology, and in the second the result of knowledge transfer, that is, the transfer of an existing term into another linguistic community resulting in term creation in a different language.

As Fischer (2010) elaborates, in the primary term creation of a multilingual terminology, the same concept is being lexicalized simultaneously in more languages, thus excluding the need for translation. In practice, however, multilingual primary term creation takes place in two steps: primary term creation in one or some languages followed by secondary term creation in the other languages (translation). Whereas the process of translating terminology ideally takes an onomasiological approach, based on 'comparing first the two conceptual systems and then finding or creating the equivalent target term for a source term', in practice it more often becomes semasiologically oriented (2010: 26–7).

Primary and Secondary Term Creation in the EU Context

In several of her works (1988, 2010) Šarčević discusses the problem of conceptual incongruence between different legal systems, which in EU multilingual terminology can be identified as a problem of conceptual mismatching, and suggests the need for a thorough conceptual analysis as a starting point for determining the adequacy of potential equivalents. Accordingly, Fischer explains that the process of secondary term creation based on the translation of existing terms indeed often involves one or more conceptual systems. Two basic processes are commonly at work here: the designation of new EU concepts in some languages (multilingual primary term creation of EU terms) and the translation of the existing terms into the other languages (secondary term creation) (2010: 26).

EU concepts are often intentionally vague in order to facilitate their application in the different legal and political systems of the Member States, not yet fully harmonized on European level. This results in the use of rather vague terms and additionally contributes to the lack of terminological precision. The proper functioning of EU law presupposes the autonomy of EU concepts, which has been established by the case law.[2] However, the assumption of EU-specific concepts and an autonomous EU conceptual system is not fully realistic since in practice the EU and national conceptual systems interact, and with 24 languages involved a large number of combinations is possible. Furthermore, since the same official language is sometimes used in two or more Member States, in such cases it is linked to more than one national conceptual system. In addition, EU terms and terms of the national conceptual system(s) are sometimes used in the same EU text (Fischer 2010: 27). Such a network of potential links between EU and national concepts allows room for term variability on various levels.

Interestingly, legal experts often find this kind of overlapping welcome and the polysemy of EU and national terms not problematic. This is probably due to the fact that, in their understanding, such lexical overlapping points only to the

2 On the autonomy of EU concepts, see chapters 6 and 10 in this volume by Kjær and Engberg.

relatedness of concepts, not to their identical reference. Such a situation however inevitably leads to potential misunderstandings by insufficiently knowledgeable translators. This confirms the long established assumption that the relation of language and law is very specific and bears little resemblance to concept–term relation in most other domains since the concept–term relation tends to be more arbitrary than in other disciplines. As Brækhus once put it: 'If the legislator, in a new law, describes a legal phenomenon otherwise than in an earlier law, then the legal reality changes: law only exists in human language' (Brækhus 1956: 14 cited in Mattila 2013: 137).

Lack of Terminological Consistency in Translations of the *Acquis*

Terminological inconsistency in translations of the *acquis* occurs at the level of the term when different terms are used in the target language to designate the same EU concept, as well as at the level of the concept when the term used in the target language is linked to more than one concept, either on EU level or on EU and national levels. The following is an attempt to identify some of the causes of terminological inconsistency in translations of the *acquis* in Croatia prior to accession.

Pragmatic Reasons for the Lack of Terminological Consistency

Terminological inconsistency can be caused by reasons not closely related to language proper or terminology deficiency in itself. For example, the translation of the *acquis* in Croatia was carried out under pressure by numerous translators of various degrees of expertise and experience. Since the entire EU terminology had to be created from scratch, this resulted in the lack of terminological consistency, especially in the initial phase when translation aids in the form of glossaries, dictionaries or term bases were not yet in place. Although the *acquis* itself is often perceived as static, by its very nature it is dynamic as it grows on a daily basis, while other parts are amended or repealed. Apart from the fluid accession date, the fact that the body of EU law intended for translation constantly varies and fluctuates inevitably had an impact on the process of translation and finalization of the *acquis*.

This can be illustrated by noting the changes in the 'priority list' of the documents assigned for translation during Croatia's accession procedure (see Table 12.1). Shortly after Croatia submitted its request for full membership in 2003, the entire number of OJ pages of the *acquis* at that time totalled roughly one third of the bulk of documents received for translation by April 2013, two months before accession.[3]

3 This information was made available to us in oral communication with the Translation Coordination Unit of the Croatian Ministry of Foreign and European Affairs. More than 214,000 OJ pages or around 21,300 documents were sent to the

Table 12.1 ***Acquis*** **(OJ number of pages) changing in time**

	Number of OJ pages
June 2003	75,448
April 2013 (received altogether)	215,702
Excluded altogether (validity ended; already translated)	61,386
Priority list final	161,523

By the formal end of the translation process more than 68,000 OJ pages, most of which had already been translated by Croatian translators, had been repealed and excluded altogether because the validity of the documents had expired. Sometimes documents would be withdrawn and later returned to the priority list. For example, the Commission Directive 2004/6/EC of 20 January 2004[4] changed its status eight times. Due to the extreme volatility of the priority list, the Ministry of Foreign and European Affairs launched an internal joke referring to it as a 'moving target', a metaphor which was eventually adopted by all EU institutions. Taking account of all changes, the final number of OJ pages delivered by the accession date, to our knowledge, surpassed 160,000.

Croatia's fluid accession date was another pragmatic reason that contributed to the pressing deadlines towards the end. Contrary to earlier enlargements, the accession date (1 July 2013) was not fixed until very late in the process. Without a final deadline to work around, the translation service did not engage a sufficient number of lawyer-linguists to carry out the final legal-linguist revision of the translations. Instead, the finalization of all documents was left to the small group of Croatian lawyer-linguists recruited by the EU institutions for this purpose starting in 2010, thus making it necessary to finalize too many pages in a short period of time. No procedures had been established for cases when mistakes were detected and too many last-minute changes were introduced by the lawyer-linguists.

EU Translation Aids

Since specific translation tools for the Croatian translators of the *acquis* did not exist at the time preparations for accession began and are still rather scarce, the translators had to rely on all translation aids available. However, EU translation tools are not always fully reliable in terms of harmonization. Term bases (IATE in

EU after 1 December 2004, when the first documents were uploaded to TAIEX CCVista (ccvista.taiex.be).

4 Commission Directive 2004/6/EC of 20 January 2004 derogating from Directive 2001/15/EC to postpone the application of the prohibition of trade to certain products.

particular, but Euramis as well)[5] are not strictly normative but rather descriptive. IATE entries often turn out to be term-based instead of concept-based. As a consequence, concepts are not consistently handled as single terminological entries, which is easily noticed when examining the term *general government*, a single concept for which there are six different entries depending on the domain (see Table 12.2). Although the IATE domain classification system is based on the *EuroVoc* thesaurus, unfortunately it does not eliminate polyhierarchy, as *EuroVoc* does by assigning concepts which could be classified under several subject fields only to the field that seems the most logical for users.

Table 12.2 Term *general government* in IATE

TERM	DOMAIN
general government	Administrative structures [COM] Accounting [COM] Administrative law [EP] Executive power and public service [COM] ECONOMICS, Statistics [Council] Community finance, FINANCE, Accounting, ECONOMICS [ECA]

Linguistic Sources of Disharmonization

EU multilingual lawmaking is not based on co-drafting where all the language versions are drafted simultaneously or alternately. Instead, EU legislation is currently drafted primarily in English and then translated into the other official languages. It is at that point that secondary term formation takes place. At the level of the text the *de facto* translation in each of the official languages becomes *de iure* an authentic text. Despite the presumption that all equally authentic texts of EU legislation have the same meaning, this proves to be an illusion in reality. The EU principle of equal authenticity of legal texts should theoretically be based on multilingual primary term formation; however, the production of EU multilingual legislation largely entails the process of secondary term formation based on English or, less commonly these days, French. According to Temmerman, this situation has resulted in EU texts being drafted in 'Euro-English' which in turn are increasingly being produced by Europeans of different linguistic and cultural origins. As a result, if 'Euro-English has become the *lingua franca* and if Europeans continue to have the right to information in all official European languages, the issue of approximate meaning will have to be tackled all the time' (2011: 114).

5 Euramis, the European Advanced Multilingual Information System, is the translation memory of the European Commission.

Lexical variation: Two or more terms for one concept
Despite the clear instructions that 'identical concepts shall be expressed in the same terms' (*Joint Practical Guide* 6.2.), the EU legislator sometimes uses synonyms even in the same text. Using more than one term to designate the same concept is misleading because it suggests that the underlying concepts are also different. For example, in the consolidated versions of the Treaty on European Union (TEU) and Treaty on the Functioning of the European Union (TFEU), the term *third country* occurs 18 times and *third State* four times. In the Croatian version there is a trend of unification with *treća zemlja* (third country) occurring 21 times, and *treća država* (third State) only once.

Ironically, inappropriate solutions in the authenticated translations of the *acquis* sometimes result in the creation of more suitable terms in everyday usage. For example, the official Croatian term for *member of the European Parliament* is *član Europskoga parlamenta*, which is a literal translation from English, and not the standard Croatian collocation used in this context. In the Croatian administrative language it is more common to associate the term *zastupnik* with the Parliament. As a result, the term used almost exclusively in daily practice is *zastupnik Europskoga parlamenta* instead of the official term cited above.

Another example of an inappropriate Croatian solution is the term *Sud* for the *Court of Justice*. Since this designation is considered too general to be used as the name of that specific judicial institution, the attribute *European* is usually added. This in turn raises another issue because the name *Europski sud* is used by some authors as a designation for the *Court of Justice of the European Union* and by others for the *Court of Justice*. This ambiguous usage results in confusion due to insufficient distinction of the terms in question.

Sometimes the lawyer-linguists replaced established terms with new ones. For example, the Croatian term *opća država*, the established term for *general government* in the system of public finances, was for unknown and apparently unnecessary reasons changed during the final legal-linguistic revision into *ukupna država*, thus creating a new term for the same concept. The same thing happened with the Croatian terms for *State government* (*regionalna država* changed to *savezna država*) and *Social security funds* (*fondovi socijalnog osiguranja* changed to *fondovi socijalne sigurnosti*). The 'new' terms are used, for example, in Council Regulation 2223/96.[6] On the other hand, the original term is used in Guideline ECB/2013/23,[7] which was translated later by the Croatian lawyer-linguist of the European Central Bank. This situation of co-existence of more terms for the same concept is not welcome and should be avoided by all means.

On the other hand, some terms that had already been established in national harmonized legislation were given preference over new Croatian terms which

6 Council Regulation (EC) No 2223/96 of 25 June 1996 on the European system of national and regional accounts in the Community.

7 Guideline ECB/2013/23 of the European Central Bank of 25 July 2013 on government finance statistics.

are considered more adequate from a linguistic standpoint and their degree of transparency (for example, *žig Zajednice* for *Community trade mark* instead of *zaštitni znak Zajednice*).

Two closely related terms for different concepts

Sometimes similar terms are used in the English text to designate different concepts. For instance, *border control*, *border checks* and *border surveillance*[8] denote three different concepts, the first of which is superordinate to the latter two. The use of similar terms may lead to the false assumption that they denote the same concept. In Croatian, on the other hand, the terms for *guarantee* (*garancija*) and *warranty* (*jamstvo*) are sometimes considered to be synonymous, although they denote two different legal concepts.

Confusion arises when different concepts are frequently used without making a distinction between them, as is the case in regard to *undertaking* (*poduzetnik*), *enterprise* (*poduzeće*) and *company* (*trgovačko društvo*). One of the reasons for the failure to distinguish between these terms lies in the fact that there are six different Croatian terms for *company* in Euramis, each of which represents a different concept. As a result, the Croatian translation for *Law relating to undertakings*, the title of Chapter 17 of the Directory of European Union legislation, has been revised three times, resulting in three different translations. First it was confused with Company law and mistranslated as *Pravo trgovačkih društava*. At the date of Croatian accession it was called *Pravo poduzeća* and since then preference has been given to the rather confusing term *poduzetnik*, thus resulting in *Pravo koje se odnosi na poduzetnike*.[9]

Albeit similar, the terms *public service* (*javna služba*) and *official authority* (*javna ovlast*) are used differently depending on the context: *public service* in the context of free movement of workers (Art. 45(4) TFEU), and *official authority* in the context of freedom to provide services and right of establishment (Art. 51 TFEU). Similarly, the term *mandatory requirement* (*obvezni uvjet*) is used in the context of free movement of goods and *overriding reason relating to the public interest* (*prevladavajući razlog od općeg interesa*) in the context of freedom to provide services and right of establishment. Introduced by the Court of Justice of the European Union, the two terms are used indiscriminately, thus raising the question whether they can be regarded as referring to distinct concepts at all. This is a particularly delicate area since case law introduces new concepts and thus potential new items in need of harmonization.

It is sometimes difficult to determine whether two terms represent two different concepts or a single one. There are many examples of such indeterminate relationships. For example, *public policy* (*javni poredak*) and *public interest* (*javni*

8 Regulation (EC) No. 562/2006 of the European Parliament and of the Council of 15 March 2006 establishing a Community Code on the rules governing the movement of persons across borders (Schengen Borders Code).

9 See, for example, eur-lex.europa.eu/eu-enlargement/hr/special.html.

interes) are different concepts in private international law, but some Croatian lawyers regard them as synonyms in EU law.

Some EU terms are in a complex mutual relationship. Over time the legislator has introduced new terms but has changed the underlying concepts as well, thus leading to confusion. For instance, it is not clear whether *common market*, *single market* and *internal market* are different terms for the same concept or different concepts altogether. Namely, the merging of the national markets of the Member States forms a single market in the area of the internal market. This dilemma, which was caused by the inconsistent use of the terms *common market* and *internal market* in the Treaties, was resolved by the entry into force of the Treaty of Lisbon. To date, *internal market* is the only term used in the Treaties; however, uniform terminology has still not been established because the term *single market* is used in other documents where it is often identified as *internal market* as well.

Two terms for a single EU term: two Croatian concepts

There are cases where a single English term can be translated by two different Croatian terms representing two related, but not identical, concepts. For example, the term *public health* can refer in Croatian to *javno zdravlje* (condition) or *javno zdravstvo* (system) depending on the context. The problem arose when the Croatian Ministry of Health for no obvious reason changed its name from the linguistically more appropriate *Ministarstvo zdravstva* into *Ministarstvo zdravlja*, probably following the model of English and some other languages.

The confusion relating to the term *consolidated version* and its underlying concept illustrates the case of dangerous mismatching that can occur when existing national terms with a different meaning are used to designate EU concepts. The source of the confusion may be insufficient knowledge of the meaning of the national or the EU term or both. In this case, the two Croatian terms *konsolidirana verzija* and *pročišćena inačica* were at first used indiscriminately as synonyms for *consolidated version* but were later assigned to two different concepts as distinguished by (the majority but not necessarily all) the Croatian translators of the *acquis*. This resulted in the first term bearing the usual meaning 'a version of a text into which subsequent amendments have been incorporated, but which has no legal effect', while the second term acquired the meaning of a 'version of a document which in national system undergoes a certain procedure of verification, usually legislative'. Currently, the Croatian equivalent for *consolidated version* in IATE is *pročišćeni tekst*, although the respective definitions differ considerably.

Diachronic reasons

Terms and names change over time. Like many other expressions, the earlier name 'Official Journal of the European Community' was changed to 'Official Journal of the European Union' when the Treaty of Nice entered into force on 1 February 2003. With the entry into force of the Treaty of Lisbon on 1 December 2009, the European Union acquired the status of a legal person and officially replaced the European Community. Similarly, the three-pillar structure was dissolved, as a result of which Community law officially became EU law or Union law. Although the term *Community* is now obsolete, it is still used in many other terms and collocations (*Community trade mark*, *Community design*, *Community plant variety right*, etc.). The question that logically arises in this situation is whether all terms and expressions containing *Community* (*Zajednica*) should be changed to *Union* (*Unija*) during the harmonization of national legislation or whether *Community* should be kept although it refers to the Union (and no longer exists).

Orthographic reasons
A dilemma initiated by the Croatian translators in the Council reveals yet another rather obvious source of discordance but with potentially less obvious consequences. The official language equivalents for *EU Council Presidency* listed in *EuroVoc* show considerable discrepancy among languages in the use of capitalization, as well as some variation in wording (Presidency of the Council) found in IATE. The problem concerns not only orthographic convention but also the fact that, in Croatian and perhaps in the majority of other EU official languages, a capital letter is used for the name of a body or an institution, while an initial lower-case letter indicates the function itself. Since the specific name of the EU Council Presidency, for example, the Lithuanian Presidency, can refer to the composition of the presidency, this led the Croatian translators to use the capital letter (*Predsjedništvo*), as is usually the case in English, and to revert to lower case, or an entirely different term altogether (*predsjedanje*/*predsjedavanje*) when referring to the act of presiding. After a lengthy discussion among translators and lawyer-linguists of several EU institutions, it was decided that the term always refers to the function and should therefore be written in lower case in Croatian.

Final Remarks

Recent developments in terminology theory drawing on sociolinguistics, cognitive semantics, discourse analysis, corpus linguistics and some other applied linguistic disciplines take into account the phenomenon of term variability and the dynamics of terms in specialized communication. Although the concept of dynamics in terminology is usually understood and interpreted in a wide spectrum of approaches, it generally points to the fact that even special languages, by definition highly standardized, demonstrate the creative potential resulting in variation and reflecting the dynamics of cognition. Such insights will certainly have an impact on the future understanding of the processes in special-language communication particularly in multilingual and multicultural settings. Some of the examples discussed above speak in favour of this view. Legal language and legal terminology are generally less prone to change than most other disciplines; however, the 'Europeanization' of law and its multiplication in an already impressive number of national terminologies certainly make room for uncontrolled variation in spite of the ongoing controlled processes of concept and term harmonization mentioned earlier.

Variation, as Temmerman points out, is often cognitively motivated and should not be too easily dismissed as unnecessary in expert discourse. She predicts that the traditional meaning of terminology standardization will possibly have to be redefined 'as a dynamic societal process in which many factors come into play' (2011: 109). In her opinion, there is a great deal of variation in IATE although the EU inter-institutional term base is primarily aimed at achieving terminology standardization in the EU institutions (2011: 106). While this can certainly support some of the above claims, on the other hand, it is probably not intentional but rather the accidental result of the way terminology is presented in IATE. In the context of the problem tackled in this chapter and from the point of view of a new EU language having recently completed the strenuous task of translating the entire *acquis*, we should not forget the translators' position and their daily needs. As interesting and intriguing as it may be to view the inevitability of lack of harmonization in a multilingual special-language setting like the EU as a cognitive phenomenon, it should also be understood that this phenomenon poses much less of a problem when manifested on discourse level (especially monolingual) where context plays an important role. In daily practice, however, as Bononno (2000: 646) emphasizes in more pragmatic terms, terminology is often 'an *ad hoc* affair [for translators], more a matter of filling in the blanks in their knowledge than systematically studying a constellation of terms in a given universe of discourse'. In a multilingual, multicultural and 'multilegal' context (such as the EU translation services), where legal certainty remains an imperative, EU translators continue to rely on consolidated and coordinated terminology resources. In our view, such resources need to clearly reflect the fact that the EU legal language is a genre in itself and that, despite its often intentional vagueness, EU legal terminology does not represent a conglomerate of concepts wide enough to cover both EU and national legal, ideological or linguistic idiosyncrasies – but rather a coherent legal system.

References

Bononno, R. 2000. Terminology for translators: an implementation of ISO 12620. *Meta*, XLV(4), 646–69.

Ćapeta, T. 2009. Multilingual law and judicial interpretation in the EU, in *Curriculum, Multilingualism and the Law*, edited by L. Sočanac, C. Goddard and L. Kremer. Zagreb: Nakladni zavod Globus, 89–110.

Fischer, M. 2010. Language (policy), translation and terminology in the European Union, in *Terminology in Everyday Life*, edited by M. Thelen and F. Steurs. Amsterdam: John Benjamins, 21–33.

ISO 860:2007. *Terminology Work: Harmonization of Concepts and Terms.*

Joint Practical Guide of the European Parliament, the Council and the Commission for persons involved in the drafting of European Union legislation. 2013. Available at: eur-lex.europa.eu/content/pdf/techleg/joint-practical-guide-2013-en.pdf.

Mattila, H.E.S. 2013. *Comparative Legal Linguistics*. 2nd edition. Farnham: Ashgate.

Sager, J.C. 1990. *A Practical Course in Terminology Processing*. Amsterdam: John Benjamins.

Šarčević, S. 1988. The challenge of legal lexicography: implications for bilingual and multilingual dictionaries, in *ZüriLEX '86 Proceedings*, edited by M. Snell-Hornby. Tübingen: Francke Verlag, 307–14.

Šarčević, S. 2010. Legal translation in multilingual settings, in *Translating Justice*, edited by I. Alonso Araguár, J. Baigorri Jalón and H.J.L. Campbell. Granada: Comares, 19–45.

Temmerman, R. 2011. Ways of managing the dynamics of terminology in multilingual communication. *SCOLIA*, 25, 105–22.

Chapter 13

The Way Forward for Court Interpreting in Europe

Martina Bajčić

Introduction

In accordance with Article 6 of the European Convention on Human Rights (hereinafter: ECHR), anyone facing a criminal charge must be provided with the services of an interpreter (free of charge) if he or she does not understand the language of the proceedings. Although all EU Member States are signatories to the ECHR, not all of them meet the above requirement, at least not in a satisfactory way (Morgan 2011: 6). At the same time, the growing mobility of EU citizens and the enlargement of the EU has increased the number of criminal proceedings involving a non-national citizen, and in turn the need for court interpreting. Therefore, the EU has started exploring ways to bridge the differences in court interpreting in the Member States.

The profession of court interpreters varies in the Member States with regard to training, accreditation, rates of pay and even official status. With the intention of proposing minimum requirements for court interpreters, the Commission held an experts' meeting in 2002, followed by a Green Paper in 2003, and subsequently put forward a proposal for European legislation guaranteeing the right to interpretation and translation in criminal proceedings. Since no unanimous agreement was reached – a requirement in criminal matters in the pre-Lisbon Treaty period – the proposal was shelved until 2009 when the Commission proposed a Framework Decision with a view to achieving mutual recognition of court decisions and introducing minimum standards for court procedures to safeguard uniform protection level for suspects. Thereafter, based on Article 82 of the Treaty on the Functioning of the European Union (hereinafter: TFEU),[1] the Commission finally proposed the first legislative instrument in the field of criminal law adopted after the entry into force of the Lisbon Treaty, namely, Directive 2010/64/EU.[2] As noted

1 Consolidated Version of the Treaty on the Functioning of the European Union, OJ 2012/C 326/01.

2 Directive 2010/64/EU of the European Parliament and of the Council on the Right to Interpretation and Translation in Criminal Proceedings of 20 October 2010, OJ L 280/1. With the entry into force of the Lisbon Treaty, Framework Decisions were replaced by Directives.

by Morgan (2011: 7), the Directive had to be 'Strasbourg-proof' in the sense that it meets the standards of the ECHR and settled case law of the European Court of Human Rights[3] (hereinafter: ECtHR). Therefore, it was held that the Directive should not only address the growing need for court interpreting in criminal matters, but also ensure that the interpretation and translation provided is of 'sufficient quality' throughout the EU, which is a formidable task indeed.

Departing from this background, the first two sections of this chapter examine how to cope with the implications of the Directive for the profession of court interpreters. Its implementation provides ample opportunity to review the status of court interpreters in the EU and seek ways of improving it. The latter should proceed on two tracks: the educational or institutional and the professional, with the purpose of establishing a roadmap of general qualifications for court interpreters and making the profession more uniform throughout the EU, as is elaborated in the last two sections. This, in turn, can improve the quality of court proceedings and enhance the mutual recognition of judicial decisions in Europe.

Directive 2010/64/EU on the Right to Interpretation and Translation in Criminal Proceedings

In response to the growing demand for court interpreting and the need to establish minimum standards throughout the Union, Directive 2010/64/EU was adopted by the European Parliament and the Council on 20 October 2010. The deadline for transposition of the Directive by the Member States was 27 October 2013. Unlike regulations, directives must be transposed into national legislation, whereby the Member States have the choice of the form and method by means of which the result of a given directive is to be achieved. Directive 2010/64/EU sets minimum standards to be observed, which means that the Member States have the option of offering greater protection, especially if additional protection would be necessary in practice. However, the standards of protection must not fall below the rights guaranteed under the ECHR and the EU Charter of Fundamental Rights. As regards Directive 2010/64/EU, the minimum rules to be adopted by all Member States concern the right to interpretation and the translation of essential documents, as well as the quality of the interpreting, translation and training. As stated in the introduction, Directive 2010/64/EU aims to facilitate the application of the right to interpretation and translation for those who do not speak or understand the language of the proceedings by ensuring free and adequate language assistance. This means that any person who has been charged with a criminal offence in a Member State has the right to a court interpreter if he or she does not understand the language of the proceedings.

Despite its Strasbourg-proof character, the wording of the Directive is sometimes vague or unclear, thus calling for caution by the Member States when

3 On relevant case law of the ECtHR, see Ortega Herráez et al. (2013: 91–3).

transposing and implementing the Directive. It is interesting to note that even the basic concept of criminal proceedings is not defined in the Directive; instead, it is to be interpreted in the light of ECtHR case law. Legal practitioners should also be aware that interpreters are not required to be present in cases of minor offences such as traffic offences. Nevertheless, the Directive applies to appeals before courts following the imposition of sanctions for minor offences (Art. 2(2): 'during appeal or any other procedural application'). For this reason, the provisions of the Directive have been transposed in national criminal legislation and in legislation concerning minor offences, for example, in Croatia in the Criminal Procedure Act and the Minor Offences Act.[4]

Equally unclear are the Directive's provisions on 'remote interpretation' in Article 2(6), which provides that remote interpreting can be used if the physical presence of an interpreter is not required to safeguard the fairness of the proceedings. Remote interpreting can be defined as simultaneous interpretation where the interpreter is not in the same room as the speaker or his/her audience, or both (Mouzourakis 1996: 22–3; cited in Fowler 2012). To date, video-conferencing has been used by conference interpreters, however, not by court interpreters. The possibility of using remote interpreting is problematic in several aspects. First, it assumes that courts are equipped with all the necessary technology to enable remote interpreting, and second, that court interpreters are skilled in working via video links. Both assumptions are far from realistic. Most importantly, remote interpreting is not suitable for the specific context of criminal proceedings. Although it might cut costs or eliminate delays, remote interpreting can seriously impact the smooth functioning of the court because of the tendency for the participants to speak fast, which is characteristic of trials subject to time restrictions, and due to problems with sound amplification and other technical glitches. Moreover, the language of criminal proceedings is particularly dense in legal terminology (see Fowler 2012). With this in mind, remote interpreting could have the opposite effect of undermining the fairness of the proceedings and even lead to higher costs as a result of possible appeals on the ground of poor interpreting quality. Therefore, the national authorities should consider all possible ramifications of remote interpreting.

The broadly formulated provisions in Article 3 are also problematic. Paragraph 1 lays down the general rule requiring written translation of all documents which are essential for the accused to exercise his or her right to defence and to a fair trial. As to the question, which documents are deemed essential, paragraph 2 explicitly restricts these documents to 'any decision depriving a person of his liberty, any charge or indictment and any judgment', while paragraph 3 authorizes the competent authority to decide whether any other document is to be deemed essential in a given case. Going a step further, paragraph 7 admits an exception to the general rule by providing for the possibility of an oral summary of essential

4 *Zakon o kaznenom postupku* (Croatian Official Gazette Nos. 121/11, 143/12), *Prekršajni zakon* (Croatian Official Gazette Nos. 39/13, 107/07).

documents if such summary would not jeopardize the fairness of the proceedings. The competent authorities are cautioned against making such decisions lightly and are advised to consider the possible consequences of allowing the written translation of essential documents to be replaced by an oral summary. Although oral summaries would perhaps result in lower costs, possible repercussions might lead to a violation of procedural rights or even occasion a national court to refer a preliminary question to the Court of Justice concerning violation of the Directive.[5] Article 3(5) stipulates that the accused has the right to challenge a decision finding that no translation of documents or passages thereof is needed. In such cases, the costs would inevitably increase for the Member States.[6]

The Need for Concretization

In light of the concerns raised above, we turn our attention to the German Act on Strengthening Procedural Rights of Accused Persons in Criminal Proceedings (Gesetz zur Stärkung der Verfahrensrechte von Beschuldigten im Strafverfahren, hereinafter: BeVReStG),[7] which aims to ensure a more concrete transposition of Directive 2010/64/EU. Even before transposition of the Directive, §187(1) of the German Court Constitution Act (*Gerichtsverfassungsgesetz*, hereinafter: GVG)[8] provided an accused or convicted person with the right to translation and interpretation services free of charge. The German Code of Criminal Procedure (*Strafprozessordnung*, hereinafter: StPO)[9] also contained provisions concerning translation and interpretation. However, in order to concretize the right to interpretation, the German *Bundestag* adopted the above-mentioned BeVReStG, transposing Directive 2010/64/EU, as well as Directive 2012/13/EU on the right to information in criminal proceedings.[10] The BeVReSTG, which entered into force on 6 July 2013, amended relevant provisions of the GVG and the StPO.

In order to concretize the Directive's vague provision on essential documents, amended subparagraph 2 of §187 GVG requires the indictment, charge and judgment to be translated in line with the Directive. An oral translation or oral summary of the content of such documents is possible only if it guarantees the

5 Under Article 267 TFEU, the Court of Justice has jurisdiction to give preliminary rulings concerning the interpretation of the Treaties and secondary law such as directives. Accordingly, there could be some interesting case law in regard to Directive 2010/64/EU in the future.

6 See the communication of 20 February 2013 on questions raised during the transposition of Directive 2010/64/EU in Germany at: http://www.neuerichter.de/fileadmin/user_upload/fg_interkulturelle_kommunikation/FG-IK-2013-02.20_PM_Umsetzung_der_EU-Richtlinie.pdf [accessed September 2013].

7 BeVReStG of 2 July 2013 (German Official Gazette I, 1938 No. 34).

8 *Gerichtsverfassungsgesetz* of 9 May 1975 (German Official Gazette I, at 1077).

9 *Strafprozessordnung* of 7 April 1987 (German Official Gazette I 1074, at 1319).

10 Directive 2012/13/EU of the European Parliament and of the Council on the right to information in criminal proceedings of 22 May 2012, OJ L 142/1.

criminal procedural rights of the accused. Most importantly, it stresses that, as a rule, such solution should be accepted only if the accused has a defence attorney. Thus the amended provision lays down more precise guidelines for the national authorities than the Directive itself. Furthermore, subparagraph 3 of §187 GVG provides that the accused may waive the right to written translation only if he or she has been properly informed of the consequences of such a waiver.[11]

Written translations of judgments are important for filing appeals and exploring possibilities for other remedies. In this regard, BeVReStG amends the StPO by adding subparagraph 3 to §37, which provides that both the judgment and its translation shall be submitted to the persons participating in the proceedings. In accordance with Article 2 of Directive 2010/64/EU, the StPO is further amended to extend the right to interpretation during criminal proceedings before investigative and judicial authorities to include police questioning as well. This is done in subparagraph 1 of §168b by replacing the term *staatsanwaltschaftliche Untersuchungshandlungen* (investigations by the public prosecution) with the broader term *Untersuchungshandlungen der Ermittlungsbehörden* (investigations by investigation authorities).

The final issue to be addressed concerns the failure of the Directive to specify who is qualified to interpret and translate. This is all the more surprising in light of the common desire of the protégées of the Directive to create a common platform for court interpreters in all Member States. In this regard, the Directive simply requires Member States to establish registers of 'independent translators and interpreters' who are 'appropriately qualified' (Art. 5(4)) and to take concrete measures to ensure that the interpreting and translation provided is of 'sufficient quality to safeguard the fairness of the proceedings' (Arts. 2(8) and 3(9)). How and by whom this is to be done is not clear. However, the Directive guarantees the accused the right to complain if he or she regards the quality of translation to be insufficient to safeguard the fairness of the proceedings (Art. 3(5)). Moreover, the Directive requires Member States to ensure that a procedure is in place for ascertaining whether the suspect or accused person speaks and understands the language of the proceedings (Art. 2(4)).

In light of these obligations, it would be advisable for Member States to introduce procedural guidelines or a *lex specialis* to give their competent judicial authorities more detailed guidance and to concretize certain obligations imposed by the Directive, as the German BeVReStG does. Doing so would facilitate the task of the judicial staff in all dealings with court interpreters. In broad terms, Article 6 of the Directive stipulates that Member States shall request 'those responsible for the training of judges, prosecutors and judicial staff involved in criminal

11 §187(3) GVG reads as follows: 'Der Beschuldigte kann auf eine schriftliche Übersetzung nur wirksam verzichten, wenn er zuvor über sein Recht auf eine schriftliche Übersetzung nach den Absätzen 1 und 2 und über die Folgen eines Verzichts auf eine schriftliche Übersetzung belehrt worden ist. Die Belehrung nach Satz 1 und der Verzicht des Beschuldigten sind zu dokumentieren.'

proceedings to pay special attention to the particularities of communicating with the assistance of an interpreter'.

With this in mind, in the aftermath of Directive 2010/64/EU, professional associations and training institutions could play a significant role by introducing needed changes in the profession of court interpreters. Professional associations should also keep and update registers of properly qualified court interpreters, assuming that a general agreement is reached on the qualifications required for court interpreters to be entered into such registers. Taking into account the obligations imposed by the Directive, the following sections of this chapter focus on the quality of court interpreting in the EU and the need for its further professionalization.

Court Interpreting in the EU: Looking for Quality

In a 1909 appeal case *Emery – R.* v. *Governor of H.M. Prison* (UK),[12] a man who was deaf had been found not to be capable of understanding the proceedings brought against him and was detained without a trial under the Criminal Lunatics Act. In *R* v. *Iqbal Begum* (1985, UK),[13] the wrong language interpreter was summoned. Instead of a Punjabi interpreter, the solicitor of the accused tried to use a Pakistani accountant, as a result of which the trial was annulled. Therefore, one can conclude that the mere presence of an interpreter does not satisfy the requirements of a fair trial; the interpreting provided must be of sufficient quality. These two examples show that interpreters play a vital role in ensuring a fair trial.

In retrospect, it is safe to say that court interpreting has come a long way; however, there is still considerable room for improvement. The obligations imposed by Directive 2010/64/EU on the Member States make it clear that it is high time to professionalize court interpreting and improve its quality. Therefore, professional associations representing court interpreters are advised to take advantage of this opportunity by taking immediate action to strengthen links with the relevant institutions and obtain greater control over the market. Most importantly, in order to gain professional status, court interpreters need to raise awareness of their significant role in court.

The notion of court interpreting is somewhat blurred in the European context because of the country-specific differences in the qualifications and authorization of court interpreters. As a recent study of the Commission shows (Pym et al. 2012), the title itself is not used consistently throughout the EU. In the framework of this chapter, we define court interpreters as certified or sworn translators who are authorized to designate their translations as legally valid. The government or state body competent to issue the authorization varies. For example, in Austria, Belgium, the Czech Republic, Croatia, France and Germany, local or regional

12 *Emery – R.* v. *Governor of H.M.* Prison at Stafford, ex parte Emery [1909] 2 K.B. 81.

13 *R.* v. *Iqbal Begum*; Court of Appeal, 22 April 1985 [1991] 93 Cr. App. R. 96.

courts are responsible for such authorization, whereas in Estonia, Poland, Romania, Slovenia and Slovakia, the Ministry of Justice authorizes court interpreters. The prerequisites for becoming a sworn translator also differ. In Finland, the status of certified translator is acquired by passing an exam organized by the Authorized Translator's Board or by completing a degree in Translation. In Norway, exams are organized by the Norwegian School of Economics, while in Bulgaria the Ministry of Foreign Affairs accredits companies to provide certified translation. In Luxembourg, five years of working experience is required to become a court interpreter (see Pym et al. 2012). Though not mandatory in most Member States, there seems to be a growing tendency towards such requirements. In fact, a proposal has been made to establish a voluntary European certification system for translators (TransCert),[14] which, among other things, would require a certain number of mandatory working hours for certification. Whether such requirements should be included is debatable; however, there is no denying that the EU needs more uniform qualification requirements for court interpreters, especially in the context of Directive 2010/64/EU.

It should be noted that some Member States do not even have an official system of sworn translators. For instance, in the United Kingdom, there is no official requirement that legal documents be accompanied by a certification stating the qualifications of the translator. In such cases, it is difficult to determine who is authorized to provide court interpreting that would be of sufficient quality in the sense of Directive 2010/64/EU. After all, interpreting and translation quality may be a ground for requesting a review procedure. On the other hand, some countries with sworn court interpreters allow non-interpreters to be summoned if a court interpreter cannot be found (for example, Spain under the *Ley de Enjuciamento Criminal* 1882/2004).

Furthermore, the fact that different terms are used in the Member States to designate sworn or certified translators makes it difficult to determine who can translate or interpret, especially because this is not explicitly specified by the Directive. Terminological inconsistency is also present in national legislation where different national acts sometimes use different terms. For instance, no fewer than three different terms are used in Croatian legislation: *interpreter, court interpreter* and *sworn court interpreter* (*tumač, sudski tumač, prisegnuti sudski tumač*), whereas the Directive only uses the term *interpreter*. Unlike *court interpreter*, the term *interpreter* in Croatian and other languages includes a sign language interpreter as well. For this reason, the term *Gerichtsdolmetscher* (court interpreter) is usually used in Germany, although some acts use *Dolmetscher* (interpreter) only

14 TransCert (Trans-European Voluntary Certification for Translators) is a European project which addresses the urgent need for further development of the profession and proposes a European-wide certification for translators. The main goal of TransCert is to address these needs jointly, that is, with the involvement of all stakeholders in the translation sector, with the aim of establishing a complete certification for the job profile 'Translator'.

(*inter alia*, the *Justizvergütungs- und Entschädigungsgesetz*, hereinafter: JVEG).[15] The transposition of Directive 2010/64/EU offers an opportunity to remove such terminological inconsistencies and introduce uniform terminology in all relevant legislation concerning the activities of court interpreters.

Despite the different starting positions of the Member States, the goal of Directive 2010/64/EU is to introduce a uniform system of qualification and to improve the quality of court interpreting throughout the EU with a view to ensuring a fair trial in all Member States. Given the evident lack of specialized training programmes for court interpreters, uniform programmes are needed, especially ones focusing on the development of interdisciplinary skills. Similarly, court interpreters need to be made aware of their important role and responsibility in court proceedings. The specific task of a court interpreter is to enable the administration of justice in more than one language. In order to guarantee a fair trial in multilingual proceedings, court interpreters must be qualified. Moreover, they need to be aware of the legal consequences of mistranslations. For instance, a miscommunication between an interpreter and a doctor testifying during proceedings may lead to new lawsuits. Therefore, in light of the obligations imposed by the Directive, court interpreters should be obliged to have liability insurance covering all professional duties. This includes interpreting and translation out of court. For example, as a result of cross-border healthcare services,[16] more patients are seeking medical treatment in other Member States, which could increase the need for the services of court interpreters in and out of court.

As already mentioned, Articles 2(8) and 3(9) of the Directive specify that the translation or interpreting provided must be of sufficient quality to ensure that suspects or accused persons are informed about the charges against them and are able to exercise their right of defence. Also, according to Articles 2(5) and 3(5), review procedures may be initiated to check quality. However, it is unclear how and by whom such procedures should be conducted. Video recording or recording of interpreting in situations covered by the Directive would enable subsequent quality checks; however, each Member State should first introduce procedural provisions stipulating who can conduct quality control. The latter should be done in cooperation with training institutions and professional associations, and not by legal practitioners alone. Needless to say, interpreters will be reluctant to be recorded in such a stressful working environment, especially without appropriate remuneration.

Despite its imperfections, Directive 2010/64/EU marks a significant step forward in the quest to improve the quality of court interpreting. While some national provisions (for example, in Croatia and Germany) go further by making it possible to sanction unconscientious work by court interpreters, the Directive

15 *Justizvergütungs- und -entschädigungsgesetz* of 5 May 2004 (Judicial Remuneration and Compensation Act) (German Official Gazette I, at 718, 776).

16 Directive 2011/24/EU of the European Parliament and of the Council of 9 March 2011 on the application of patients' rights in cross-border healthcare, OJ L 88/45.

takes the initial step by explicitly requiring interpreting and translation to be of sufficient quality. Furthermore, the Directive provides for the possibility to question the quality of the services provided and even to challenge the quality in a review procedure.

In this context, the project on the Quality of Legal Translation (hereinafter: Qualetra) funded by the European Commission should be mentioned. Set up in response to Directive 2010/64/EU, Qualetra focuses on training, testing and evaluating legal translators and training legal practitioners taking part in criminal proceedings.[17] For this purpose court interpreting includes legal translation as a specific instance of court interpreting (Pym et al. 2012: 20). Although legal translation activities are frequently referred to without distinction, only court interpreters can produce certified translations, that is, official documents accompanied by seals or stamps attesting the authority of the translator (Pym et al. 2012: 23; see also Mayoral Asensio 2003: 81), whereas legal translators translate various documents of a legal nature for different judicial systems. EU projects such as Qualetra and cross-language training (see Kadrić 2005) focusing on the development of interdisciplinary skills play an important role in improving the quality of court interpreting and creating a common training platform for interpreters. Such a platform is a precondition for court interpreters to achieve mutual recognition, allowing them to exercise the freedoms of the internal market. Unfortunately, to date, there has been very little cross-border recognition of the status of sworn translators. In a ruling of 17 March 2011 (Joined Cases C-372/09 and C-373/09 *Josep Peñarroja Fa*), the Court of Justice stated that the duties of court expert translators 'are not covered by the definition of "regulated profession" set out in Article 3(1)(a) of the Directive 2005/36/EC of the European Parliament and of the Council of 7 September 2005 on the recognition of professional qualifications'.[18] In fact, Spain is the only EU country which recognizes the professional qualifications of sworn translators from other European countries. That is regrettable; however, mutual recognition can be promoted only if we can rely on the legal translations and interpreting provided by accredited court interpreters with a uniform official status throughout the EU.

As indicated above, further professionalization is needed to improve the quality of court interpreting. In light of Directive 2010/64/EU, professionalization should proceed on two parallel tracks: the educational or institutional and the professional. The former includes the introduction of specialized programmes or training for

17 The project proposal falls within the context of the European Convention on Human Rights, the EU Charter, the Stockholm Programme and Directive 2010/64/EU, in particular, its Articles 3, 5 and 6.

18 Directive 2005/36/EC of the European Parliament and of the Council of 7 September 2005 on the recognition of professional qualifications, OJ L 255; judgment of the Court (Fourth Chamber) of 17 March 2011 (reference for a preliminary ruling from the Cour de cassation – France) – proceedings brought by Josep Peñarroja Fa (Joined Cases C-372/09 and C-373/09).

court interpreters, preferably within the framework of existing programmes for translation and interpreting, or as part of lifelong learning translator training. Such programmes should enable the participants to acquire interdisciplinary knowledge and develop interdisciplinary skills, thus ensuring a high level of language, legal, terminology and translation competence. On the professional track, associations of court interpreters and translators should offer greater protection and regulate the status of court interpreters, as well as provide the framework for legislative changes in terms of the remuneration and protection of interpreters.

Training for Court Interpreters

Despite the professional challenges facing court interpreters, there is a general lack of specialized qualification programmes for court interpreters throughout Europe. Contrary to the United States and Canada, European interpreters are usually trained in more general fields and obtain generic qualifications in legal public service interpreting, for example, in the United Kingdom. This is alarming in light of the significant role played by education and training in furthering the professionalization of court interpreting. Therefore, existing translator training programmes should be modified and new ones established which are tailored to meet the specific needs of court interpreters. Furthermore, instead of competing with each other, the programmes should be more uniform so as to ensure that future court interpreters will be properly prepared in all Member States to meet the professional challenges before them.

However, it is difficult to create universal programmes throughout the Union. Even in graduate programmes there are still considerable differences although the Bologna process[19] has been introduced in all Member States. Nonetheless, a general roadmap for unifying programmes should be provided at EU level. In this context, it is important to mention the European Master's of Translation (EMT) network, which currently connects 54 university translation programmes in Europe. Most of the programmes offer a general translation qualification[20] with legal translation

19 The Bologna process was initiated by the Bologna Declaration of 19 June 1999 of the European Ministers of Education. Its objectives include introducing a system of academic degrees which are easily recognizable and comparable, thus promoting the mobility of students, teachers and researchers, ensuring high quality teaching, etc.

20 For instance, the programme in Cologne (Germany) offers the following general modules: foundations of specialized translation including seminars/lectures on translation studies, languages for special purposes (LSP), computer linguistics and terminology; tools and methods including seminars/lectures on technical writing, desktop publishing, business practice, management of translation projects, liaison interpreting for translators; knowledge base for specialized translation in the fields of science and technology, law and economics; specialized translation (scientific and technical translation, legal translation, economic translation and medical translation). Available at http://www.f03.fh-koeln.de/fakultaet/itmk/studium/studiengaenge/master/fachuebersetzen/00587/index.html [accessed September

or court interpreting being taught as part of specialized translation. An exception is the *Máster en Traducción Jurídica-Financiera* in Madrid (Universidad Pontificia Comillas, Departamento de Traducción e Interpretación), which focuses on legal and financial translation.

In light of the specific legal context of court interpreting, specialist training for court interpreters should aim at developing a solid set of interdisciplinary competences. The following subsection attempts to single out interdisciplinary competences considered indispensable for court interpreters. Note that the term *competence* refers to both knowledge and skills, that is, 'the combination of aptitudes, knowledge, behaviour and know-how necessary to carry out a given task under given conditions' (EMT Expert Group's Report,[21] hereinafter: EMT Report 2009: 3). In other words, key competences for court interpreters should be anchored on theoretical grounds that facilitate the development of practical skills. The link between theory and practice is very transparent in the area of court interpreting and legal translation. Gaining a basic understanding of theoretical problems such as legal equivalence is just as important for court interpreters, as is practical experience in legal drafting and communicating in the courtroom, all of which prepare future interpreters to cope with the challenges of the profession in the real world.

Interdisciplinary Knowledge and Skills

Before defining the specific competences of court interpreters, it is useful to mention the general competences of translators. In the EMT Report (2009: 4–7), the Expert Group identifies six main general competences: (1) translation service provision competence (marketing, social role of the translator); (2) language competence; (3) intercultural competence (includes a sociolinguistic and a textual dimension); (4) information mining competence (*inter alia*, knowing how to identify information and documentation requirements, terminological research); (5) thematic competence (knowing how to search for appropriate information to gain a better grasp of the thematic aspects of a document) and (6) technological

2013]. The Master's programme in Vienna also covers a variety of specialized translation fields such as legal translation, technical translation, economic translation, medical and pharmaceutical translation, localisation, terminology management, translation technology, translation of different text types, including literary translation. It also includes developing translation technology and terminology management skills. Available at: http://transvienna.univie.ac.at/studieninformation/studienplaene/studienplan-2007-bama/ma-uebersetzen/ [accessed September 2013]. Such programmes are undoubtedly well designed; however, court interpreters would benefit more from specialized programmes.

21 Set up by the Commission's Directorate-General for Translation in April 2007, the main task of the EMT expert group is to make specific proposals with a view to implementing a European reference framework for a European Master's in Translation (EMT) throughout the EU. More information available at: http://ec.europa.eu/dgs/translation/programmes/emt/index_en.htm [accessed September 2013].

competence (mastery of tools). The following discussion deals only with aspects of these competences relevant for a specialization in court interpreting.

According to the EMT Report (2009: 5), language competence includes knowing how to understand grammatical, lexical and idiomatic structures, as well as the graphic and typographic conventions of language A and the other working languages (B, C). In addition, translators must possess the know-how to use the same structures and conventions in languages A and B and develop sensitivity to changes in language(s).

In the legal context, language competence includes familiarity with different text types and legal drafting practices, both of which also take account of the sociolinguistic and textual dimensions, that is, intercultural competence. The sociolinguistic dimension concerns knowing how to recognize function and meaning in language variations; knowing how to identify the rules for interaction relating to a specific community, including non-verbal elements; and knowing how to produce a register appropriate to a given situation, for a particular document (written) or speech (oral) (EMT Report 2009: 6). In the context of court interpreting, the textual dimension includes the know-how to recognize and identify the structure and parts of texts, especially legal texts (judgments, indictments), as well as the know-how to draft texts containing the same legal information in other languages in accordance with the conventions of the genre. Although court interpreters translate other text types as well,[22] it is essential for them to master the specific features of legal texts and to understand how the legal status of a text (binding or non-binding) affects its usage in legal processes.

For our purpose, the sociolinguistic dimension constitutes part of the wider language competence involving the ability to adapt to different situations and recipients of interpreting. Interpreting at a wedding is not the same as interpreting at a police interrogation or in court proceedings. As a rule, a court interpreter translates not only for the party (victim, suspect, accused) but also for the judge, public prosecutor or police. The court interpreter's role is to transfer legal information so as to enable effective communication throughout the proceedings, without attempting to explain the meaning of specific legal concepts.

In addition to language competence, court interpreters must develop basic legal competence by acquiring in-depth knowledge of the legal systems of their working languages. Among other things, this includes familiarity with different court systems and court proceedings. Since court interpreters can be engaged at different stages of the proceedings, from police questioning and detention to pre-trial and trial, it is important that they can differentiate between these stages and understand the basic procedural differences. Not surprisingly, the proposal was made back in October 2002 to include visits to courts, police stations and prisons in training programmes for court interpreters (Morgan 2011). Such visits would familiarize court interpreters with their future working surroundings. Furthermore,

22 On the main text types of translation in criminal proceedings, see Ortega Herráez et al. (2013: 103–4).

special attention could be devoted to social aspects of interpreting in cases involving youth, victims, etc.

Another legal aspect of training future court interpreters is the need to acquaint them with the relevant national and EU legislation regulating their activities, in particular their rights and obligations under Directive 2010/64/EU. Providing broader training in EU law is also advisable, as it would contribute to a better understanding of the EU criminal justice system (including documents such as the European Arrest Warrant and general information such as the jurisdiction of the CJEU). For example, post-Lisbon changes (Art. 82(2)(b) TFEU) enable the EU to adopt directives establishing minimum rules regarding the rights of individuals in criminal procedures with a view to facilitating the mutual recognition of judgments and to promoting police and judicial cooperation in criminal matters. In addition to the right to interpretation and translation, these rights include the right to information, access to defence counsel, protection of suspects, communication with family, etc. All of these legal aspects would familiarize court interpreters with their working environment and help them develop the sensitivity needed to meet the specific challenges of their profession.

Terminology competence instrumental for all court interpreters encompasses not only in-depth knowledge of the relevant specialized terminology but also skills in terminology management and the use of databases. In the legal context, special attention needs to be devoted to legal terminology. For example, court interpreters need to differentiate the terms used to designate the suspect during different stages of the proceedings and to know at which stage the suspect becomes the accused. Furthermore, interpreters must differentiate between terms and concepts; it often occurs that the same term refers to two or more different legal concepts, which could lead to different legal effects depending on the context. It is also important to distinguish between national and European legal terminology, keeping in mind that the same term may denote different concepts in EU law and national law. For instance, the terms *crime* and *criminal proceedings* have different meanings in EU and national law. As regards Directive 2010/64/EU, this problem is circumvented by referring to the case law of the ECtHR, which explains the meaning and scope of criminal proceedings, as well as the meaning of other relevant legal concepts.

Finally, a specialized interdisciplinary programme for court interpreters should focus on developing translation competence by ensuring that the participants acquire a solid knowledge of General Translation Studies and legal translation scholarship, while developing skills in legal translation and oral interpretation (note-taking technique, simultaneous and consecutive interpretation, etc.). As mentioned earlier, court interpreters are often required to perform both interpreting and translating tasks (Ortega Herráez et al. 2013: 98). In light of Directive 2010/64/EU, techniques such as remote interpreting and working via video links should also be incorporated into translation training. It is absolutely essential to develop an interdisciplinary approach to all of these competences by placing them in a legal context. This requires including both lawyers and linguists as trainers in courses for court interpreters. The set of desired competences for court interpreters described here does not purport to be exhaustive and should therefore be regarded as a starting point.

To provide court interpreters with the knowledge and practical skills needed to be effective participants in court proceedings, specialized programmes focusing on the above interdisciplinary competences should be offered at the postgraduate level or as part of lifelong learning programmes for translators already holding a degree. A rare example is the programme Translating and Interpreting for Courts and Public Services,[23] which was launched in 2013 at the Hochschule Magdeburg-Stendal in Germany.[24] Upon completion of the programme, participants obtain a certificate qualifying them to become sworn interpreters appointed by the Ministry of Sachsen-Anhalt. The appointment is recognized throughout Germany and all sworn interpreters are listed in the federal data bank.[25] The programme lasts two semesters (112 hours) and offers three different orientations: interpreting for the economy, interpreting for the public sector and court interpreting.

Admission requirements include an above-average command of German and very good knowledge of the respective working language (C1). In addition to a university degree or a corresponding qualification and completed interpreter and translator training in the working language, prospective candidates must pass an aptitude test and have two years of working experience as an interpreter or translator.

The programme consists of the following mandatory modules:

a. introduction to the legal and public service procedures and area (public administration and civil law);
b. criminal law and criminal procedure law, police and court expert systems (administrative law, public notaries);
c. introduction to the legal translation technique (introduction to terminology management, legal translation and translation of documents); and
d. interpreting.

As mentioned above, it would be advisable for the mandatory modules to cover relevant aspects of EU law, especially Directive 2010/64/EU and national legislation transposing the Directive, as well as other legal and terminological aspects of court interpreting. Nevertheless, the launch of such a programme opens

23 See details of the study programme at: https://www.hs-magdeburg.de/weiterbildung/angebote/zertifikat/dolmetschen-und-uebersetzen-1/spo-duue [accessed September 2013].

24 In light of the influential body of German translation theory and the long tradition of German translator training institutions such as Heidelberg (1930), Germersheim (1947) and Saarbrücken (1948), it is not surprising that Germany is a frontrunner in specialized programmes for interpreters.

25 Available at: http://www.gerichtsdolmetscherverzeichnis.de/aufgelistet [accessed September 2013].

a small window of opportunity for court interpreters, paving the way for other specialized programmes based on interdisciplinary skills.

In short, the education of court interpreters calls for an urgent shift to a more specialized training focusing on developing interdisciplinary skills. Institutions of higher learning hold the key to the professionalization of court interpreting by introducing specialized training programmes. They could also play an important role in monitoring the quality of interpreting, ensuring that it is in line with Directive 2010/64/EU. To this end, greater cooperation is required between educational institutions, the judiciary and professional associations. Just as specialized training programmes are needed to educate highly qualified interpreters, professional associations are needed to regulate their work.

Role of Associations of Court Interpreters and Translators in Protecting Court Interpreters and Regulating their Status

While institutions of higher learning have the task of providing adequate training programmes to meet the standards imposed by Directive 2010/64/EU, it is up to the relevant professional associations to regulate the professional status of court interpreters. After all, the main criteria for a group to qualify as a profession are the existence of an association that controls its members and the assumption that only those members are qualified to provide particular services. Furthermore, a professional status is established by a set of social signs confirming the presumption of expertise and the presumed value of that expertise (Pym et al. 2012: 11). The professional associations of court interpreters need to work on both aspects so that the expertise of court interpreters is duly recognized and also valued by those using their services.

There is no denying that today's society attaches greater value to high-earning professions whose knowledge seems shrouded in mystery. The fact that we do not always understand the technical jargon of some professionals, for example, in the field of medicine, puts certain specialists in a position of power and control. Although translators and interpreters have the advantage of knowing more than their clients, they enjoy neither the control nor the prestige often attached to the expertise of other professions. I can confirm this with an anecdote from my own experience that occurred at the beginning of my career. At least from my point of view, I found it humiliating to be introduced as the secretary when I was interpreting at a high calibre meeting.[26] Such experiences are probably not isolated events but paint a realistic picture of how interpreters are perceived in the professional community.

26 Regretfully, secretarial and translation activities are often placed in the same group, for example, in the 2008 'General Industrial Classification of Economic Activities within the European Communities' (see Pym et al. 2012: 13). Similarly, very few countries have a separate census category for translators (Pym et al. 2012: 18).

As regards remuneration, the rates charged by interpreters differ significantly within the EU. Under the above-mentioned JVEG, interpreters in Germany currently earn at least 70 EUR per hour, whereas interpreters in Italy earn 14.68 EUR for the first *vacazione* (period of two hours) and 8.15 EUR for each subsequent *vacazione* (Garwood 2012: 179). In Poland interpreters charge 9 EUR per hour (Rybinska and Mendel 2012) and in Croatia 20 EUR per hour (pursuant to the Croatian Ordinance on Permanent Court Interpreters),[27] although the rates of conference interpreters are significantly higher in both countries.[28]

As a general conclusion, it can be said that commensurate pay is needed to ensure quality interpreting, as demonstrated by a recent debacle involving the UK interpreters' community. In 2012 the UK Ministry of Justice concluded a five-year contract with a private company to supply all English and Welsh courts with language services. The private contract almost halved the hourly rates of interpreters, as a result of which 60 per cent of the interpreters listed in the National Register of Public Service Interpreters refused to work for the company. Since the company could not provide sufficient interpreters, trials were postponed, suspects released and compensation claims filed (Bowcott and Midlane 2012). Therefore, paying lower fees may end up being more costly in the long run and undermine the quality of interpreting.

A transparent sign of professional status is membership in a professional association, especially an association of authority. Such associations can raise the professional bar in terms of remuneration and status. In the field of translation several factors contribute to the authority of an association and its members, such as admission criteria restricting its membership, how many years the association has existed, its size, whether it is active in a wider or parent association, the degree of specialization of its members, etc. (Pym et al. 2012: 33). The main roles of an interpreter and translator association are to represent the profession in dealings with the government and to confer considerable professional standing on its members, as does the German Federal Association of Translators and Interpreters (*Bundesverband der Dolmetscher und Übersetzer*, hereinafter: BDÜ).

---

27 In Croatia, judges, public prosecutors and other judicial bodies are known to question and even reduce the price of interpreting and translation, as a result of which court interpreters often have to explain the fees charged by referring to the Ordinance of Permanent Court Interpreters or their respective associations. Receiving less pay than a court interpreter originally charged is especially irritating as it happens after the service has already been provided.

28 It is interesting to compare the above rates with the fees for contract interpreters in the United States. Certified and professionally qualified interpreters charge $388 for a full day, and $210 for half a day, which is double the price charged by non-certified interpreters. Available at: http://www.uscourts.gov/FederalCourts/UnderstandingtheFederalCourts/DistrictCourts/CourtInterpreters/ContractInterpretersFees.aspx [accessed October 2013].

Lessons to be Learned

Founded in 1950s, the BDÜ functions as an umbrella association for 14 regional associations and one commercial organization. It provides its 7,000 members powerful representation, while encouraging local interaction (Pym et al. 2012: 45). The BDÜ can serve as an example for other professional associations, especially by its close cooperation with various institutions important for the profession, such as EULITA (European Legal Interpreters and Translators Association), which takes a leading role in promoting cooperation and best practices in working arrangements with the legal services and legal professionals throughout Europe. Following Germany's lead, Portugal established a National Translation Council (*Conselho Nacional de Tradução*) in 2011 as a forum for exchanging ideas between institutions of higher education and translators, professionals and translation companies (Pym et al. 2012: 68). Established with the same objective in 2013, Croatia's fledgling Translators Association (*Zajednica za prevoditeljstvo*) serves as an umbrella organization for private companies, freelancers, smaller associations and members of academia.

Such state-level associations should strive to cooperate at EU level and organize conferences or workshops for court interpreters. Given the scarcity of conferences for court interpreters, this would promote cooperation among professional interpreters and encourage the exchange of experiences. With this in mind, professional associations should organize seminars to familiarize their members with Directive 2010/64/EU and national measures transposing the Directive. Before greater uniformity can be achieved at EU level, fragmentation or the existence of a large number of small associations should be eliminated in various Member States and replaced by umbrella associations.[29]

Moreover, court interpreter associations can learn valuable lessons from court expert witnesses in terms of their professional representation, remuneration and protection. Unlike expert witnesses, court interpreters in many Member States still do not have mandatory liability insurance. Strong umbrella associations could assist in this regard and propose changes to existing legislative regulations. Similarly, they should be in charge of setting up and maintaining registers of court interpreters as envisaged by Directive 2010/64/EU. It is advisable to include more information in the registers on the qualifications and experience of court interpreters. A tiered system of labels (such as expert or qualified) would indicate different levels of competence, providing the judicial authorities with more information when looking for a qualified interpreter.

29 Today there are eight translator associations in Croatia (with 726 members); five are court interpreter associations. On the other hand, Slovenia has four (with 809 members), Slovakia three (with 611 members) and Germany only five (with 8,878 members) (Pym et al. 2012: 36).

Concluding Remarks

Achieving a common European platform for court interpreting will not happen by itself. As suggested in the preceding sections of this chapter, in the aftermath of Directive 2010/64/EU, the Member States, that is, their training institutions and professional associations, need to take collective action to find the best way forward for court interpreters in the EU.

First, the transposition of Directive 2010/64/EU calls for concretization on the part of Member States by providing adequate procedural measures to ensure proper implementation of the Directive in practice. Even after its transposition in national legislation, a Directive still constitutes a source of law. In other words, the Directive continues to have an indirect or interpretative effect and may even replace the provisions of national law (Ćapeta and Rodin 2011: 62).

Second, Directive 2010/64/EU raises the quality standards of court interpreting in the EU. In order to meet these standards, the Member States must provide adequate training at national level, while striving for greater uniformity of different programmes at EU level. To fill the existing gap due to the lack of specialized programmes, institutions of higher learning must establish training programmes for court interpreters focusing on interdisciplinary competences, including language, legal, terminology and translation knowledge and skills.

Finally, in addition to institutionalized training, professional associations must ensure further professionalization of court interpreting by securing better working conditions for their members in terms of adequate remuneration and protection. Establishing authoritative umbrella associations is instrumental for successful implementation of the desired legislative changes and for bridging significant differences in the remuneration of court interpreters in the Member States.

The described strengthening of the profession of court interpreters would increase the quality of interpreting in court proceedings, thereby guaranteeing the right to a fair trial, which in turn would also enhance the mutual recognition of judicial decisions throughout the EU.

References

Bowcott, O. and Midlane, T. 2012. Interpreters stay away from courts in protest at privatised contract. *Guardian* (Online, 2 March). Available at: http://www.theguardian.com/law/2012/mar/02/interpreters-courts-protest-privatised-contract [accessed October 2013].

Ćapeta, T. and Rodin, S. 2011. *Osnove prava Europske unije*. Zagreb: Narodne novine.

EMT Expert Group's Report. 2009. Competences for Professional Translators, Experts in Multilingual and Multimedia Communication, 16–17 March 2009. Available at: http://ec.europa.eu/dgs/translation/programmes/emt/key_documents/emt_competences_translators_en.pdf [accessed August 2013].

Fowler, Y. 2012. Interpreting into the ether: interpreting for prison/court video link hearings, in Proceedings of the Critical Link 5 Conference held in Sydney, 11–15 April 2007. Available at: http://criticallink.org/wp-content/uploads/2011/09/CL5Fowler.pdf [accessed August 2013].

Garwood, C. 2012. Court interpreting in Italy: the daily violation of a fundamental human right. *The Interpreters' Newsletter*, 17, 173–89.

Kadrić, M. 2005. Court interpreter training in a European context, in EU-High-Level Scientific Conference Series MuTra 2005 – Challenges of Multidimensional Translation: Conference Proceedings. Available at: http://www.euroconferences.info/proceedings/2005_Proceedings/2005_Kadric_Mira.pdf [accessed August 2013].

Mayoral Asensio, R. 2003. *Translating Official Documents*. Manchester: St. Jerome.

Morgan, C. 2011. The new European Directive on the right to interpretation and translation in criminal proceedings, in *Videoconference and Remote Interpreting in Criminal Proceedings*, edited by S. Braun and J.L. Taylor. Guildford: University of Surrey, 5–10.

Ortega Herráez, J.M., Giambruno, C. and Hertog, E. 2013. Translating for domestic courts in multicultural regions: issues and new developments in Europe and the United States of America, in *Legal Translation in Context, Professional Issues and Prospects*, edited by A. Borja Albi and F. Prieto Ramos. Bern: Peter Lang, 89–121.

Pym, A., Grin F., Sfreddo, C. and Chan, A.L.J. 2012. *The Status of the Translation Profession in the European Union. Final Report*, 24 July 2012. EU: DGT/2011/TST.

Rybinska, Z. and Mendel, A. 2012. Polish survey: quality of interpreting and translation as seen by users (pre-trial proceedings). Paper presented at the TRAFUT Workshop, Antwerpen, 18–20 October 2012. Available at: http://www.eulita.eu/sites/.../rybinska_TRAFUT_AN.pps [accessed April 2013].

Index

FSC
www.fsc.org
MIX
Papier | Fördert
gute Waldnutzung
FSC® C083411

Kolibri 360 GmbH
Ferdinand-Jühlke-Straße 7
99095 Erfurt, Deutschland
produktsicherheit@kolibri360.de